Straight

Answers

Straight Answers

Answers to 100 Questions about
the Catholic Faith

By

Rev. William P. Saunders, Ph.D.

Marie + Bob,

May God bless you,

Fr. William P. Saunders

Printed and bound in the United States of America.

Nihil Obstat:
Rev. Robert J. Rippy, J.C.L.
Censor deputatus

Imprimatur:
Most Rev. John R. Keating, D.D., J.C.D.
Bishop of Arlington
June 29, 1997

The nihil obstat and imprimatur are official declarations that a book or pamphlet is free of doctrinal or moral error. No implication is contained therein that those who have granted the nihil obstat and imprimatur agree with the contents, opinions, or statements expressed.

Library of Congress Cataloging-in-Publication Data

Saunders, William P., 1957-
      Straight answers: answers to 100 questions about
the catholic faith / by William P. Saunders
             p. 398   cm.
      ISBN 1-885938-25-X (HC) / ISBN 1-88-5938-14-4 (PBK)
        1. Catholic Church--Doctrines--Miscellanea. I. Title.
BX1754.3.S28 1998
282--dc21   98-50058
                                          CIP

Published in 1998 by

Cathedral Foundation Press
P.O. Box 777
Baltimore, Maryland 21203

Publisher: Daniel L. Medinger
Assistant Manager: Patti Medinger
Cover & Book Design: Dave Schall
Printed by: Catholic Printing Services

Dedicated to the loving memory
of my parents Joseph and Pauline Saunders
who gave me life and shared their faith with me.

TABLE OF CONTENTS

Sacred Scripture

Jesus Christ, Our Savior

The Church

Sacraments and Liturgy

The Last Things

Mary, Our Blessed Mother

Saints, Angels, and the Devil

Moral Issues

Special Topics

ABOUT THE AUTHOR

Father William P. Saunders was born on March 9, 1957 in Washington, D.C. to Dr. Joseph F. and Pauline C. Saunders. In 1959, his family moved to Springfield, Virginia where he was raised. He has one older brother, Joseph F. Saunders, Jr.

After graduating from West Springfield High School as the class valedictorian in 1975, he attended the College of William and Mary, Williamsburg, Virginia. He graduated in 1979 with a Bachelor of Business Administration degree in Accounting and with membership in Beta Gamma Sigma Honor Society.

During the summer after college graduation, Father Saunders focused on the vocation to the priesthood, with which he had been wrestling since college. He applied to the Diocese of Arlington, Virginia for admission into the seminary, and was assigned to St. Charles Borromeo Seminary, Philadelphia, Pennsylvania. In 1984, Father Saunders graduated from St. Charles Seminary with a Master of Arts in Sacred Theology, *Summa cum laude*, and was ordained to the Holy Priesthood on May 12.

As a priest, Father Saunders has served as the Assistant Pastor at St. Mary Catholic Church in Alexandria, VA (1984-1988), the Campus Chaplain and Adjunct Professor of Theology for Marymount University, Arlington, VA (1988-1993), and the Assistant Pastor (1993-95) and subsequently the Pastor (1995 to present) at Queen of Apostles Catholic Church in Alexandria, Virginia.

During this time, Father Saunders pursued studies at Catholic University, receiving a Doctor of Philosophy in Education Administration in 1992.

He was appointed as President of the Notre Dame Institute for Catechectics in 1992, a graduate school offering a Master of Arts in Catechectics, Sacred Scripture, and Spirituality. On February 1, 1997, the Notre Dame Institute officially merged with Christendom College, Front Royal, Virginia, becoming the Notre Dame Graduate School. At that time, Father Saunders was appointed Dean of the Graduate School.

AN INTRODUCTION

Straight Answers has its origins in Father Saunders' column of the same name (which appears weekly in the) *Arlington Catholic Herald*, the newspaper of the Diocese of Arlington. The purpose of the column was to respond to questions about the Catholic faith. Living in an age of confusion where truth has become blurred and challenges abound, many faithful Catholics want a "straight answer"– answers that are substantive and clear, and devoid of personal opinion or trendiness.

As a pastor and educator, Father Saunders responds to a variety of questions about the faith– Some answers concern very timely issues, such as "What is the Church's teaching on euthanasia?" Others focus on points of Catholic tradition, such as "Why do priests use incense at Mass?" And others provide explanations for beliefs which are commonly misunderstood by non-Catholics, such as "What is the Immaculate Conception?"

Although succinct, each answer is well-grounded in the magisterial documents, and the history and tradition of the Roman Catholic Church. This book is designed to be instructive to the regular Catholic reader and to empower him to defend the faith.

Pope John Paul II, in an address to seminarians at St. Joseph's Seminary of the Archdiocese of New York in 1995, asserted, "If there is one challenge facing the Church and her priests today, it is the challenge of transmitting the Christian message whole and entire without letting it be emptied of its substance." *Straight Answers* strives to meet that challenge.

SACRED

SCRIPTURE

ARE CATHOLICS FORBIDDEN FROM READING THE BIBLE?

Unfortunately, some misguided individuals' including some popular television evangelists – have wrongfully accused the Catholic Church of forbidding the faithful to read the Bible. Such accusations could not be further from the truth. One must always remember that the Roman Catholic Church, guided by the Holy Spirit, preserved the writings of Sacred Scripture, and also formed and approved the canon (the official set of books which constitute the Bible). The Church has also tried to provide good, vernacular translations of the Bible for the faithful to read. The examples are many: St. Jerome (d. 420) translated the Bible into Latin, producing the *Vulgate* version in the year 381. Cardinal Allen guided scholars in the year 1594 to produce the English translation known as the *Douay-Rheims*. In 1948, Pope Pius XII in his encyclical *Divino Afflante Spiritu* charged scholars to go again to the original texts of Sacred Scripture and produce good, modern translations in the vernacular languages. The results of this work resulted in the *New American Bible* printed in 1968; in its introduction, Pope Paul VI wrote, "We are gratified to find in this new translation of the Scriptures a new opportunity for men to give themselves to frequent reading of, and meditation on, the living Word of God. In its pages we recognize His voice, we hear a message of deep significance for every one of us."

The Church does caution the faithful reader that the Bible is a complex piece of literature, written over many centuries by many different authors inspired by the Holy Spirit. To fully appreciate the texts of Sacred Scripture which teach the truths of salvation, one would need knowledge of the historical background, the literary forms and images used, and the understanding of the revelation in the Tradition of the Church. While each person may read a passage and reflect on how it pertains to his particular life circumstances, any official interpretation concerning doctrine would be the responsibility of the Magisterium (the teaching authority) of the Church. Whenever a heresy has arisen in the Church, it is usually because someone misinterpreted Sacred Scripture and presented the findings as "gospel" truth.

Nevertheless, Catholics ought to have a familiarity with Sacred Scripture. St. Jerome said, "Ignorance of Scripture is ignorance of Christ." Vatican II exhorted "all the faithful, especially those who live the religious life, to learn 'the surpassing knowledge of Jesus Christ' (Philemon 3:8) by frequent reading of the divine Scriptures" (*Dogmatic Constitution on Divine Revelation*, #25). In recent times, many parishes have established Bible Study groups. The number of guides beneficial for Bible study have increased, such as William Barclay's *The Daily Study Bible Series* (Westminster Press, 1975), and *The Navarre Bible* (Four Courts Press, 1992). Particular "study" Bibles include *The New Catholic Study Bible* (Thomas Nelson Publishers, 1985) and *The Catholic Study Bible* (Oxford University Press, 1990). All of these are ways to help the faithful to know the Word of God.

Moreover, the Church does see the value of the reading and study of Sacred Scripture in healing the soul, making reparation for sin, and satisfying partially or fully the temporal punishment due for sin. According to the *Enchiridion of Indulgences* (1968), "a partial indulgence is granted to the faithful, who with the veneration due to the Divine Word make a spiritual reading from Sacred Scripture. A plenary indulgence is granted, if this reading is continued for at least one half an hour" (#50).

WHY DOES THE CATHOLIC VERSION OF THE BIBLE HAVE MORE BOOKS THAN THE PROTESTANT VERSION?

To appreciate this question and its answer, one must first remember that almighty God never handed anyone a complete Bible and said, "Here it is." Rather, over the centuries of salvation history, the Holy Spirit inspired the authors of Sacred Scripture to write down God's revelation to us. As time went on, the Church compiled these books to form a Canon' an authoritative set of Sacred Scripture' and declared it "God's Word."

The books of the Old Testament were written probably between 1000 and 100 BC, and are usually distinguished as four sets: The Law (or Torah, our first five books of the Old Testament), the Historical Books, the Prophets, and the Writings. Even in the New Testament itself, we find references to the reading of the Law and the Prophets in synagogue services (e.g. Luke 4:16-19, Acts 13:15). After the Fall of Jerusalem in AD 70, the Jewish rabbis convened the Council of Jamnia (90-100), at which time they established what books would be considered their Sacred Scripture. At this time, some controversy still existed over what are called the seven "deuterocanonical books " (Tobit, Judith, Wisdom, Sirach, Baruch, and I & II Maccabees) although they had been incorporated in their entirety or at least partially in versions of the Septuagint, the official Greek translation of the Old Testament by the year 100 BC. Part of the reason for the controversy was because these were the latest writings of the Old Testament and were written in Greek rather than Hebrew; the other books of the Old Testament – the "protocanonical books" – were older and originally written in Hebrew. Modern scholars note that Jamnia did not exclude any books definitively; a rigid fixing of the Jewish canon does not occur until at least 100 years later, and even then other books – including the deuterocanonical books – were read and honored. Many Scripture scholars, however, have no doubt that the apostolic Church accepted the deuterocanonical books as part of its canon of Sacred Scriptures. For instance, Origen (d. 245) affirmed the use of these books among Christians even though some of the Jewish leaders did not officially accept them.

Meanwhile, the writing of the New Testament books occurred between the time of our Lord's death and the end of the first century. (Recent studies of the Dead Sea Scrolls by some scholars suggest a date of the earliest writings closer to the time of our Lord's death, whereas much scholarship seems to place the writings between AD 50 and 100). After the legalization of Christianity in 313, we find the Church striving to formalize what writings of the New Testament were truly considered inspired and authentic to the teachings of our Lord. St. Athanasius in his *Paschal Epistle* (367) presented the complete list of 27 books of the New Testament saying, "These are the sources of salvation, for the thirsty may drink deeply of the words to be found here. In these alone is the doctrine of piety recorded. Let no one add to them or take anything away from them." This list of 27 books along with the 46 books of the Old Testament (including the deuterocanonical ones) was affirmed as the official canon of Sacred Scripture for the Catholic Church by the synods of Hippo (393), and Carthage I & II (397 and 419). The letter of Pope St. Innocent I in 405 also officially listed these books.

Although some discussion arose over the inclusion of other books into the Church's canon of Sacred Scripture after this time, the Council of Florence (1442) definitively established the official list of 46 books of the Old Testament and 27 of the New Testament.

With this background, we can now address why the Protestant versions of the Bible have less books than the Catholic versions. In 1534, Martin Luther translated the Bible into German. He grouped the seven deuterocanonical books of the Old Testament under the title "Apocrypha," declaring, "These are books which are not held equal to the Sacred Scriptures and yet are useful and good for reading." Luther also categorized the New Testament books: those of God's work of salvation (John, Romans, Galatians, Ephesians, I Peter, and I John); other canonical books (Matthew, Mark, Luke, Acts, the rest of Pauline epistles, II Peter, and II & III John); and non-canonical books (Hebrews, James, Jude, Revelation, and the seven books of the Old Testament). Many Church historians speculate that Luther was prepared to drop what he called the "non-canonical books" of the New Testament but refrained from doing so because of possible political fall-out. Why Luther took this course of action is hard to say. Some scholars believe Luther wanted to return to the "primitive faith," and therefore accepted only those Old Testament books written in Hebrew originally; others speculate he wanted to remove anything which disagreed with his own theology. Nevertheless, his action had the permanent consequence of omitting the seven deuterocanonical books of the Old Testament in Protestant versions of the Bible.

The Thirty-nine Articles of Religion (1563) of the Church of England asserted that these deuterocanonical books may be read for "example of life and instruction of manners," although they should not be used "to establish any doctrine" (Article VI). Consequently, the King James Bible (1611) printed the books between the New Testament and Old Testaments. John Lightfoot (1643) criticized this arrangement because he thought the "wretched Apocrypha" may be seen as a bridge between the two. The Westminster Confession (1647) decreed that these books, "not being of divine inspiration, are no part of the canon of Scripture, and therefore are of no authority of the Church of God; nor to be in any otherwise approved, or made use of than other human writings." The British and Foreign Bible Society decided in 1827 to remove these books from further publications and labeled these books "apocryphal." However, many Protestant versions of the Bible today will state, "King James version with Apocrypha."

The Council of Trent, reacting to the Protestant Reformers, repeated the canon of Florence in the *Decree on Sacred Books and on*

Traditions to be Received (1546) and decreed that these books were to be treated "with equal devotion and reverence." The *Catechism* repeats this same list of books and again affirms the apostolic Tradition of the canon of Sacred Scripture.

WHO WROTE THE GOSPELS?

To answer this question we must first be clear on how the gospels were formed and what constitutes authorship. Citing Vatican II's *Dogmatic Constitution on Divine Revelation*, the *Catechism* has a very succinct presentation on the formation of the gospels (cf. #125-127). The foundational premise is that "Holy Mother Church has firmly and with absolute constancy maintained and continues to maintain, that the four Gospels [Matthew, Mark, Luke, and John], whose historicity she unhesitatingly affirms, faithfully hand on what Jesus, the Son of God, while He lived among men, really did and taught for their eternal salvation until the day when He was taken up" (*Dogmatic Constitution on Divine Revelation,* #19). After the ascension of Jesus, the apostles went forth preaching the gospel, handing on to others what our Lord had done and taught. Having been instructed by the Lord and then enlightened by the Holy Spirit, they preached with a fuller understanding. Eventually, the "sacred authors" wrote the four gospels. Each author, guided by the Holy Spirit, selected from the events and teachings of our Lord which perhaps they had witnessed or which had been handed on either orally or in written form. Sometimes the authors may have synthesized some of these events or teachings, may have underscored parts, or explained parts with a view to a certain audience. This is why the gospels oftentimes tell the same story, but each will have certain details not included by the others. In a similar way, if each member of a family had to write a family history, each one would tell basically the same story, but each member would also highlight certain details he considered important and would keep in mind who would be reading the family history. Nevertheless, the sacred authors wrote "in such a fashion that they have told us the honest truth about Jesus" (#19). Therefore to suggest, as some misguided individuals do, that the third century Church "wrote" the gospels in some kind of vacuum, almost to "create" Jesus, is without foundation.

So did Sts. Matthew, Mark, Luke and John write the gospels? Is the sacred author also the saint? Remember only St. Matthew and St. John were among the twelve apostles. We must keep in mind that in the ancient world, authorship was designated in several ways: First, the author was clearly the individual who actually wrote the text with his own pen. Second, the individual who dictated the text to a secretary or scribe was still considered the author. Third, the individual was still considered the author if he only provided the ideas or if the text were written in accord with his thought and in his spirit even though a "ghost writer" did the actual composition. In the broadest sense, the individual was even considered the author if the work was written in his tradition; for example, David is given credit for the psalms even though clearly he did not write all of them.

Whether the final version of the gospels we have is the word-for-word work of the saints is hard to say. Nevertheless, tradition does link the saints to their gospels. St. Mark, identified with John Mark of Acts 12:12 and the Mark of I Peter 5:13, is mentioned in a quote contained in a letter from St. Papias (c. 130), Bishop of Hierapolis: "When Mark became Peter's interpreter, he wrote down accurately, although not in order, all that he remembered of what the Lord had said or done." St. Irenaeus (d. 203) and Clement of Alexandria (d. 215) supported this identification. The Gospel of Mark is commonly dated about the year 65-70 in conjunction with the destruction of the Temple of Jerusalem.

St. Matthew is identified with the tax collector called as an apostle (Matthew 9:9-13). Papias again attested to the saint's authorship and indicates that he was the first to compile a collection of Jesus' sayings in the Aramaic language. For this reason, the Gospel of Matthew, at least in a very basic form in Aramaic, is considered the first gospel and placed first in the New Testament, although the Gospel of Mark is probably the first in a completed form. St. Irenaeus (d. 203) and Origin (d. 253) again supported this authorship. Nevertheless, some scholars doubt the saint's direct authorship because we only have the Greek version, not the Aramaic, and no citations are made from the Aramaic version in Church literature. The version of the gospel we have was probably written between 70-80.

St. Luke, the beloved physician and disciple of St. Paul (Colossians 4:14), has consistently been recognized in Christian tradition as the author of the third gospel, beginning with St. Irenaeus, Tertullian (d. 220), and Clement of Alexandria. The gospel was written about 70-80.

St. Irenaeus identified the author of the fourth gospel as St. John the apostle. He does so based on the instruction of his teacher, St. Polycarp (d. 155), who himself was a disciple of St. John. Throughout this gospel, the numerous details indicate the author was an eyewitness. Also scholars generally agree that "the beloved disciple" mentioned in the gospel is St. John. This gospel was written probably about 80-90.

Whether the actual saint wrote word-for word, whether a student did some later editing, or whether a student actually wrote what had been taught by the saint, we must remember the texts "whole and entire" are inspired by the Holy Spirit. Yes, the human authors used their skills and language with a view to an audience; however, they wrote what God wanted written. The *Dogmatic Constitution on Divine Revelation* clearly asserted, "Since, therefore, all that the inspired authors, or sacred writers, affirm should be regarded as affirmed by the Holy Spirit, we must acknowledge that the books of Sacred Scripture firmly, faithfully, and without error, teach that truth, which God, for the sake of our salvation, wished to see confided to the Sacred Scriptures" (#11). So no matter who actually put the finishing touches on the Sacred Scriptures, each is inspired.

Interestingly, with the recent scholarship on the Dead Sea Scrolls, new evidence points to the authorship of the traditional authors. Rev. Reginald Fuller, an Episcopalian and Professor Emeritus at Virginia Theological Seminary, with Dr. Carsten Thiede, have analyzed three papyrus fragments from the 26th chapter of the Gospel of Matthew; the fragments date to the year 40, which would indicate that the author was an eyewitness to our Lord's public ministry. Father Jose O'Callaghan, S.J., studying fragments of the Gospel of Mark and using paleographic means, dated them at 50, again indicating an eyewitness author. Finally, Episcopalian Bishop John Robinson also posited from his research that all four gospels were written between 40 and 65, with John's being possibly the earliest. This new research is not only questioning some of the modern scholarship but also supporting the traditional authorship.

Perhaps some mystery surrounds these texts and the identity of the authors. Nevertheless, we hold them as sacred, as inspired, and as truly the Word of God.

JESUS CHRIST, OUR SAVIOR

DID JESUS ALWAYS KNOW WHO HE WAS?

The answer, as best as we can derive one, rests in the Church's understanding of the Incarnation. We firmly believe that Jesus Christ, second person of the Holy Trinity, consubstantial with the Father, truly divine, entered this world taking on human flesh through Mary, who had conceived by the power of the Holy Spirit. The gospels clearly reveal this belief: The gospel of St. Matthew attests, "When [Jesus'] mother Mary was engaged to Joseph, but before they lived together, she was found with child through the power of the Holy Spirit" (Matthew 1:18) and then quoting Prophet Isaiah, "The virgin shall be with child and give birth to a son, and they shall call him 'Emmanuel' a name which means 'God is with us'" (Matthew 1:23). Archangel Gabriel in the Gospel of St. Luke said to Mary, "The Holy Spirit will come upon you and the power of the Most High will overshadow you; hence, the holy offspring to be born will be called Son of God" (Luke 1:35). Lastly, emphasizing the divine union of Father and Son (the Word) from all eternity, the Gospel of St. John records, "In the beginning was the Word, and the Word was in God's presence, and the Word was God" (John 1:1) and then presents the incarnation, "The Word became flesh and made His dwelling among us, and we have seen His glory: The glory of an only Son coming from the Father, filled with enduring love" (John 1:14). In these few verses, we find the ineffable mystery of Jesus Christ, true God who became also true man.

Because we face a mystery of faith, a mystery in the sense that our limited human reason will never fully comprehend it, various errors, especially in the early centuries of the Church arose concerning Christ. The heresy of Docetism denied the humanity of Christ, while Arianism denied the divinity of Christ. Later heresies also arose: Nestorianism, which asserted that Christ was a divine person joined to a human person; monophysitism ("one nature") which posited that the divine nature of Christ absorbed the human nature of Christ; monothelitism ("one will") posited that the divine will of Christ absorbed the human will. The Church condemned these heresies in its first six ecumenical councils.

The Council of Chalcedon (451), the fourth ecumenical council, provided a very precise declaration: "Following the holy Fathers, we unanimously teach and confess one and the same Son, our Lord Jesus Christ: the same perfect in divinity and perfect in humanity, the same truly God and truly man, composed of rational soul and body; consubstantial with the Father as to His divinity and consubstantial with us as to His humanity; 'like us in all things but sin.' He was begotten from the Father before all ages as to His divinity and in these last days, for us and for our salvation, was born as to His humanity of the Virgin Mary, the Mother of God. We confess that one and the same Christ, Lord, and only-begotten Son, is to be acknowledged in two natures without confusion, change, division, or separation. The distinction between the natures was never abolished by their union, but rather the character proper to each of the two natures was preserved as they came together in one person and one hypostasis."

Given this understanding, Christ, true God and true man, has a genuine human knowledge and a genuine divine knowledge. Again, we must be careful not to confuse, change, divide, or separate them. The human knowledge would have the limits imposed by our Lord living in this time and space at a particular time of history. For this reason, after Jesus is found in the temple at age twelve and returns to Nazareth, the Gospel states, "[He] progressed steadily in wisdom and age and grace before God and men" (Luke 2:52). Moreover, Jesus asks questions of the apostles, genuinely seeking an answer; for example, He asks, "How many loaves have you?" or "Who do people say that I am?" The Catechism explains, "This corresponded to the reality of His voluntary emptying of Himself, taking the form of a slave" (#472).

Nevertheless, our Lord also had a divine knowledge. Jesus had an intimate and immediate knowledge of the Father, as evidenced in the Farewell Discourse of the Gospel of St. John (cf. 14:1ff). He also could read the souls of individuals: "Jesus was immediately aware of their reasoning, though they kept it to themselves and He said to them: "Why do you harbor these thoughts?" (Mark 2:8). St. Maximus the Confessor (d. 662) stated in his *Quaestiones et dubia*, "The human nature of God's Son, not by itself but by its union with the Word, knew and showed forth in itself everything that pertains to God."

The Catechism summarizes the point as follows: "By its union to the divine wisdom in the person of the Word incarnate, Christ enjoyed in His human knowledge the fullness of understanding of the eternal plans He had come to reveal. What He admitted to not knowing in this area, He elsewhere declared Himself not sent to reveal" (#474).

Father Bertrand de Margerie, S.J. in his *The Human Knowledge of Christ* provided further clarification: "Classical Christology teaches, and the Magisterium also, that, long before Easter, Jesus enjoyed in His human intelligence a three-fold knowledge: acquired, infused, and beatific. The first kind came to Him as it does to other men, from the exercise of His senses and His reason; the second was immediately communicated to His human soul by His Divine Person; and the third gave Him immediate knowledge of His Father. This classical Christology is anxious to emphasize not only what Jesus knew as a man, but further and above all that He knew all that was necessary for the perfect carrying out of His mission as Savior and Redeemer."

Immediately, we can still see we are left with a mystery surrounding Christ's divine and human knowledge. Ironically, some theologians still "tip" the scale to one side or the other, usually today emphasizing the human knowledge and its limitations to the extent of de-divinizing Christ. Rather than try to dissect Christ, which we will never be able to do, we must appreciate what His knowledge means for us. Christ entered this world, true God becoming true man. In His divine knowledge, He revealed to us perfectly the ways of God, and lighted a path for us to follow to gain salvation. In His human knowledge, Christ knew fully well the human condition that each of us experiences, our joys yet sorrows, pleasures yet pains, successes yet failures. Therefore, each of us must turn to our Lord, believing in His Word, trusting in His will, and relying on His strength.

WHY IS JESUS CALLED THE "LAMB OF GOD?"

To understand why the title "Lamb of God" is used for Christ, we must first appreciate the celebration of Passover. Recall that at about 1250 BC, the Israelites were slaves of Egypt. Almighty God heard the cry of His people: Exodus 2:24 stated, "He heard their groaning and was mindful of His covenant with Abraham, Isaac, and Jacob." God sent Moses to deliver His people from their bondage. After Moses had performed nine signs, Pharaoh's heart was still unmoved. Finally, God told Moses to have each family take a one-year-old, male, unblemished lamb; slaughter the lamb; and paint the door posts and lintel of every house where they would eat its roasted flesh with unleavened bread and bitter herbs. That night, the Angel of Death would "passover" the homes protected by the blood, but take the lives of the first born children unprotected by the blood of the lamb. Because of that blood sacrifice, Pharaoh let the people go: they went from slavery to freedom, from a land of sin to the Promised land, and from death to new life.

The prophets used this image of the lamb to describe the Messiah. Isaiah prophesied, "Though he was harshly treated, he submitted and opened not his mouth; like a lamb led to the slaughter or a sheep before the shearer, he was silent and opened not his mouth" (Isaiah 53:7). However, the image is twofold: the Messiah would be both the sacrificial lamb to atone for sin and the suffering servant. Interestingly, when speaking to the Ethiopian eunuch who was reading this exact passage from Isaiah, St. Philip told how it referred to Christ and how He fulfilled it (Acts 8:26ff).

Nevertheless in the Gospels, Jesus is specifically identified as "the lamb of God" in the sense of both the sacrificial offering for sin and the suffering servant. As John the Baptizer was proclaiming the coming of the Messiah at the River Jordan, he saw Jesus and proclaimed, "Look! There is the Lamb of God who takes away the sin of the world!" (John 1:29). After foretelling His passion, death, and resurrection for the third time, Jesus asserted, "Anyone among you who aspires to greatness must serve the rest, and whoever wants to rank first among you must serve the needs of all. Such is the case of the Son of Man who has come, not to be served by others, but to serve, to give His own life as a ransom for the many" (Matthew 20:26-28).

The imagery of "Lamb of God" becomes clear in the Passion Narratives of the Gospels. In St. John's gospel, Pilate condemned Jesus to death on the preparation day for Passover at noon (John 18:28, 19:14), the hour when the priests began to slaughter Passover lambs in the temple. After the crucifixion, the Gospel recorded that they did not break any of Jesus' bones in fulfillment of Scripture (John 19:36); this reference corresponds to Exodus 12:46 and Numbers 9:12 where none of the Passover lamb's bones were to be broken. After our Lord's death, the soldier thrust forward his lance, piercing the heart of our Lord; out flowed blood and water (John 19:34), always interpreted as signs of the life-giving sacraments of Holy Eucharist and Baptism.

Ponder the depth of what is happening in the passion narratives! At the crucifixion, Jesus, the innocent and sinless victim, takes all of our sins unto Himself. He though does not just bear our sins and suffer the punishment for us that is due for them; no, Jesus Himself expiates the sins. He as Priest offers Himself on the altar of the cross. Through His blood He washes away sin. However, unlike the Passover lamb that was slaughtered, roasted, and eaten, our Lord rose from the dead, conquering both sin and death. He has truly delivered us from the slavery of sin, shown us the path of salvation, and given us the promise of everlasting life. He has made a new, perfect, and everlasting covenant with His own blood. Therefore St. Peter exhorted, "Realize that you were delivered from the futile way of life your fathers handed on to you, not by any diminishable sum of silver or gold, but by Christ's blood beyond all price, the blood of a spotless, unblemished lamb ... " (I Peter 1:19).

We must not forget that this image evokes victory. The Book of Revelation highlights this notion picturing the Lamb surrounded by angels, the "living creatures," and elders, who cried out, "Worthy is the Lamb that was slain to receive power and riches, wisdom and strength, honor and glory and praise!" (Revelation 5:12). Jesus is the King of kings, and Lord of lords (Revelation 17:14) who will be victorious against the powers of evil and will invite the righteous to the wedding feast of the Lamb (Revelation 19:9), the union of the Church, the new Jerusalem, in heaven with the Lord.

For this reason, the *Agnus Dei* is sung during the fraction, the breaking of the consecrated Host. St. John Chrysostom (d. 407) preached of how the fraction symbolized the Passion of Christ: "What Christ did not suffer on the Cross, He suffers in the sacrifice for thee." The hymn itself invokes Christ and recalls His sacrificial death with overtones of a hymn of victory of the triumphal Lamb. This belief is then emphasized again when the priest holds up the fractured Host and says, "This is the Lamb of God who takes away the sins of the world, happy are those who are called to His supper." (Or, in a literal translation of the Latin, "Happy are those who are called to the supper of the Lamb," better reflecting the imagery of Revelation.)

As we celebrate the mysteries of the Mass, we look to the Lamb who suffered, died, and rose for our salvation. We must gather around the altar of the Lamb, offering to Him our own hearts and pledging to be His servants, so that we may welcome Him and become wedded to Him in the Holy Eucharist.

WHAT DO WE MEAN BY THE *"PASSION"* OF CHRIST? WHAT IS CRUCIFIXION?

The Passion of Christ, from the Latin *patior* meaning "to suffer," refers to those sufferings our Lord endured for our redemption from the agony in the garden until His death on Calvary. The Passion Narratives of the gospels provide the details of our Lord's passion, and at least to some extent, they are corroborated by contemporary Roman historians, Tacitus, Seutonius, and Pliny the Younger. Archeological discoveries combined with modern medical examination provide an accurate picture of what our Lord endured. In an age where the "risen" Jesus appears on the cross and "suffering" and "sacrifice" have become unpopular terms, we must not lose sight of the reality of the passion.

After the Last Supper, Jesus went to the Garden of Gethsemane at the Mount of Olives. Our Lord prayed, "Father, if it is your will, take this cup from me; yet not my will but yours be done" (Luke 22:42). Jesus knew the sacrifice He faced. He prayed so intensely that "His sweat became like drops of blood falling to the ground" (Luke 22:44). Medical science testifies that people may emit a bloody sweat when in a very highly emotional state (a condition called hematidrosis or hemohidrosis), the result of hemorrhaging into the sweat glands. Little wonder the Father sent an angel to strengthen our Lord (Luke 22:43).

Our Lord was then arrested and tried before the Sanhedrin, presided over by the High Priest Caiphas. Responding to their questions, He proclaimed, "Soon you will see the Son of Man seated at the right hand of the Power and coming on the clouds of Heaven" (Matthew 26:64). For this statement, He was condemned to death for blasphemy, and was then spat upon, slapped, and mocked. While the Sanhedrin could condemn our Lord to death, it lacked the authority to execute; only Pontius Pilate, the Roman governor, could order an execution.

The Jewish leaders, therefore, took Jesus to Pilate. Notice how the charge changed: The Jewish leaders told Pilate, "We found this man subverting our nation, opposing the payment of taxes to Caesar, and calling Himself the Messiah, a king" (Luke 23:2). What happened to the charge of blasphemy? Pilate did not care if Jesus wanted to be a messiah, a prophet, or a religious leader; however, if Jesus wanted to be a king, He threatened the authority of Caesar. Any act of rebellion, treason, or subversion had to be punished quickly and severely. So Pilate asked, "Are you the king of the Jews?" (Luke 23:3).

Pilate could not find conclusive evidence to condemn Jesus. Pilate challenged the chief priests, the ruling class, and the people, "I have examined Him in your presence and have no charge against Him arising from your allegations" (Luke 23:14). When offering to release a prisoner, Pilate asked the crowd about Jesus: "What wrong is this man guilty of? I have not discovered anything about Him that calls for the death penalty" (Luke 23:22). Even Pilate's wife pleaded with him not to interfere in the case of "that holy man" (Matthew 27:19).

Pilate then had Jesus scourged (John 19:1). The Romans used a short whip (*flagrum* or *flagellum*) with several single or braided leather thongs. Iron balls or hooks made of bones or shells were placed at various intervals along the thongs and at their ends. The person was stripped of his clothing and whipped along the back, buttocks, and legs. The scourging ripped the skin and tore into the underlying muscles, leaving the flesh in bloody ribbons. The victim verged on circulatory shock, and the blood loss would help determine how long he would survive on the cross. To enhance the scourging of our Lord, the soldiers added other tortures: crowning Him with thorns, dressing Him in a purple cloak, placing a reed in His right hand, spitting upon Him, and mocking Him, "All hail, king of the Jews!" (Matthew 27:27-31).

After the scourging, Pilate again presented Christ to the crowd who chanted, "Crucify Him, crucify Him!" Fearing a revolt, Pilate capitulated and handed over Jesus to be crucified. The Romans had perfected crucifixion, which probably originated in Persia, to produce a slow death with the maximum amount of pain. Crucifixion was reserved for the worst of criminals. This punishment was so awful that Cicero (d. 43 BC) introduced legislation in the Roman Senate exempting Roman citizens from crucifixion; this is why St. Paul was beheaded rather than crucified for being a Christian.

The victim carried his own cross to further weaken him. Since the entire cross weighed around 300 pounds, he usually carried only the horizontal beam (*patibulum*) (75-125 pounds) to the place of execution where the vertical beams (*stipes*) were already in place. A military guard headed by a centurion led the procession. A soldier carried the *titulus* which displayed the victim's name and his crime, and was later attached to the cross (Matthew 27:37). For our Lord, the path from the praetorium to Golgatha was about 1/3 of a mile, and He was so weak Simon of Cyrene was forced to assist Him (Matthew 27:32).

Upon arriving at the place of execution, the law mandated the victim be given a bitter drink of wine mixed with myrrh (gall) as an analgesic (Matthew 27:34). The victim was then stripped of his garments (unless this had already occurred). His hands were stretched over the *patibulum* and either tied, nailed, or both. Archeological evidence reveals the nails were tapered iron spikes approximately 7 inches in length with a square shaft about 3/8 of an inch. The nails were driven through the wrist between the radius and the ulna to support the weight of the person. The *patibulum* was affixed to the stipes, and the feet were then tied or nailed directly to it or to a small footrest (*suppedaneum*).

As the victim hung on the cross, the crowds commonly tormented him with jeers (cf. Matthew 27:39-44). The Romans oftentimes forced the family to watch to add psychological suffering. The soldiers divided the man's garments as part of their reward (Matthew 27:35). The victim would hang on the cross anywhere from three hours to even three days. As he hung in agony, insects would feed on the open wounds or the eyes, ears, and nose, and birds in turn would prey on the victim. With the combined effects caused by the loss of blood, the trauma of scourging, and dehydration, the weight of the body pulled down on the outstretched arms and shoulders impeding respiration. The person died from a slow asphyxiation. Perhaps this is why Jesus spoke only tersely from the cross. If the person tried to lift himself up on his feet to breathe, incredible pain would be felt at the nail wounds and the back wounds from the scourging. To hasten death, the soldiers would break the legs of the victim (John 19:32-33). When he appeared dead, the soldiers insured the fact by piercing the heart with a lance or sword; when Jesus' heart was pierced out flowed blood and water (pericardial fluid) (John 19:34). Commonly, the corpse was left on the cross until decomposed or eaten by birds or animals; however, Roman law allowed the family to take the body for burial with permission of the Roman governor. In our Lord's case, Joseph of Arimathea asked Pilate for Christ's body, and He was then buried (John 19:38).

As we contemplate the Mass, we must remember what our Lord endured for our salvation. He offered Himself as the perfect sacrifice for sin on the altar of the cross and washed away our sins with His blood. We also must recognize our responsibility to repent of sin: The *Catechism* (#589), quoting the old *Roman Catechism*, asserts, "Sinners were the authors and the ministers of all the sufferings that the divine Redeemer endured" and "Since our sins made the Lord Christ suffer the torment of the cross, those who plunge themselves into disorders and crimes crucify the Son of God anew in their hearts (for He is in them) and hold Him up to contempt." Our crucified Lord on the cross is a vivid image of His love for each of us. Meditating on His passion will strengthen us against temptation, move us to frequent confession, and keep us on the path of salvation. By embracing our crucified Lord and His cross we will come to the glory of the resurrection.

WHAT DO WE MEAN WHEN WE SAY IN THE APOSTLES' CREED THAT JESUS DESCENDED INTO HELL?

In approaching this question, we must first examine the word *Hell*. Usually, when we hear the word *Hell*, we immediately think of the place of eternal damnation for those who have rejected God in this life and have committed mortal sins without repentance.

However, in the Old Testament, *Hell* (or *Sheol* in the Hebrew texts or *Hades* in Greek texts) referred to "the place of the dead." (Interestingly, our English word *Hell* is derived from a Germanic name for the place of the dead in Teutonic mythology.) This Hell was for both the good and the bad, the just and the unjust. It was the nether world, a region of darkness. In the later writings of the Old Testament, a clear distinction was made between where the good resided in Hell versus where the bad were, the two being separated by an impassable abyss. The section for the unjust was named Gehenna, where the souls would suffer eternal torment by fire.

Gehenna was the name of the valley at the boundary between the territories of Judah and Benjamin. Here was the shrine to the pagan god Molech, to whom human sacrifice was offered. The prophet Jeremiah cursed the place, denouncing it as a "Valley of Slaughter" stinking of death, decay, and corruption. (Cf. Jeremiah 19:6ff.)

Our Lord attested to this "land of the dead" understanding of Hell: Recall the parable of Lazarus, the poor beggar, who sat at the gate of the rich man, traditionally called Dives (cf. Luke 16:19ff). Lazarus dies and is taken to the "land of the dead" (the original Greek text uses the word *Hades*) and is comforted at the bosom of Abraham. Dives also dies and goes to the "land of the dead"; however, he finds eternal torment, being tortured in flames. Dives sees Lazarus and cries out to Abraham for relief. However, Abraham replies, "My child, remember that you were well off in your lifetime, while Lazarus was in misery. Now he has found consolation here, but you have found torment. And that is not all. Between you and us there is fixed a great abyss, so that those who might wish to cross from here to you cannot do so, nor can anyone cross from your side to us."

Our Lord also emphasized the "eternal punishment" of Hell: When Jesus spoke of the last judgment and separating the righteous from the evil, He said to the latter, "Out of my sight you condemned, into that everlasting fire prepared for the devil and his angels" (cf. Matthew 25:31ff). Jesus also spoke of "risking the fires of Gehenna" for serious sins, like anger and hatred (Matthew 5:21ff), and adultery and impurity (Matthew 5:27ff).

Given this understanding, we believe that the sin of Adam and Eve had closed the Gates of Heaven. The holy souls awaited the Redeemer in the land of the dead, or Hell. Our Lord offered the perfect sacrifice for all sin by dying on the cross, the redemptive act that touches all people of every time, past, present, and future. He was then buried. During that time, He descended among the dead: His soul, separated from His body, joined the holy souls awaiting the Savior in the land of the dead. Remember St. Paul wrote, "'He ascended' what does this mean but that He had first descended into the lower regions of the earth? He who descended is the very one who ascended high above the heavens, that He might fill all men with His gifts" (Ephesians 4:9-10). His descent among the dead brought to completion the proclamation of the Gospel and liberated those holy souls who had long awaited their Redeemer. The Gates of Heaven were now open, and these holy souls entered everlasting happiness enjoying the beatific vision. Please note: Jesus did not deliver those souls damned to eternal punishment in Hell nor did He destroy Hell as such. The *Catechism* highlights the importance of this event: "This is the last phase of Jesus' messianic mission, a phase which is condensed in time but vast in its real significance: the spread of Christ's redemptive work to all men of all times and all places, for all who are saved have been made sharers in the redemption" (#634).

An "Ancient Homily" of the early Church for Holy Saturday captured this event: "The whole earth keeps silence because the King is asleep. The earth trembled and is still because God has fallen asleep in the flesh and He has raised up all who have slept ever since the world began ... . He has gone to search for Adam, our first father, as for a lost sheep. Greatly desiring to visit those who live in darkness and in the shadow of death, He has gone to free from sorrow Adam in his bonds and Eve, captive with him – He who is both their God and the Son of Eve ... . 'I am your God, who for your sake have become your Son ... . I order you, O sleeper, to awake. I did not create you to be held a prisoner in Hell. Rise from the dead, for I am the life of the dead.'"

WHAT IS THE DEVOTION TO THE SACRED HEART OF JESUS?

The *Catechism*, quoting Pope Pius XII's beautiful encyclical on the devotion to the Sacred Heart of Jesus, *Haurietis Aquas* (1956), states, "[Jesus] has loved us all with a human heart. For this reason, the Sacred Heart of Jesus, pierced by our sins and for our salvation, 'is quite rightly considered the chief sign and symbol of that ... love with which the divine Redeemer continually loves the eternal Father and all human beings' without exception" (#478).

To appreciate this rich symbolism of the heart, we must remember in Judaism that the word *heart* represented the core of the person. While recognized as the principle life organ, the heart was also considered the center of all spiritual activity. Here was the seat of all emotion, especially love. As the psalms express, God speaks to a person in his heart and there probes him. This notion of the heart is clear when we read the words of Deuteronomy 6:5-6: "Therefore, you shall love the Lord, your God, with all your heart, and with all your soul, and with all your strength. Take to heart these words which I enjoin on you today."

The heart has even greater depth when contemplated in light of the incarnation. We believe that Jesus Christ, second person of the Holy Trinity and consubstantial with the Father, entered this world taking on our human flesh, true God became also true man. While Jesus' heart obviously served a physiological function, spiritually His Sacred Heart also represents love: the divine love our Lord shares with the Father and Holy Spirit in the Trinity; the perfect, divine love which God has for us; and the genuine human love Christ felt in His human nature. One of the most beautiful passages of the Gospels is our Lord saying, "Come to me, all you who are weary and find life burdensome, and I will refresh you. Take my yoke upon your shoulders and learn from me, for I am gentle and humble of heart. Your souls will find rest, for my yoke is easy and my burden light" (Matthew 11:28-30). Therefore, while meditating on the Sacred Heart of Jesus, we are called to share in the love of the Lord and strive to express our own genuine love for God, ourselves, and our neighbors.

Throughout the gospel, we see the outpouring of Jesus' love from His heart, whether in the miracle stories, the reconciliation of sinners, or the compassion for the grieving. Even on the cross, our Lord poured out His love for us: there the soldier's lance pierced His side and out flowed blood and water (John 19:34). St. Bonaventure said the Church was born from the wounded side of the Lord with the blood and water representing the Sacraments of the Holy Eucharist and Baptism.

The early Church Fathers clearly cherished this meaning of the Sacred Heart of our Lord. St. Justin Martyr (d. 165), in his *Dialogue with the Jew Trypho* said, "We Christians are the true Israel which springs from Christ, for we are carved out of His heart as from a rock." Likewise, St. Irenaeus of Lyons (d. 202) said, "The Church is the fountain of the living water that flows to us from the Heart of Christ" (*Adversus Haereses*). St. Paulinus of Nola (d. 431) in his *Letters* (#21) added, "John, who rested blissfully on the breast of our Lord, was inebriated with the Holy Spirit, from the Heart of all creating Wisdom he quaffed an understanding which transcends that of any creature." Although these are just a few brief examples from the times of the early Church, we find a profound respect for the Sacred Heart of our Lord as a font of His love which gave birth to the Church and continues to nourish its members.

The devotion continued to grow during the Middles Ages, and in 1353 Pope Innocent VI instituted a Mass honoring the mystery of the Sacred Heart. During the age of the Protestant movement, devotion to the Sacred Heart was practiced in hope of restoring peace to a world shattered by political and religious persecution.

Shortly thereafter, the devotion escalated due to the fervor surrounding the apparitions of our Lord to St. Margaret Mary Alacoque (1647-90). For example, on December 27, 1673, our Lord revealed, "My Divine Heart is so passionately inflamed with love ... that, not being able any longer to contain within Itself the flames of Its ardent charity, It must let them spread abroad through your means, and manifest Itself to man, that they may be enriched with Its precious treasures which I unfold to you, and which contain the sanctifying and salutary graces that are necessary to hold them back from the abyss of ruin." The four apparitions provided the catalyst for the promotion of the devotion to the Sacred Heart: a feast day in honor of the Sacred Heart, and the offering of our Lord's saving grace and friendship if the individual attended Mass and received Holy Communion on nine consecutive first Fridays of the month.

In 1899, Pope Leo XIII consecrated the world to the Sacred Heart of Jesus. Since then, his successors have exhorted the faithful to turn to the Sacred Heart and make acts of personal consecration. They have also begged the faithful to offer prayers and penances to the Sacred Heart in reparation for the many sins of the world. Considering our present day and age, the temptations and sins of this world, the growing apathy and secularism, we too should turn again in loving devotion to the Sacred Heart of Jesus and ask Him to pour forth His grace. We must strive to make our hearts like His own, for He said, "Blessed are the pure of heart, for they shall see God" (Matthew 5:8). May we remember the words of the Preface of the Mass in honor of the Sacred Heart of Jesus: "Lifted high on the Cross, Christ gave His life for us, so much did He love us. From His wounded side flowed blood and water, the fountain of sacramental life in the Church. To His open heart the Savior invites all men, to draw water in joy from the springs of salvation."

THE CHURCH

DID JESUS ESTABLISH THE PAPACY AND WAS ST. PETER THE FIRST POPE?

In Catholic tradition, the foundation for the office of the Pope is rooted primarily in Matthew 16:13-20. Here Jesus asked the question, "Who do people say that the Son of Man is?" The apostles responded, "Some say John the Baptizer, others Elijah, still others Jeremiah or one of the prophets." Our Lord then turned to them and point-blank asked them, "And you, who do you say that I am?"

St. Peter, still officially known as Simon, replied, "You are the Messiah, the Son of the living God." Our Lord recognized that this answer was grace-motivated: "No mere man has revealed this to you, but my heavenly Father."

Because of this response, our Lord first said to St. Peter, "You are 'Rock,' and on this rock I will build my church and the Gates of Hell shall not prevail against it." The name change itself from "Simon" to "Peter" indicates the apostle being called to a special role of leadership. Recall how Abram's name was changed to Abraham, or Jacob's to Israel, or Saul's to Paul when each of them was called to assume a special role of leadership among God's people.

The word *rock* also has special significance. On one hand, to be called "rock" was a Semitic expression designating the solid foundation upon which a community would be built. For instance, Abraham was considered "rock" because he was the father of the Jewish people (and we too refer to him in the First Eucharistic Prayer of the Mass as "our father in faith") and the one with whom the covenant was first made.

On the other hand, no one except God was called specifically "rock," nor was it ever used as a proper name except for God. To give the name "rock" to St. Peter indicates that our Lord entrusted to him a special authority. Some anti-papal parties try to play linguistic games with the original Greek gospel text where the masculine gender word *petros*, meaning a small, moveable rock, refers to St. Peter while the feminine gender word *petra*, meaning a massive, immoveable rock, refers to the foundation of the Church. However, in the Aramaic language, which is what Jesus spoke and which is the original language of St. Matthew's gospel, the word *kephas*, meaning rock, would be used in both places without gender distinction or difference in meaning. The gender problem arises when translating from Aramaic to Greek and using the proper form to modify the masculine word *Peter* or feminine word *Church*.

The "Gates of Hell" is also an interesting Semitic expression. The heaviest forces were positioned at the gates, so this expression captures the great war-making power of a nation. Here this expression refers to the powers opposed to what our Lord is establishing, the Church. (A similar expression is used in reference to our Lord in Acts 2:24: "God freed Him from the bitter pangs of Hell, however, and raised Him up again, for it was impossible that death should keep its hold on Him.") Jesus associated St. Peter and his office so closely with Himself that he became a visible force for protecting the Church and keeping back the power of Hell.

Second, Jesus says, "I will entrust to you the keys of the kingdom of heaven." In the Old Testament, the "number two" person in the Kingdom literally held the keys. In Isaiah 22:19-22 we find a reference to Eliakim, the master of the palace of King Hezekiah (II Kings 18:17ff) and keeper of the keys. As a sign of his position, the one who held the keys represented the king, acted with his authority, and had to act in accord with the king's mind. Therefore, St. Peter and each of his successors represent our Lord on this earth as His Vicar and lead the faithful flock of the Church to the Kingdom of Heaven.

Finally, Jesus says, "Whatever you declare bound on earth shall be bound in heaven; whatever you declare loosed on earth shall be loosed in heaven." This is rabbinic terminology. A rabbi could bind, declaring an act forbidden or excommunicating a person for serious sin; or, a rabbi could loose, declaring an act permissible or reconciling an excommunicated sinner to the community. Here Christ entrusted a special authority to St. Peter to preserve, interpret, and teach His truth.

In all, this understanding of Matthew 16 was unchallenged until the Protestant leaders wanted to legitimize their rejection of papal authority and the office of the Pope. Even the Orthodox Churches recognize the Pope as the successor of St. Peter; however, they do not honor his binding jurisdiction over the whole Church but only grant him a position of "first among equals."

St. Peter's role in the New Testament further substantiates the Catholic belief concerning the papacy and what Jesus said in Matthew 16. St. Peter held a preeminent position among the apostles. He is always listed first (Matthew 10:1-4; Mark 3:16-19; Luke 6:14-16; Acts 1:13) and sometimes the only one mentioned (Luke 9:32). He speaks for the apostles (Matthew 18:21; Mark 8:28; Luke 12:41; John 6:69). When our Lord selects a group of three for some special event, such as the Transfiguration, St. Peter is in the first position. Our Lord chose St. Peter's boat in which to teach. At Pentecost, St. Peter preached to the crowds and told of the mission of the Church (Acts 2:14-40). He performed the first miraculous healing (Acts 3:6-7). St. Peter also received the revelation that Gentiles were to be baptized (Acts 10:9-48) and sided with St. Paul against the need for circumcision (Acts 15). At the end of his life, St. Peter was crucified, but in his humility asked to be crucified upside down.

As Catholics, we believe that the authority given to St. Peter did not end with his life, but was handed on to his successors. The earliest writings attest to this belief. St. Irenaeus (d. 202) in his *Adversus haereses* described how the Church at Rome was founded by St. Peter and St. Paul and traced the handing on of the office of St. Peter through Linus, Cletus (also called Anacletus), and so on through twelve successors to his own present day, Pope Eleutherius. Tertullian (d. 250) in *De praescriptione haereticorum* asserted the same point, as did Origen (d. 254) in his *Commentaries on John*, St. Cyprian of Carthage (d. 258) in his *The Unity of the Catholic Church*, and many others.

Granted, the expression of papal authority becomes magnified after the legalization of Christianity, and especially after the Fall of the Roman Empire and the ensuing political chaos. Nevertheless, our Church boasts of an unbroken line of legitimate successors of St. Peter who stand in the stead of Christ. We must always remember that one of the official titles of the Pope, first taken by Pope St. Gregory I, the Great (d. 604), is "Servant of the Servants of God." As we think of this answer, may we be mindful of our Holy Father, Pope John Paul II, and pray for his intentions.

WHAT IS INFALLIBILITY?

Before delving into the topic of infallibility, we must first be certain as to how we understand truth. As Catholics, we believe in an absolute, immutable truth rooted in God. This truth has been perfectly revealed in Christ, for He is the Word who became flesh (John 1:14), and "the way, and the truth, and the life" (John 14:6). Jesus also promised the apostles that He would send the Holy Spirit, whom He identified as the Spirit of Truth, who would instruct them in everything and remind them of all that He had revealed (cf. John 14:17, 26). Pope John Paul II beautifully underscored this notion of truth in the opening of his encyclical *The Splendor of Truth*: "The Splendor of Truth shines forth in the works of the Creator and, in a special way, in man, created in the image and likeness of God. Truth enlightens man's intelligence and shapes his freedom, leading him to know and love the Lord."

Our Lord entrusted His teaching office to the apostles, in particular to St. Peter, the first Pope, and their successors. Vatican II in The *Dogmatic Constitution on Divine Revelation* asserted, "The task of authentically interpreting the Word of God, whether in its written form or in that of Tradition, has been entrusted only to those charged with the Church's living Magisterium, whose authority is exercised in the name of Jesus Christ" (#10). The purpose of the Magisterium, the teaching authority of the Church, is thereby to preserve the deposit of faith handed onto us from Christ Himself and to apply its principles of truth to our modern day situation so that each Catholic can live an authentically Christian life. The *Catechism* highlighted that "it is the Magisterium's task to preserve God's people from deviations and defections and to guarantee them the objective possibility of professing the true faith without error" (#890).

To fulfill this task of teaching the faith without error, Christ granted to the Church the charism of infallibility in faith and morals: "In order to preserve the Church in the purity of the faith handed on by the apostles, Christ who is the Truth willed to confer on her a share in His own infallibility" (*Catechism*, #889). In essence, the charism of infallibility is the Magisterium's ability to know the truth of God and to teach without error.

As explained in Vatican II's *Dogmatic Constitution on the Church* (#25), this charism of infallibility is exercised in two ways: First, the college of bishops united with the Holy Father authoritatively teach on matters of faith and morals and can proclaim an infallible teaching when they agree that a particular teaching is to be held definitively and absolutely. The exercise of the charism of infallibility ordinarily occurs during an ecumenical council (a formal meeting of all of the bishops with the Holy Father). For instance, the Ecumenical Councils of Nicea I (325) and Constantinople I (381) promulgated what we call today the Nicene Creed, an infallible testament of our faith; the articles of the creed are true and certain, and to deny any or part of them is heresy. These decisions of the councils on matters of faith and morals "must be adhered to with the loyal and obedient assent of faith" (*Dogmatic Constitution on the Church*, #25).

Second, the Pope, as successor of St. Peter'the one declared as rock and given the keys of the Kingdom of Heaven along with the authority of binding and loosing (Matthew 16:13ff), by virtue of his office as supreme pastor and teacher of the faithful, enjoys the charism of infallibility. Note that the emphasis is on the office of the Pope, not on his human person. When the Pope teaches infallibly, he is said to speak *ex cathedra* ("from the chair"), meaning by the authority given to the office of Pope by our Lord.

When the Pope renders an infallible teaching, he clearly states that he is teaching as the successor of St. Peter on an issue of faith and morals and that this teaching is binding for the universal church, irreformable (meaning it will not change) and infallible (meaning it is without error). In the recent history of our Church, the Holy Father by himself has exercised the charism of infallibility: first when Pope Pius IX pronounced the dogma of the Immaculate Conception (1854) and second when Pope Pius XII pronounced the dogma of the Assumption (1950). Interestingly, in both cases, these beliefs were long held by the Church, but after seeing the crisis of faith in the world and after polling the bishops, the Holy Father in both instances decided to put forth a truth to bolster the faith of the people.

Nevertheless, even when the Pope does not speak *ex cathedra*, Vatican II reminded us that, "loyal submission of the will and intellect must be given, ... that his supreme teaching authority be acknowledged with respect, and sincere assent be given to decisions made by him ... " (*Dogmatic Constitution on the Church*, #25). Therefore, when the Pope issues a teaching on a moral issue, the Church respects it as a true teaching guided by the Holy Spirit even though it is not technically declared "infallible" and may later undergo further clarification. For instance, our Church has moral teachings on euthanasia and bioethics which provide true guidance to the faithful, but probably will be further clarified, not changed, as the parameters of these issues evolve.

In a world where so many people think truth fluctuates or is simply a matter of personal whim –"Whatever I decide, goes"– we should rejoice that we have truth and a Magisterium that courageously teaches the truth. The charism of infallibility is a tremendous gift from our Lord to the Church. In conforming to this truth, each of us finds genuine freedom in living the life God has called us to live. St. Paul captured this notion well in his first letter to St. Timothy: "I am writing you about these matters so that ... you will know what kind of conduct befits a member of God's household, the Church of the living God, the pillar and bulwark of truth" (3:14-15).

WHAT IS A CARDINAL?

The evolution of the position of cardinal and its duties is reflected in its two possible word roots: On the one hand, scholars think the title is derived from the Latin word *cardo*, meaning hinge, thereby referring to an individual entrusted with an important administrative ecclesiastical office. On the other hand, some scholars suggest that the title is derived from the Latin *incardinare*, a term found first in the *Letters* of Pope St. Gregory I (d. 604), which refers to the incardination of those clerics who serve a diocese other than the one for which they were actually ordained. Both meanings come to play in the history we have about this office.

The title of cardinal emerges following the barbarian invasions, about the year 500. During these years of turmoil, bishops were transferred to serve another diocese if their own dioceses had been overrun and the Church suppressed. In this situation, these bishops were incardinated into the new diocese and would remain there as "cardinal bishops" unless their own diocese revived.

About the 10th century in Rome, the senior clergy attached to the basilicas and the 27 "title" Churches of Rome –the original parishes– were called "cardinals" to indicate a certain prestige of their position. To some extent, this privilege extended to priests serving at several other major cathedral churches, such as Cologne, Trier, Magdeburg, and Santiago de Compostela. Nevertheless, in Rome, these cardinals became a privileged body and were more involved in the liturgical and administrative duties of the Church.

By the time of Pope Leo IX (d. 1054), the title "cardinal" was reserved to the Pope's principal counselors and assistants living in Rome. In 1059, Pope Nicholas II made them the papal electors as well. In 1084, not only were bishops and priests granted the title "cardinal" but also deacons; for instance, during the pontificate of Pope Urban II, 7 cardinal deacons existed. Also at this time, the title of cardinal and right to elect the Pope was conferred on bishops living outside of the vicinity of Rome and presiding over their own dioceses. Later, Pope Alexander III (d. 1181) reserved the selection of cardinals exclusively to the Pope in 1179.

Over the years, the number of cardinals has varied. Pope Sixtus V (d. 1590) set the number of cardinals at 70 in 1586, after the number of the 70 Elders of the Old Testament. Pope John XXIII (d. 1963) revoked this rule and increased the number of cardinals. In his apostolic letter *Ingravescentem Aetatem* (1970), Pope Paul VI placed certain age restrictions on cardinals: At age 75, a cardinal must submit his resignation as head of an administrative post in the Curia, and at age 80, he loses his right to vote for the next successor of St. Peter. With the induction of the new cardinals (and after the sudden death of two), the College now has 163 members, 120 of whom are under the age of 80.

As an aside, the Holy Father may name cardinals *in pectore*, meaning he reserved the man's name in his heart. The purpose of keeping a cardinal's identity secret is to protect him from harm because of the political or other circumstances in which he lives. Such a cardinal is not bound by the duties of cardinals and does not possess any of their rights or privileges; however, the situation reverses once the Holy Father reveals his name and his seniority is dated from his naming *in pectore*.

We must remember that the Pope selects those men as cardinals who are "especially outstanding for their doctrine, morals, piety, and prudence in actions" (*Code of Canon Law*, Canon 351). Usually archbishops are appointed as cardinals since they head very large dioceses, i.e. archdioceses. (If one is not a bishop, he must receive episcopal consecration.) Especially since the pontificate of Pope Paul VI, the selection of cardinals has better reflected the whole Church throughout the world.

Together the cardinals form a special "college" which has the responsibility to provide for the election of the Pope. As the Holy Father stated in his address to the new cardinals, "[They] constitute the senate of the Church, the first collaborators of the Pope in his universal pastoral service." The head of the College of Cardinals is the Dean who is elected by the other cardinals and approved by the

Pope. The cardinals assist the Pope collegially when they gather in a consistory at his invitation to address questions of major importance. Individual cardinals also preside over an office of the Curia or serve on a papal commission. For example, Cardinal Ratzinger is Prefect of the Sacred Congregation for the Doctrine of the Faith.

Officially, the cardinals still hold ranks which reflect the origin of the office: episcopal (bishop), presbyteral (priest), and diaconal (deacon). Cardinal bishops include the six titular bishops of the suburban sees of Rome (Ostia, Palestrina, Porto-Santa Rufina, Albano, Velletri-Segni, and Frascati) and the Eastern Rite Patriarchs. Three of the Cardinal bishops are active full-time in Curia. Cardinal priests, formerly serving in the original 27 parish churches in Rome, are bishops whose dioceses are outside of Rome. Cardinal deacons, who were formerly chosen according to regional divisions of Rome, are titular bishops assigned to full-time service in the Curia. Therefore, each of the cardinals is assigned a titular Church in Rome as a symbol of being members of the clergy of Rome; moreover, each cardinal receives a ring, which as the Holy Father explained, is "a sign of the special spousal bond which now unites them to the Church of Rome, which presides in charity."

While the position of cardinal is clearly a great honor, it is also a grave responsibility. In Spring 1998, the Holy Father exhorted the new cardinals and the whole college: "May the Paraclete [Holy Spirit] be able to dwell fully in each one of you, fill you with divine consolation, and thus make you, in turn, consolers of all those who are afflicted, especially the members of the Church who are most tried, of the communities which suffer the greatest tribulations because of the Gospel. ... You are called to help the Pope to lead Peter's boat toward this historic goal. I am counting on your support and your enlightened and expert counsel to guide the Church in the last phase of preparation for the Holy Year. Looking along with you beyond the threshold of 2000, I invoke from the Lord an abundance of gifts of the divine Spirit for the entire Church, so that the 'springtime' of Vatican Council II may find its 'summer,' that is, its mature development, in the new millennium.

The mission to which God call us today requires attentive and constant discernment. For this reason, I exhort you to be more and more men of God, who listen deeply to His Word, capable of reflecting His light in the midst of the Christian people and among all men of goodwill."

One last minor point concerning why the cardinals wear red. The Holy Father stated at the last investiture: "Red is a sign of the dignity of the office of a Cardinal, signifying that you are ready to act with fortitude, even to the point of spilling your blood for the increase of the Christian faith."

WHAT DOES CHURCH MEAN?

The English word *church* (or the Scottish *kirk* or the German *kirche*) is derived from the late Greek *kyriakon* which meant "the Lord's house." This word is in turn derived from an earlier version of the Greek used for Sacred Scripture, where we find the word *ekklesia*. When the Old Testament was translated into Greek to produce the Septuagint version, the word *ekklesia* was used for the Hebrew word *kahal*, meaning the religious assembly of God. *Kahal* also distinguished God's covenant people from all others.

In the New Testament, we also find the usage of *ekklesia* for church for the same reason. Our Lord called the apostles to follow Him, and with other disciples formed a distinct group of followers. They were personally committed to Him even at the cost of separation from family and friends. Moreover, they were commissioned to make disciples of all the nations and to carry on the mission of Jesus.

More clarity is given to the idea of church in Acts of the Apostles and the epistles. Here we see *ekklesia* used to describe both local churches and the Church as a whole, but the local church is always seen as inherently part of the overall Church. Membership in the church involves baptism and a clear acceptance of Jesus as the Lord and Savior who suffered, died, and rose from the dead. With the admission of the Gentiles and the Fall of the Temple in AD 70, the Church has a clear distinction from Judaism. This Church has a hierarchical organization with bishops, presbyters, and deacons. Through the Church, the divine will of the Lord is revealed; for example, the Church guided by the Holy Spirit has preserved the writings of the Old Testament and recorded the revelation of the New Testament, and then set the canon of Sacred Scripture to produce the Bible. Not forgetting the communal dimension, the Church has had a genuine concern for the needs of each member, and each member plays a role in continuing the mission of Christ. Interestingly, in the year 100, St. Ignatius of Antioch in his *Letter to the Smyrnaeans* used the term Catholic (meaning "universal") to describe the unity of this church.

The *Dogmatic Constitution on the Church* of the Second Vatican Council stated, "The Church in Christ is in the nature of sacrament'a sign and instrument, that is of communion with God and of unity among all people ...'" (#1). Using images found in Sacred Scripture, the Council described the Church in many ways: The Church is a sheepfold or flock, entrusted to the care of human shepherds by the Good Shepherd, Jesus, who gave His life for His sheep (John 10:1ff). Just as Christ is the vine and the faithful the branches who receive life from Him, through the Church the life of Christ flows to us (John 15:1ff). St. Paul described the Church as the body of Christ: just as a body has many organs with various functions under the direction of the "head," so the Church has many members each sharing in the mission of Christ in various ways and ministries all under the "head," Christ (I Corinthians 12:1ff). Finally, St. Paul speaks of the Church as the Bride of Christ: Through our baptism into the Church, we, as individuals and as a community of believers, share in that covenant of love and life sealed by the blood of Christ.

In all, the beautiful significance of the word church can be best understood by reflecting on the "Four Marks of the Church": First, the Church is one, in that all members are united in their belief, worship, sacraments, tradition, and leadership. For instance, a person can travel anywhere in the world and find the same exact Mass, same beliefs preached, and same leadership.

Second, the Church is holy because our Lord established it and continues to share His divine life, His grace, with its members. In turn, the Church continues the mission of Christ with each member striving to live a Christ-like life in accord with His teachings and with the help of His grace.

Third, the Church is Catholic (meaning "universal") because it is destined to last for all time, and all the faithful on earth are united with the faithful in Heaven and the souls in Purgatory.

Finally, the Church is apostolic because Christ founded it upon the apostles, giving the authority to St. Peter, the first Pope, and the other apostles, the first bishops. This authority has been handed on to their successors as in the case of the choosing of St. Matthias to replace Judas. Because of these distinctive marks, Vatican II affirmed, "This Church, constituted and organized as a society in the present world, subsists in the Catholic Church, which is governed by the successor of Peter and by the bishops in communion with him" (#8). Therefore, even though a visitor might not be a regular part of the community of that particular parish, in a sense he is because of his membership in the one, holy, Catholic, and apostolic Church. Therefore, the word *church* evokes a beautiful image intrinsically linked to the mystery of salvation.

WHY BE A CATHOLIC?

Each Catholic should be able to provide a solid, well-thought answer in response to the question, "Why are you a Catholic?" Granted, for each individual, the answer is very personal and may be somewhat different from another person's answers. Hopefully, none of us who are adults and confirmed would simply state, "Well, my parents baptized me Catholic," or "I was raised Catholic," or "My family has always been Catholic." No, for each of us, the answer must be personal, heart-felt, and full of conviction. Therefore, I will give you my answer to this question.

First, I would say I am a Catholic because the Roman Catholic Church is the Church that Jesus Christ founded. Any good historian worth his salt must admit that the first Christian Church existing since the time of Christ is the Roman Catholic Church. The first major rupture in Christianity did not occur until 1054 when the Patriarch of Constantinople had a dispute with the Pope over who had more authority; the Patriarch excommunicated the Pope, who returned the favor, and the "Orthodox" Churches were born. Then in 1517, Martin Luther sparked the Protestant movement, and he was followed by Calvin, Zwingli, and Henry VIII. Since then, Protestantism has splintered into many other Christian Churches.

Nevertheless, the one Church that Christ founded is the Roman Catholic Church. This statement does not mean that goodness does not exist in other Christian Churches. It does not mean other Christians cannot go to heaven. However, it does mean that there is something special about the Catholic Church. Vatican Council II in the *Dogmatic Constitution on the Church* stated that the fullness of the means of salvation subsists within the Catholic Church because it is the Church Christ founded (#8).

The second reason I am a Catholic is because of apostolic succession. Jesus entrusted His authority to His apostles. He gave a special authority to Peter, whom He called "rock" and to whom He entrusted the keys of the Kingdom of Heaven. Since the time of the apostles, this authority has been handed down through the Sacrament of Holy Orders from bishop to bishop, and then extended to priests and deacons. If possible, each bishop could trace his authority as a bishop back to the apostles. This handing-on of apostolic succession becomes clear at ordinations to priesthood. In that sacred ordination rite, the bishop imposes his hands on the heads of the men to be ordained. In the quiet of the moment, the apostolic succession is handed on. In the vision of faith, one can see not just the bishop, but St. Peter and St. Paul, even Jesus Himself conferring the Holy Orders. No bishop, priest, or deacon in our Church is self-ordained or self-proclaimed; the authority comes from Jesus Himself and is guarded by the Church.

The third reason I am a Catholic is because we believe in truth, an absolute, God-given truth. Christ identified Himself as "the way, and the truth, and the life" (John 14:6). He gave us the Holy Spirit, whom He called the Spirit of truth (John 14:17) who would instruct us in everything and remind us of all that He taught (John 14:26). The truth of Christ has been preserved in Sacred Scripture, the Bible. Vatican Council II in the *Dogmatic Constitution on Divine Revelation* stated that "that which has been asserted by the human authors of Sacred Scripture must be said to have been asserted by the Holy Spirit so that the words of Sacred Scripture teach firmly, faithfully, and without error that truth Christ wanted put into Sacred Scripture for our salvation" (#11). This truth is guarded and applied to a particular time and culture by the Magisterium, the teaching authority of the Church. As we face issues like bioethics or euthanasia, issues that the Bible never specifically addressed, how fortunate we are to have a Church that says, "This way of life is right or this way is wrong in accordance with the truth of Christ." No wonder the Catholic Church makes the headlines of *The Washington Post* or *New York Times*! We are the only Church to take a stand and say, "This teaching is true in accord with the mind of Christ."

Another reason I am a Catholic is because of our sacraments. We believe in seven sacraments which Jesus gave to the Church.

Each sacrament captures an important element of Christ's life, and by the power of the Holy Spirit gives us a share in the divine life of God. For example, just think what a precious gift we have to receive the Holy Eucharist, the Body and Blood of our Lord, or to know that our sins truly are forgiven and our soul is healed each time we receive absolution in the Sacrament of Penance.

Finally, I am a Catholic because of the people who make up the Church. I think back to so many saints: St. Peter and St. Paul kept the gospel alive in the earliest times. During the Roman persecution, the early martyrs of the Church, like St. Anastasia, St. Lucy, St. Justin, or St. Ignatius (who in the year 100 called the Church "Catholic"), defended the faith and suffered torturous deaths for it. In the Dark Ages when many things were truly "dark," there were the great lights of St. Francis, St. Dominic, and St. Catherine of Sienna. During the Protestant movement when heresy was ripping the Church apart, the Church was defended by St. Robert Bellarmine or St. Ignatius Loyola, genuine reformers. I think of living saints like Pope John Paul II, who just day in and day out do God's holy work. There are so many saints that inspire each of us to be good members of the Church.

But there are others too. At Mass, look around your Church. See married couples who strive to live the sacrament of marriage in an age of self-indulgence and infidelity. See the parents who want to hand on their faith to their children. See the young people who struggle to live the faith despite a world of temptations. See the elderly who have remained faithful despite changes in the world and the Church. See the priests and religious who have dedicated their lives to the service of the Lord and His Church. So many good people make up our Church.

Yes, none of us is perfect. We sin. That is why one of the most beautiful prayers in the Mass occurs before the sign of peace; we pray, "Lord, look not on our sins, but on the faith of your Church." Yes, despite human frailty, the Church, as that institution founded by Christ continues to carry on His mission in this world.

In a nutshell, these are the reasons I am a Catholic and a member of the Roman Catholic Church. These reasons are not flippant. Rather, they reflect much careful thought and struggle. I hope that each Catholic can proudly provide a solid, clear answer to the question, "Why are you a Catholic?"

WHAT IS EXCOMMUNICATION?

Excommunication is the Church's most severe penalty imposed for particularly grave sins. Through baptism, a person is incorporated into the body of the Church through which there is a "communication" of spiritual goods. By committing a particularly grave sin and engaging in activities which cause grave scandal and fracture the body of the Church, that communication ceases, and the person is deprived of receiving the sacraments and other privileges.

The practice of excommunication arose in the early Church. In his First Letter to the Corinthians, St. Paul castigated that community for tolerating the practice of incest, "a man living with his father's wife" (I Corinthians 5:1). He admonished the Corinthians for not removing the offender from their midst. St. Paul said, "I hand him over to Satan for the destruction of his flesh, so that his spirit may be saved on the day of the Lord" (5:5). St. Paul further warned against associating with anyone who bears the title "brother" (indicating being a believer and part of the Church) but who is immoral, covetous, an idolater, an abusive person, a drunkard, or a thief. He then closed the passage by quoting from the Torah, "Expel the wicked man from your midst" (Deuteronomy 6:13).

Note, however, that St. Paul also expressed hope. He imposed the sanction upon the offender "so that his spirit may be saved on the day of the Lord," indicating a hope for repentance, conversion, and a readmittance into the community. (This motive is affirmed also in II Thessalonians 3:15 and II Corinthians 2:5-11.) Nevertheless, until such time, the obstinate sinner had to be removed to prevent both the infection of the rest of the believers and the appearance of condoning such a sinful action.

Later, excommunication became clearly associated with the Sacrament of Penance. At this time, the Sacrament of Penance was generally received once. Seeking forgiveness, serious sinners presented themselves to the bishop, who assigned them to a class of penitents (*ordo paenitentium*). The penitents were liturgically excommunicated from the Church and assigned to perform a penance, which usually lasted weeks, even months. Once the penance was completed, the bishop formally lifted the excommunication, absolved the sinners, and welcomed them back into full communion with the Church. By the seventh century, the Sacrament of Penance was repeatable and became more as we know it today, while the idea of excommunication became a severe Church penalty imposed for only the most serious offenses. Nevertheless, the lifting of the penalty of excommunication still was linked with the making of a good sacramental confession and the reception of absolution.

The *Code of Canon Law* (1983) specifies that an excommunicated person is forbidden to participate in a ministerial capacity (celebrant, lector, etc.) in the Sacrifice of the Mass or in any other form of public worship; to celebrate or to receive the sacraments; to celebrate the sacramentals; to exercise any ecclesiastical office or ministry; and to issue any act of governance (#1331.1). An excommunicated person also cannot be received into a public association of the Christian faithful (#316.1).

On one hand, the penalty of excommunication can be imposed by a proper authority (*ferendae sententiae*) or incurred automatically (*latae sententiae*). A bishop may directly impose the penalty of excommunication, but only for the most serious offenses and after giving due warning (#1318). Following the same rationale of the early Church, this severe penalty intends to correct the individual and to foster better church discipline (#1317). As the shepherd of his diocese, a bishop must protect both the souls of the faithful from the infection of error and sin, and of those who are jeopardizing their salvation. The bishop or his delegate may remit the penalty when the sinner has repented and has sought reconciliation.

On the other hand, a person can also incur automatic excommunication. A person who is an apostate from the faith, a heretic, or a schismatic (#1364); or one who procures a successful abortion (#1398) is automatically excommunicated. In these cases, the local ordinary or a delegated priest can remit the penalty.

In some very grievous cases, only the Holy See can lift the ban of an automatic excommunication: if a person desecrates the Blessed Sacrament or uses it for a sacrilegious purpose (#1367); if a person uses physical force against the Pope (#1370); if a priest absolves an accomplice in a sin against the Sixth Commandment (#1378); if a bishop consecrates someone as a bishop without permission of the Holy Father (#1982); and if a priest directly violates the seal of confession (#1388).

We must keep in mind that the purpose of excommunication is to shock the sinner into repentance and conversion. Excommunication is a powerful way of making a person realize his immortal soul is in jeopardy. Excommunication does not "lock the door" of the Church to the person forever, but hopes to bring the person back into communion with the whole Church. Moreover, this penalty awakens all of the faithful to the severity of these sins and deters them from the commission of these sins. This line of thought is highlighted in the *Catechism* when it speaks of the automatic excommunication for abortion: "The Church does not thereby intend to restrict the scope of mercy. Rather, she makes clear the gravity of the crime committed, the irreparable harm done to the innocent who is put to death, as well as to the parents and the whole of society" (#2272). In all, while the Church imposes this severe penalty for just cause, she also remembers, "A heart contrite and humbled, O God, you will not spurn" (Psalm 51:19).

WHAT IS THE NEW CATECHISM?

On October 11, 1992, Pope John Paul II officially promulgated the *Catechism of the Catholic Church* with his apostolic constitution *Fidei Depositum*. The idea of a catechism is not new. About the year 100, the *Didache* was compiled, which was a compendium of the teachings of the Apostles on doctrine, morals, and liturgy. The most famous universal catechism was that of the Council of Trent in 1566. In the United States, one easily remembers the *Baltimore Catechism* produced in 1885 at the Third Plenary Council of Baltimore. All of these catechisms had the same objective: to authentically teach the Catholic faith. All of these catechisms were published in times of great controversy, when forces of disbelief, confusion, and heresy attacked the Church. For this same reason, Pope John Paul II encouraged the issuance of a new catechism for the entire Church.

On January 25, 1985, Pope John Paul II summoned an extraordinary assembly of the Synod of Bishops to mark the twenty-fifth anniversary of the conclusion of the Second Vatican Council. The purpose of this synod was not only to celebrate the graces and fruits of the council, but also to clarify and deepen an understanding of its teachings. As with any previous council, the aftermath of Vatican II saw much disbelief, confusion, and even heresy. So the synod stated "that a catechism or compendium of all Catholic doctrine regarding both faith and morals be composed as a source text for the catechisms or compendia composed in the various countries. The presentation of doctrine should be biblical and liturgical, presenting sure teaching adapted to the actual life of Christians." From 1985 until 1992, the Holy Father and the Sacred Congregation of the Clergy guided by Cardinal Ratzinger assiduously dedicated themselves to composing the new *Catechism*.

The *Catechism* has a "four pillar format": what the Church believes (an explication of the Creed), what the Church celebrates (the sacraments), what the Church lives (the moral teachings of the

Church) and what the Church prays (the spiritual life of the Church). In one sense the *Catechism* is old, reiterating beliefs long held and defined by the Church, such as the mystery of the Holy Trinity. In another sense, the *Catechism* is new, addressing moral issues like nuclear war and questions of bioethics.

To date, the *Catechism* has been published in most major languages. It was first released in French because that was the common working language of the many scholars assigned to this task. Rather than using a "question and answer format" like the *Baltimore Catechism*, the new *Catechism* reads in narrative form. The *Catechism* is well indexed with many citations from Sacred Scripture, Church documents, and the writings of the Popes, Church Fathers, and the Saints. In all, the *Catechism* provides a beautiful expression of the living faith handed down to us through the generations.

Keep in mind that the *Catechism* is meant to be studied and used by the person in the pew. The *Catechism* is not meant to be just a reference work in libraries or a tool for theologians, priests, or scholars. For instance, shortly after its release, over 500,000 copies of the *Catechism* were sold in both the French and the Italian translations, attesting to its wide reception by faithful Catholics and the current hunger for the authentic teachings of the Church. I would encourage every Catholic home to have a good English translation of the Bible and the *Catechism*. Together these two sources represent what we believe as Catholics.

Moreover, the new *Catechism* is a remarkable teaching tool. Parents, as the primary educators of their children, can utilize the *Catechism* in handing the faith onto their children. Here is a reference for any question that a child may have. Whenever posed a question by a child or when conversation arises which takes one by surprise, the parent, like any good teacher, ought to go to the *Catechism*, study, and then return to the child with a clear and accurate answer. Moreover, the parents can use the *Catechism* not only as a resource to supplement the religious education materials of a school or CCD program, but also as a standard to hold those programs accountable. In all, the new *Catechism* will be a unifying force in the Church. What is presented in the *Catechism* ought to be preached from the pulpit, taught in Catholic schools and CCD programs, and lived and reinforced in the family.

Pope John Paul II declared the new *Catechism* to be a gift to the universal Church. The Holy Father stated, "The *Catechism of the Catholic Church* lastly is offered to every individual who asks us to give an account of the hope that is in us and who wants to know what the Catholic Church believes."

WHAT IS THE DIFFERENCE BETWEEN AN ENCYCLICAL, AN APOSTOLIC CONSTITUTION, A PAPAL BULL, AND A PASTORAL LETTER?

Each of these titles has a certain nuance which distinguishes them from each other. An apostolic constitution represents a very solemn pronouncement issued by the Pope on a doctrinal or disciplinary question. For example, Pope Paul VI's apostolic constitution *Missale Romanum* (1969) promulgated for the whole Church the new missal to be used at Mass. (A less weighty matter may also be addressed by a *motu proprio* which is similar to an executive order.)

A papal "bull" is a very dramatic way of presenting such a solemn pronouncement. Written on parchment, a lead seal (*bulla*) is attached with cords of silk. On one side of the seal would be the image of the reigning pope, and the other side would bear the images of St. Peter and St. Paul. For example, the dogma of the Assumption of our Blessed Mother was issued through the apostolic constitution, *Munificentissimus Deus* (1950) in the form of a papal bull. Even the wording indicates the solemn and definitive nature of the teaching: The document begins, "The Apostolic Constitution by which is defined the dogma of faith that Mary, the Virgin Mother of God, has been assumed into Heaven in Body and Soul, Pius the Bishop, Servant of the Servants of God, for everlasting remembrance."

Broader in scope and less solemn, an encyclical denotes a pastoral letter written by the Holy Father for the entire Church. This document focuses on a pastoral issue concerning a matter of doctrine, morality, devotion, or discipline. Since the earliest days of the Church, Popes have issued this kind of letter. However, Pope Benedict XIV was the first in modern times to specifically use "an encyclical" with his *Ubi primum* (1740) which dealt with the duties of bishops. (Note that the official title of an encyclical is generally the first two or three words of the text's Latin translation, the official language of issuance.) Since that time, the Popes have used encyclicals as the normal medium for teaching to the whole Church. Even the salutation of an encyclical captures the broadness of the audience to which it is addressed. For example, Pope John Paul II's recent encyclical *The Gospel of Life* (1995) begins with the salutation, "John Paul II to the Bishops, Priests, and Deacons, Men and Women Religious, Lay Faithful, and All People of Good Will on the Value and Inviolability of Human Life." Sometimes the encyclical may be addressed to a particular audience: For example another recent encyclical *The Splendor of Truth* (1993) begins, "Venerable Brothers in the Episcopate, Health and the Apostolic Blessing!" indicating its primary audience as the Bishops throughout the world who in turn will teach the people entrusted to their care.

Although encyclicals are not the normal medium through which the Pope would issue an infallible statement (although he could), the teaching contained in the encyclical represents a part of the ordinary magisterium of the Church held by the Holy Father and therefore commands respect and assent. The *Dogmatic Constitution on the Church* of the Second Vatican Council asserted clearly the role of the Pope as the "supreme pastor and teacher of all the faithful" (#25). Even though the teaching may not be formally declared infallible, Vatican II exhorted that "his supreme teaching authority be acknowledged with respect, and sincere assent be given to decisions made by him, conformably with his manifest mind and intention ... " and that "loyal submission of the will and intellect must be given ... " to the teaching.

Just as the Pope holds universal teaching authority for the whole Church throughout the world, a bishop may write a pastoral letter to instruct the faithful of his diocese. Vatican II stated, "[The Bishops] are authentic teachers ... endowed with the authority of Christ, who preach the faith to the people assigned to them, the faith which is destined to inform their thinking and direct their conduct" (*Dogmatic Constitution on the Church*, #25). Like the encyclical, the subject matter may be doctrinal, moral, devotional, or disciplinary. For example, Bishop John Keating has written several pastoral letters during his tenure as Bishop of the Diocese of Arlington: *A Pastoral Letter on Morality and Conscience* (1994) was more doctrinal, *A Pastoral Letter on Parish Councils* (1985) was more disciplinary, and *A Pastoral Letter on Reverence for the Eucharist* (1988) was doctrinal, devotional, and disciplinary. In turn, the faithful of the diocese are called "to adhere to [the teaching] with a ready and respectful allegiance of mind" (#25).

Several bishops may jointly issue a pastoral letter. For example, recently the Bishops of the Provinces of Baltimore and Washington issued a pastoral letter during Lent, 1992, encouraging people to utilize the Sacrament of Penance. The National Conference of Catholic Bishops has also written numerous pastoral letters providing guidance to Catholics throughout the United States.

In all, through these various documents, the Church continues to preserve the faith and to address issues confronting the faithful today so that they can live an authentic Christian life.

WHY IS PARISH REGISTRATION IMPORTANT?

Before delving into the question of parish registration, we must first be mindful of what a parish is. The word *parish* itself originates in Judaism and identifies the body of people. "Parish" denoted the Israelites living in exile in Egypt. Later, "parish" signified the earthly existence of Israel living in this world but not as part of this world; rather, as a parish of pilgrim people of God, the Israelites looked forward to the heavenly Jerusalem.

In Christianity, the term was similarly used to denote the church community living the Kingdom of God now in this world but with a view to its fulfillment in the heavenly Kingdom. St. Peter reminded the early Church, "Conduct yourselves reverently during your sojourn in a strange land" (I Peter 1:17), highlighting that idea of a pilgrim people journeying toward Heaven. During the time of persecution, the parish was each individual community headed by a Bishop. By AD 100 , the Bishop would send priests to offer Mass in homes especially in the rural areas; moreover, each priest would also carry some of the Holy Eucharist consecrated by the Bishop to be distributed to the faithful at these sites as a sign of their unity as a whole Church.

After the legalization of Christianity, the diocesan structure soon came into existence. The bishop oversaw the care of the entire diocese, referred to as "the Church," e.g. the "Church of Arlington," and appointed priests as pastors in his stead to care for the local, smaller communities, now designated as "parishes." By the time of Popes Zosimus (417-18) and Leo, the Great (440-461), parishes were given specific geographical areas by the bishop to insure the pastoral care of the people. However, because of the politics surrounding the feudal system of the Middle Ages, sometimes the jurisdiction of the bishop as well as the territory of parishes were not so clear.

The Council of Trent (1545-63) addressed the parish structure of the diocese and established these governing principles: The bishop is the pastor of his flock. He must live within and personally govern his diocese, which includes visiting his parishes. He must insure the authentic preaching of the faith and the administration of the sacraments. Therefore, to meet the needs of the faithful, the bishop creates parishes with specific boundaries and appoints properly educated pastors and assistants.

The present *Code of Canon Law* reflects this history, stating, "A parish is a definite community of the Christian faithful established on a stable basis within a particular church; the pastoral care of the parish is entrusted to a pastor as its own shepherd under the authority of the diocesan bishop" (#515). Even if a bishop determines that the pastoral care of a parish or parishes is entrusted to a team of several priests, one priest should direct the activity and be responsible to the bishop; likewise, in the case of the death of a pastor or when no resident pastor can be appointed, the bishop must still appoint a priest with the powers and faculties of a pastor to insure the pastoral care of the faithful (#517). The pastor has grave responsibilities to his flock: He must preach the Word of God; instruct the people in the faith; promote apostolic works; see to the Catholic education of children; reach out to those either who have stopped practicing the faith or who do not believe; insure the devout celebration of the sacraments, particularly the Most Holy Eucharist and Penance; and foster family prayer and devotion (#528).

However, parish life does not depend solely on the priests. Vatican II's *Decree on the Apostolate of Lay People* asserted that the laity should be filled with an apostolic spirit and work closely with their priests: "Nourished by their active participation in the liturgical life of their community, they engage zealously in its apostolic works; they draw men toward the Church who had been perhaps very far away from it; they ardently cooperate in the spread of the Word of God, particularly by catechetical instruction; by the expert assistance they increase the efficacy of the care of souls as well as of the administration of the good of the Church" (#10). Therefore, the pastor, his assistants, and the faithful work together to build a sense of community within the parish, particularly through the celebration of the Mass. For this reason, under normal circumstances, adults are to be baptized in their parish Church and infants in the parish church of their parents, and couples are to be married in the parish where either the groom or bride live. Through the spirit and practice of the laity and the clergy working together to foster this community, the relationship of the parish to the bishop is strengthened (*Constitution on the Sacred Liturgy*, #42).

To help insure this dynamic in the parish, the Church requires registration. Parish registration creates a two-fold obligation: On one hand, the pastor is obligated to serve the spiritual needs of that individual. On the other hand, the individual is obligated to support the mission and needs of the parish.

In her wisdom, the Church has seen the practice of registering at the Church responsible for a particular territory as the best way for both priests and laity to meet these obligations. *The Code of Canon Law* stipulates, "As a general rule a parish is to be territorial, that is it embraces all the Christian faithful within a certain territory; whenever it is judged useful, however, personal parishes are to be established based upon rite, language, the nationality of the Christian faithful within some territory or even upon some determining factor" (#518). In our society today, sometimes a person may feel more comfortable at a particular parish or like the ambiance of a particular parish even though it is not the territorial parish for where the person lives. When a pastor allows these individuals to register, he then also accepts the responsibility for their spiritual care. For instance, if a person were sick or dying, that parish priest now has the responsibility for that person. The ironic part is that in cases of emergency, usually the priests of the closest parish, the territorial parish, get the call.

In all, Pope Pius X reminded us that the purpose of the parish is to gather people with their different backgrounds and talents and insert them into the universality of the Church. The parish is a microcosm of the whole Church. While nurturing the souls of the faithful members, the parish as a whole must be ready to respond to the broader needs of the diocese, and the national and international Church. The faithful must also have a sense of serving the needs of all the faithful throughout the world and of building up the Kingdom of God now.

WHAT ARE THE EASTERN RITES?

The Second Vatican Council's *Decree on the Catholic Eastern Churches* emphasized, "The Catholic Church values highly the institutions of the Eastern Churches, their liturgical rites, Ecclesiastical traditions and their ordering of Christian life. For in those churches, which are distinguished by their venerable antiquity, there is clearly evident the tradition which has come from the Apostles through the Fathers and which is part of the divinely revealed, undivided heritage of the Universal Church" (#1).

To appreciate the Eastern Churches and their rites, we must first quickly survey early Church history. At the Ascension, Jesus commanded the apostles, "Full authority has been given to me both in heaven and on earth; go, therefore, and make disciples of all the nations. Baptize them in the name 'of the Father, and of the Son, and of the Holy Spirit.' Teach them to carry out everything I have commanded you. And know that I am with you always, until the end of the world" (Matthew 28:18-20). After Pentecost, the apostles, filled with the gifts of Holy Spirit, carried the gospel message throughout the world to unknown lands and foreign peoples. Tradition holds that the different Apostles journeyed as far as Spain in the West and India in the East. From the foundation they laid, the Church continued to spread despite persecution by the Roman Empire.

Keep in mind also that the Roman Empire at that time encompassed most of western Europe, parts of eastern Europe, Asia Minor, Palestine, and northern Africa. While the Romans were severe conquerors, they did respect and tolerate the culture and customs of their subjects to insure peace. To govern this vast expanse more efficiently, Emperor Diocletian (ruling between 285-305) divided the empire in the year 292 into two main portions: Rome and Byzantium, with four prefectures. When Emperor Constantine gained control, he legalized Christianity in 313 with the promulgation of the Edict of Milan, and then in 330 established the city of Constantinople as the capital of the eastern half of the Roman Empire. From this time on, the Empire was really seen as two halves, the West and the East. The eastern half was highly influenced by Hellenistic culture introduced by Alexander the Great in the fourth century before our Lord. Eventually, Constantine would make Constantinople his home and base of government, and this city would be called, "New Rome."

Within this framework, the Church grew. Dominant centers of Christianity eventually developed: Jerusalem, the "birthplace" for Christianity; Rome, the Diocese of St. Peter and the "home base" of the Church; Antioch, in Asia Minor where Christians were first called "Christians"; Alexandria, Egypt; and Constantinople, present day Istanbul, Turkey. Each of these communities professed the same belief and were united together as one Church. As the bishops of these dominant centers appointed and ordained other bishops to lead the growing Church, the hierarchy was mindful of the authority of the Holy Father, the Successor of St. Peter.

Especially when comparing the West with the East, differences in culture and language impacted upon the expression of the faith even though essential elements remained the same. For example, Baptism always involved the invocation of the Holy Trinity and the pouring of or immersion in water; yet, other particular prayers or liturgical customs were introduced in different areas. For Mass, the West used unleavened bread while leavened bread became more of the norm for the East. Moreover, Mass was called "The Holy Sacrifice of the Mass" or simply "Mass" in the West, and "Divine Liturgy" or simply "Liturgy" in the East. In the West, the faithful genuflected before the Blessed Sacrament, while in the East bowing became customary. In the East, the sacraments of Baptism, Holy Communion, and Confirmation were administered together, whereas in the West, these sacraments eventually were separated and were administered to an individual as he matured. Another difference in religious culture was the usage of statues in the West as visible reminders to inspire devotion to the Lord, the Blessed Mother, or the saints whereas the veneration of icons evolved in the

East. While these different traditions developed and remain to this day, they reflect the beautiful depth of Roman Catholicism.

As the Church hierarchy became more stable, the position of Patriarch was recognized. A Patriarch had the highest ecclesiastical dignity after the Pope and had jurisdiction over a particular territory. The term Patriarch comes from the Greek word for the leaders of the twelve tribes of Israel. Strictly speaking, "by the term 'Eastern Patriarch' is meant the bishop who has jurisdiction over all the bishops, metropolitans (archbishops) not excepted, clergy and people of his own territory or rite, according to the rules of canon law and without prejudice to the primacy of the Roman Pontiff" (*Decree on the Eastern Churches*, #7). Therefore, the patriarch is the father and head of his patriarchate.

The oldest version of Canon Law in the Church identified three Patriarchs: The Bishops of Rome, Alexandria, and Antioch. Each Patriarch governed a territory of the Church: The Patriarch of Rome governed the whole Church in the West; the Patriarch of Alexandria, the area of Egypt and Palestine; and the Patriarch of Antioch, Syria, Asia Minor, Greece, and the remainder of the Church in the East. These three Patriarchates were recognized as having a supreme place among the bishops by the Council of Nicea in 325.

With the rise of pilgrims to the Holy Land, the Bishop of Jerusalem received greater honor. The Council of Chalcedon in 451 took the area of Palestine and Arabia from Antioch and formed the Patriarchate of Jerusalem.

Since Constantine had made Constantinople the capital of the Roman Empire in the East and called it "New Rome," the Council of Chalcedon (451) eventually elevated it as a patriarchate with jurisdiction over the territories of Asia Minor and Thrace. The New Order of the Patriarchs then became in descending order Rome, Constantinople, Alexandria, Antioch, and Jerusalem. Keep in mind that the patriarchs are considered equal in rank even though they may have a precedence of honor. Moreover, just to underscore an important point, even though the Bishop of Rome is a patriarch, as

Pope he has supreme authority and governance over the whole Church.

Given this history, the differences in culture, language, and liturgical practices, and the established hierarchy under patriarchs, the clear presence of defined "rites" arose. Rites basically refer to groups of the faithful who share the same manner of performing services for the worship of God and the sanctification of the faithful. The spiritual head of the rite is the patriarch, who in turn would be under the jurisdiction of the Pope.

During the fifth century, the barbarian invasions crippled the western Roman Empire. Rome itself declined in stature. Even though the Pope was still the Bishop of Rome, the great early Church councils were all convoked in cities of the East – Nicea, Constantinople, Ephesus, and Chalcedon. A rivalry over power, authority, and prestige developed between the Pope, Bishop of Rome, and the Patriarch of Constantinople. In the mind of the Patriarch, since Rome had declined in stature and since Constantinople was now the viable capital of the Roman Empire (or what was left of it), he thought he should be recognized as the head of the Church: in a sense, "New Rome" should be the home of the Pope. From the Pope's perspective, he was the successor of St. Peter, Bishop of Rome, who held the keys of the Kingdom. Theological issues also became subject to debate, especially the adding of the *filioque* clause to the Creed, i.e. that the Holy Spirit proceeds from the Father *and the Son*. To make a long story short, the mounting tensions finally exploded in 1054 when both the Patriarch and the Pope issued bulls of excommunication against each other.

The Eastern Church was now in formal schism with the Western Church. Although the Eastern Church acknowledged the Pope as the successor of St. Peter, it rejected his binding authority over the whole Church and considered him simply as "the first among equals." Spurning any affiliation with Rome, these Churches identified themselves as the Orthodox. The Patriarch of Constantinople was recognized as the spiritual head of the Orthodox Churches, but he did not have any juridic authority over them, except those of his own Patriarchate. (Please note that the Maronite Rite Catholic Church whose Patriarch resides in Lebanon never severed its ties with Rome.) As time continued, the Roman Catholic Church was identified with the Latin Mass and allegiance to the Holy Father, and the Orthodox Churches with the Eastern Rites and particular ethnic communities, for example the Greek Orthodox Church and the Serbian Orthodox Church.

Attempts were made to reunite these Orthodox Churches with the Roman Catholic Church. At the Council of Florence (1438-45) which both Emperor John VIII and Patriarch Joseph II of Constantinople attended, the theological questions were debated. The Eastern Orthodox Churches agreed to accept the teaching that the Holy Spirit proceeds from the Father and the Son, even though they were not required to add this phrase to the Creed. While the agreement was signed and the Churches officially reunited, a large segment of the regular clergy disdained this action. Moreover, when the Moslems conquered Constantinople in 1453, Sultan Mohammed II appointed Gennadios II as Patriarch of Constantinople, who in turn repudiated the decrees of the Council of Florence. Once again, the two Churches were officially in schism. The domination of Islam over the territory of the East made future reunification virtually impossible.

In 1596, the first successful reunion occurred between the Ruthenian Orthodox and Roman Catholic Church in Poland with the Union of Brest. Other reunifications then followed. The most recent reunion involved the Church of Malankar, India, which traces its origins to St. Thomas the Apostle; in 1930, Bishop Ivanios, two other bishops, a priest, a deacon, and a laymen reunited with the Catholic Church and the Malankar Rite of the Catholic Church was born. These reunited Eastern Rites of the Catholic Church, except the Maronite Rite, all have counterparts remaining in the Orthodox Churches.

Vatican Council II recognized in its *Decree on the Catholic Eastern Churches*, "The holy Catholic Church, which is the Mystical Body of Christ, is made up of the faithful who are organically united in the Holy Spirit by the same faith, the same sacraments and the same government. They combine into different groups, which are held together by their hierarchy, and so form particular churches or rites. Between those churches there is such a wonderful bond of union that this variety in the Universal Church, so far from diminishing its unity, rather serves to emphasize it. For the Catholic Church wishes the traditions of each particular Church or Rite to remain whole and entire, and it likewise wishes to adapt its own way of life to the needs of different times and places" (#2). Although these Eastern Rites may differ from the Western or Latin Rite in the particulars of "rite" and liturgy, ecclesiastical discipline and Canon Law, and spiritual traditions, they are fully part of the Roman Catholic Church under the leadership and pastoral care of the Pope, the successor of St. Peter.

Today, the various Eastern Rites are organized under the four eastern patriarchates. (The following information was gleaned from the *Catholic Almanac*.) The Alexandrian Rite is officially called the Liturgy of St. Mark. (St. Mark is traditionally considered the first bishop of Alexandria.) Their present liturgy contains elements of the Byzantine Rite of St. Basil and the liturgies of Sts. Mark, Cyril, and Gregory Nazianzen. This parent rite includes the Coptic Rite and the Ge'ez Rite. The Coptic Rite which is situated primarily in Egypt, reunited with Rome in 1741 and uses the Coptic and Arabic languages in its liturgies. The Ge'ez Rite, based primarily in Ethiopia, Jerusalem, and Somalia, reunited with Rome in 1846 and uses the Ge'ez language in their liturgies.

The Antiochene Rite is the Liturgy of St. James of Jerusalem. This parent rite includes the following rites: The Malankar Rite, the Maronite Rite, the Syrian Rite, the Armenian Rite, the Chaldean Rite, and the Syro-Malabar Rite. The Malankar Rite is located in India, reunited with Rome in 1930, and uses the Syriac and Malayalam languages in its liturgies.

The Maronite Rite, located primarily in Lebanon, Cyprus, Egypt, and Syria but with large populations of the faithful also in the United States, Argentina, Brazil, Australia, and Canada, has remained united with Rome since the time of its founder St. Maron, and uses the Syriac and Arabic languages in its liturgies.

The Syrian Rite is located primarily in Lebanon, Iraq, Egypt and Syria, with healthy communities in Asia, Africa, Australia, and North and South America, reunited with Rome in 1781, and uses the Syriac and Arabic languages in its liturgies.

The Armenian Rite, technically a distinct rite, arose from the Antiochene Rite and is an older form of the Byzantine Rite. Although it uses a different language, this rite is technically called the Greek Liturgy of St. Basil. This rite has jurisdictions primarily in Lebanon, Iran, Iraq, Egypt, Syria, Turkey, Ukraine, France, Greece, Romania, Armenia, Argentina, and the United States. The Armenians reunited with Rome during the Crusades, and the ritual liturgical language is Classical Armenian.

The Chaldean Rite, also technically a distinct rite, originated from the Antiochene Rite. This rite is also divided into two rites: The Chaldean Rite, located primarily in Iraq, Iran, Lebanon, Egypt, Syria, Turkey, and the United States, reunited with Rome in 1692, and uses the Syriac and Arabic languages in the liturgy. The Syro-Malabar Rite, located in India, claims to have originated with St. Thomas the Apostle, and uses the Syriac and Malayalam languages in the liturgy. Although the Syro-Malabar Rite was never in formal schism, for centuries no communication occurred between them and Rome until the time of the missionaries in the 1500s.

The Byzantine Rite, the largest Eastern Rite, is based on the Rite of St. James of Jerusalem with the later reforms of St. Basil and St. John Chrysostom. These rites employ the Liturgy of St. John Chrysostom. This parent rite comprises many rites, which are themselves highly ethnic oriented. The Albanian Rite, centered in Albania, reunited with Rome in 1628 and uses Albanian as its liturgical language. The Belarussian (formerly titled Byelorussian) Rite, centered in Belarussia with large populations in Europe, North and South America, and Australia, reunited with Rome in the 1600s and uses Old Slavonic as their liturgical language. The Bulgarian Rite, centered in Bulgaria, reunited with Rome in 1861 and uses the Old Slavonic language in the liturgy. The Croatian Rite, based primarily in Croatia with a significant population in the United States, reunited with Rome in 1611 and employs Old Slavonic as a liturgical language. The Greek Rite, which is centered in Greece and Turkey with congregations also in Asia Minor and Europe, reunited with Rome in 1829 and uses the Greek language in the liturgy. The Hungarian Rite, situated in Hungary with significant populations throughout Europe and North and South America, reunited with Rome in 1646 and uses Greek, Hungarian, and English in their liturgies. The Italo-Albanian Rite, mainly in Italy with congregations in North and South America, never separated from Rome and uses the Greek and Italo-Albanian languages in the liturgy. The Romanian Rite, centered in Romania with a significant population in the United States, reunited with Rome in 1697 and use Modern Romanian in their liturgy; in 1948, they were forced to join the Romanian Orthodox Church in Romania, but since the fall of communism, the Catholic Romanian Rite has regained independence. The Russian Rite, located mainly in Russia and China with congregations in Europe, Australia, and North and South America, reunited with Rome in 1905 and use Old Slavonic as a liturgical language. The Georgian Rite, based in the former Soviet Republic of Georgia, reunited with Rome in 1329, severed ties in 1507, then in 1917 broke with the Russian Orthodox Church and again reunited with Rome as the Georgian Byzantine Rite, and has struggled for survival ever since, especially during Communist oppression; the Georgian language is used in their liturgy. The Slovak Rite is based in Slovakia, the Czech Republic, and Canada, and uses Old Slavonik in its liturgy.

The three largest of the Byzantine Rites are the Melkite, Ruthenian, and Ukrainian. The Melkite Rite has strong congregations in Syria, Lebanon, Jordan, Israel, United States, Brazil, Venezuela, Canada, Australia, and Mexico. The Melkites reunited with Rome during the Crusades but due to impediments caused by the Moslem occupations more officially reunited in the early 1700s and use Greek, Arabic, English, Portuguese, and Spanish in the liturgy.

The Ruthenian or Carpatho-Russian Rite is based in the Ukraine and the United States with strong congregations in Ukraine, United States, Hungary, Slovakia, the Czech Republic, Australia, Canada, and South America. The Ruthenians reunited with Rome in the Union of Brest-Litovek in 1596 and the Union of Uzhorod in 1646. They employ Old Slavonic and English in the liturgy.

Finally, the Ukrainian Rite has large populations in the Ukraine, Poland, the United States, Canada, England, Australia, Germany, France, Brazil, and Argentina. The Ukrainians reunited with Rome about 1595. However, Stalin forced the Ukrainian Rite Catholics to enter the Russian Orthodox Church in 1943, but since the independence of the Ukraine, they have reunited with Rome. This rite uses Old Slavonic and Ukrainian.

In all, these rites remind us of the universality of our Roman Catholic Church and the rich liturgical traditions we share as Catholics.

SACRAMENTS
& LITURGY

WHY DO WE SAY MASS IS A SACRIFICE WHEN THE LETTER TO THE HEBREWS INDICATES THAT CHRIST OFFERED ONLY ONE SACRIFICE ON THE CROSS?

Chapter 9 of the Letter to the Hebrews addresses the sacrifice of Jesus: Verses 25-28 read, "Not that [Christ] might offer Himself there again and again, as the high priest enters year after year into the sanctuary with blood that is not his own; if that were so He would have had to suffer death over and over from the creation of the world. But now He has appeared at the end of the ages to take away sins once for all by His sacrifice. Just as it is appointed that men die once, and after death be judged, so Christ was offered up once to take away the sins of many; He will appear a second time not to take away sin but to bring salvation to those who eagerly await Him." Further, Hebrews 7:27 states, "Unlike the other high priests, [Jesus] has no need to offer sacrifice day after day, first for His own sins and then for those of the people; He did that once for all when He offered Himself." To isolate these verses from the rest of Sacred Scripture and simply take them for face value would lead one to conclude that there could be no other sacrifice – Christ sacrificed Himself, it is over and done with, and that is it period. However, such a view is myopic to say the least.

Please note that in no way do we as Catholics believe that Christ continues to be crucified physically or die a physical death in Heaven over and over again. However, we do believe that the Mass does participate in the everlasting sacrifice of Christ. First, one must not separate the sacrifice of our Lord on the cross from the events which surround it. The sacrifice of our Lord is inseparably linked to the Last Supper. Here Jesus took bread and wine. Looking to St. Matthew's text (26:26ff), He said over the bread, "Take this and eat it. This is my body"; and over the cup of wine, "This is my blood, the blood of the covenant, to be poured out in behalf of many for the forgiveness of sins." The next day, on Good Friday, our Lord's body hung on the altar of the cross and His precious blood was spilt to wash away our sins and seal the everlasting, perfect covenant. The divine life our Lord offered and shared for our salvation in the sacrifice of Good Friday is the same offered and shared at the Last Supper. The Last Supper, the sacrifice of Good Friday, and the resurrection on Easter form one saving, life-giving event.

Second, one must have a nuanced understanding of time. One must distinguish chronological time from kairotic time as found in Sacred Scripture. In the Bible, *chronos* refers to chronological time – past, present, and future'specific deeds which have an end point. *Kairos* or kairotic time refers to God's eternal time, time of the present moment which recapitulates the entire past as well as contains the entire future. Therefore, while our Lord's saving event occurred chronologically about the year AD 33, in the kairotic sense of time it is an ever-present reality which touches our lives here and now. In the same sense, this is why through Baptism we share now in the mystery of Christ's passion, death, and resurrection, a chronological event that happened almost 2,000 years ago but is still efficacious for us today.

With this in mind, we also remember that our Lord commanded, as recorded in the Gospel of St. Luke (22:14ff) and St. Paul's First Letter to the Corinthians (11:23ff), "Do this in remembrance of me." Clearly, our Lord wanted the faithful to repeat, to participate in, and to share in this sacramental mystery. The Last Supper event which is inseparably linked to Good Friday (and the resurrection) is perpetuated in the Holy Mass for time eternal.

The Mass, therefore, is a memorial. In each of the Eucharistic Prayers, the *anamnesis* or memorial follows the words of consecration, whereby we call to mind the passion, death, resurrection, and ascension of the Lord. However, this memorial is not simply a recollection of past history in chronological time, but rather a liturgical proclamation of living history, of an event that continues to live and touch our lives now in that sense of kairotic time. Just as good orthodox Jews truly live the Passover event when celebrating the Passover liturgy, plunging themselves into an event which occurred about 1200 years before our Lord, we too live Christ's saving event in celebrating the Mass. The sacrifice which Christ offered for our salvation remains an ever-present reality: "As often as the sacrifice of the cross by which 'Christ our Pasch is sacrificed' is celebrated on the altar, the work of our redemption is carried out" (*Dogmatic Constitution on the Church*, #3). Therefore, the *Catechism* asserts, "The Eucharist is thus a sacrifice because it re-presents (makes present) the sacrifice of the cross, because it is its memorial and because it applies its fruit" (#1366).

Therefore, the actual sacrifice of Christ on the cross and the sacrifice of the Mass are inseparably united as one single sacrifice: The Council of Trent in response to Protestant objections decreed, "The victim is one and the same: the same now offers through the ministry of priests, who then offered Himself on the cross; only the manner of offering is different," and "In this divine sacrifice which is celebrated in the Mass, the same Christ who offered Himself once in a bloody manner on the altar of the cross is contained and is offered in an unbloody manner." For this reason, just as Christ washed away our sins with His blood on the altar of the cross, the sacrifice of the Mass is also truly propitiatory. The Lord grants grace and the gift of repentance, He pardons wrong doings and sins. (cf. Council of Trent, *Doctrine on the Most Holy Sacrifice of the Mass*).

Moreover, the Mass also involves the sacrifice of the whole Church. Together we offer our prayers, praise, thanksgiving, work, and sufferings to our Lord, thereby joining ourselves to His offering. The whole Church is united with the offering of Christ: this is why in the Eucharistic Prayers we remember the Pope, the Vicar of Christ; the Bishop, shepherd of the local diocese; the clergy who minister *in persona Christi* to the faithful; the faithful living now; the deceased; and the saints.

The *Constitution on the Sacred Liturgy* of Vatican II summed it up well: "At the Last Supper, on the night He was betrayed, our Savior instituted the eucharistic sacrifice of His Body and Blood.

This He did in order to perpetuate the sacrifice of the Cross through the ages until He should come again, and so to entrust to His beloved Spouse, the Church, a memorial of His death and resurrection: a sacrament of love, a sign of unity, a bond of charity, a paschal banquet in which Christ is consumed, the mind is filled with grace, and a pledge of future glory is given to us" (#47). Each time we celebrate Mass, let us give thanks to our Lord for the beautiful, precious gift of the Mass and the Holy Eucharist.

IS IT BETTER TO RECEIVE HOLY COMMUNION UNDER BOTH SPECIES?

One of the most beautiful and intimate ways we participate in the Mass is through the reception of Holy Communion, the Body and Blood of our Lord Jesus Christ. The *General Instruction on the Roman Missal* asserted the "meaning" of Communion is most clearly signified when given under both species – both the Sacred Host and the Precious Blood. Here the imagery of receiving the Body and Blood of Christ, of being joined with the Messianic Banquet, becomes most clear (#240). However, no where has the Church mandated that both species must be offered.

We must remember that "the whole and entire Christ and the true sacrament are received under either species" (Council of Trent, *Doctrine on Communion Under Both Species and on Communion of Little Children*). If one receives either the Precious Blood, or the Sacred Host, or both, one receives the fullness of the grace of the sacrament. This doctrine became very clear to me when I was a deacon. At my assignment in Philadelphia, I visited an elderly lady who had lost much of her mouth to cancer. She had a permanent feeding tube through which she poured liquid nourishment. When I brought her Holy Communion, I would bring a vial of the Precious Blood which had been consecrated at the morning Mass and which she then poured down the tube, followed by water for cleansing. Did she receive Christ? Absolutely. Did she receive as much grace as those who received the Sacred Host? Absolutely.

Nevertheless, in 1970, the Sacred Congregation for Divine Worship allowed the local conferences of bishops to determine as to what extent, what motives, and what conditions Holy Communion could be received under both species. The *General Instruction* had already listed several circumstances where communion under both species was permitted, for example to the bride and groom at a nuptial Mass or the assisting extraordinary Ministers of the Eucharist (#242).

In 1984, the National Conference of Catholic Bishops in America decided that the policy was left to the local ordinary of each diocese. Each bishop must weigh the spiritual needs of his diocese with any practical concerns.

CAN WE STILL HAVE MASS IN LATIN?

Sadly, since the aftermath of the second Vatican Council, the use of Latin has virtually disappeared from parishes and dioceses throughout the world, especially the United States. However, in the *Constitution on the Sacred Liturgy*, Vatican II decreed, "The use of the Latin language, with due respect to particular law, is to be preserved in the Latin rites. But since the use of the vernacular, whether in the Mass, the administration of the sacraments, or in other parts of the liturgy, may frequently be of great advantage to the people, a wider use may be made of it, especially in readings, directives, and in some prayers and chants" (#36). Moreover, the council emphasized that the faithful be able to speak or sing in Latin the congregational parts of the Mass (#55). While the council saw the benefit of allowing the usage of the vernacular, it never meant for the vernacular to completely replace the usage of Latin. However, sometimes the "new thing" does completely replace what is "old" and perhaps viewed as "out of date," which is what happened to Latin to a great extent in the years following the council.

Perceiving this problem just two years after the close of Vatican II, Pope Paul VI himself emphasized the importance of preserving the tradition of Latin. In the *Instruction on Music in the Liturgy* (1967), the Sacred Congregation of Rites (later Sacred Congregation of Divine Worship), repeating these precepts of Vatican II, stated that "the local Ordinaries will judge whether it may be opportune to preserve one or more Masses celebrated in Latin." Actually, we are seeing the fulfillment of the vision of Vatican II with the availability of worship in both the vernacular and the traditional Latin.

Retaining the practice of offering Mass in Latin and the congregation knowing the Latin Mass parts has great value. First, we must preserve part of our Catholic heritage. Mozart, Beethoven, Vivaldi, and other great composers wrote beautiful Masses in Latin. Gregorian chant is a venerable liturgical art form. How tragic it would be if these works were lost or just confined to concert halls! I do not say this because of nostalgia because I barely remember the "old Latin Mass." Unfortunately, I can say I remember some of those '60s tunes like Ray Repp's "Sons of God," which have faded away. Rather, I come from the perspective of aesthetics as well as an appreciation of our Catholic heritage. Every Catholic ought to have such an appreciation for the richness of our Roman Rite throughout the ages.

Second, the usage of Latin is a way of expressing our unity throughout the Church. I remember once I was travelling with a priest friend in Salzburg, Austria. There we had hoped to concelebrate the Sunday High Mass at the Cathedral which would have the music of one of Franz Liszt's Masses. Unfortunately, for us, the rest of the Mass was in German. Since neither of us spoke German, we sat in the choir stalls, participated as best we could without concelebrating, and later offered Mass in English. If the Mass had been entirely in Latin, we could have effectively concelebrated. In the "old days," Catholics could travel anywhere in the world and truly participate in the Mass following their Missals.

In all, the challenge here is to preserve our Catholic tradition and heritage, rejoice in its richness, and broaden the vision of liturgical music for the present and the future generations.

SHOULD NON-CATHOLICS OR CATHOLICS WHO ARE NOT PRACTICING THEIR FAITH RECEIVE HOLY COMMUNION?

One of the great fruits of Holy Communion, according to the *Catechism*, is that the Holy Eucharist makes the Church: "Those who receive the Eucharist are united more closely to Christ. Through it, Christ unites them to all the faithful in one body – the Church. Communion renews, strengthens, and deepens this incorporation into the Church, already achieved by Baptism" (#1396). Therefore, the reception of Holy Communion truly unites in communion the Catholic faithful who share the same faith, doctrinal teachings, traditions, sacraments, and leadership.

A Catholic must be in a state of grace to receive Holy Communion, and anyone aware of being in a state of mortal sin must first receive absolution in the Sacrament of Penance (*Catechism*, #1415). Therefore, a non-practicing Catholic who has negligently not attended Mass or who has abandoned the teachings of the Church is not in a state of grace and cannot receive Holy Communion. A non-practicing Catholic who receives Holy Communion commits the sin of sacrilege – the abuse of a sacrament – and causes scandal among the faithful. St. Paul reminded the Corinthians: "Every time, then, you eat this bread and drink this cup, you proclaim the death of the Lord until He comes! This means that whoever eats the bread or drinks the cup of the Lord unworthily sins against the Body and Blood of the Lord. A man should examine himself first; only then should he eat of the bread and drink of the cup" (I Corinthians 11:26-28).

What then about non-Catholics? Sadly, since the time our Lord founded the Church upon the apostles, we have witnessed divisions, the first major one being with the Orthodox Churches in 1054 and then followed by the Protestant Churches beginning in 1517. While all Christians share many beliefs – for instance in Jesus Christ, in Baptism, and in the Bible as the Word of God – and can work and pray together in serving the mission of our Lord, major differences in beliefs still do exist, including the primacy of the Pope, the sacrificial priesthood, and the nature of sacraments, including what the Holy Eucharist is. Indeed, much progress has been made since the Second Vatican Council to discuss these differences with various Christian groups. Nevertheless, these differences still "break the common participation in the table of the Lord" (Catechism, #1398).

Here we find some distinction. Concerning the Orthodox Churches, who primarily disagree with Catholics over the authority of the Pope, Vatican II's *Decree on Ecumenism* stated, "These Churches, although separated from us, yet possess true sacraments, above all – by apostolic succession – the priesthood and the Eucharist, whereby they are still joined to us in closest intimacy." A certain communion *in sacris* including the Holy Eucharist, "given suitable circumstances and the approval of Church authority, is not merely possible but is encouraged" (#15). Along these lines, the *Code of Canon Law* stipulates that the Sacraments of Penance, Eucharist, and Anointing of the Sick may be administered to members of the Orthodox Churches if they ask on their own for these sacraments and are properly disposed (Canon 844, #3).

Besides rejecting papal authority, Vatican II recognized that the Protestant Churches "have not preserved the proper reality of the Eucharistic Mystery in its fullness, especially because of the absence of the Sacrament of Holy Orders" (*Decree on Ecumenism*, #22). For this very reason, the sharing of Holy Communion between Protestants and Catholics is not possible (*Catechism*, #1400). This statement does not suggest that Protestant Churches do not commemorate the Lord's death and resurrection in their communion service or believe that it signifies a communion with Christ. However, Protestant theology differs with Catholic theology concerning the Holy Eucharist over the real presence of Christ, transubstantiation, the sacrifice of the Mass, and the nature of the priesthood. Nevertheless, the *Code of Canon Law* makes an exception in emergency cases: "If the danger of death is present or other grave necessity, in the judgment of the diocesan bishop or the conference of bishops, Catholic ministers may licitly administer these sacraments [Penance, Eucharist, and Anointing of the Sick] to other Christians ... who cannot approach a minister of their own community and on their own ask for it, provided they manifest the Catholic faith in these sacraments and are properly disposed" (Canon 844, #4).

In regard to those who are not baptized, e.g. a member of the Jewish or Moslem faith, Catholics welcome them to share in prayer, but cannot extend to them an invitation to receive the sacraments. This restriction is obvious since the sacraments are intrinsically linked to the fundamental belief in Jesus as Lord and Savior.

We must continue to pray that the divisions which separate Christians will be healed. Until those differences are healed and out of respect for each other's beliefs, a real "intercommunion" cannot take place. I remember once I participated at the funeral of a Protestant friend, which included a communion service. The minister did indeed invite everyone to receive communion. However, I refrained out of respect for their beliefs and my own: I did not fully accept all the beliefs or practices of their particular denomination, nor did those members accept all that the Roman Catholic Church believed. Therefore, to receive communion would be to state "I am in communion with them," when in fact I was not. Worse yet, had I partaken, I would have received something sacred which should bind me as part of their communion – at least from a Catholic perspective – when in fact I have never participated in one of their services since then. We must remember that to receive communion does not depend simply on what a person individually believes; to receive communion aligns a person to a church and binds him to what that church teaches.

We must be careful not to let our hearts simply get the best of us and make blanket statements like, "Jesus loves everyone. Everyone is welcome to receive Communion." Yes, our Lord indeed loves everyone; however, we in turn must appreciate and respect the gift of the Holy Eucharist in order to receive our Lord with genuine love and devotion. I think those individuals who disregard the Church's regulations, if they are Catholic especially, have a lack of appreciation not only for Catholic theology but also for Church history. They forget the great examples of St. Edmund Campion or St. Margaret Clitherow and many others who were tortured and put to death under the reign of Elizabeth I of England because they celebrated or attended Mass, believed in transubstantiation, and were loyal to the Holy Father. They forget the examples of great saints, like St. John Neumann or St. John Vianney, who implored their congregations to use regularly the Sacrament of Penance so as to be in a state of grace when receiving the Lord. By observing these regulations concerning receiving Holy Communion we will better appreciate the gift of the Blessed Sacrament, respect each other's beliefs, and work towards unity. Ignoring these regulations will only build a false sense of communion and a shallow expression of love.

SHOULD WE FAST BEFORE RECEIVING HOLY COMMUNION?

Canon 919 of the *Code of Canon Law* states, "One who is to receive the Most Holy Eucharist is to abstain from any food or drink, with the exception of water and medicine, for at least the period of one hour before Holy Communion." Actually, this regulation merely reflects an ancient tradition in our Church, which is even rooted in Judaism. In Acts of the Apostles (13:2), we find evidence of fasting connected with the liturgy. A more normative practice of fasting before receiving Holy Communion appears throughout the Church after the legalization of Christianity in A.D. 313. St. Augustine attested to this practice in his own writings.

Granted, the specific requirements of the fast have changed over time. Prior to 1964, the Eucharistic fast was three hours. Pope Paul VI on November 21, 1964 reduced the fast to a period of one hour.

This rule has two exceptions: First, if a priest celebrates more than one Mass on the same day, as oftentimes happens on Sunday, he is only bound to the one hour fast before the first Mass. The priest may eat and drink something to keep up his strength between Masses even though a full hour fast will not occur before the next reception of Holy Communion.

Second, those who are elderly (at least sixty years of age) or sick as well as their caretakers can receive Communion even if a full hour fast has not been fulfilled. For example people in the hospital are not in control of their own schedule and may be eating or have just finished eating when visited by the Priest or Eucharistic Minister. Therefore, the period of fast before receiving Holy Communion is reduced to "approximately one quarter of an hour" for those who are sick at home or at a medical facility, those elderly confined to home or a nursing home, and those who care for these people and who are unable conveniently to observe the fast (*Immensae Caritatis*).

The most important point regarding this question concerns why we ought to fast. St. Paul reminds us, "Continually we carry about in our bodies the dying of Jesus, so that in our bodies the life of Jesus may also be revealed" (II Corinthians 4:10). We too are charged to convert our whole lives – body and soul – to the Lord. This conversion process involves doing penance, including bodily mortification like fasting, for our sins and weaknesses, which in turn strengthens and heals us. Pope Paul VI exhorted the faithful in his apostolic constitution *Paenitemini*, "Mortification aims at the 'liberation' of man, who often finds himself, because of concupiscence, almost chained by his own senses. Through 'corporal fasting' man regains strength, and the wound inflicted on the dignity of our nature by intemperance is cured by the medicine of a salutary abstinence."

Moreover, the fast before receiving Holy Communion creates a physical hunger and thirst for the Lord, which in turn augments the spiritual hunger and thirst we ought to have. In the Old Testament, fasting prepared individuals to receive the action of God and to be placed in His presence. For instance, Moses fasted 40 days atop Mount Sinai as he received the Ten Commandments (Exodus 34:28), and Elijah fasted 40 days as he walked to Mount Horeb to encounter God (I Kings 19:8). Similarly, Jesus Himself fasted forty days as He prepared to begin His public ministry (Matthew 4:1ff) and encouraged fasting (Matthew 6:16-18). Likewise, this corporal work enhances the spiritual disposition we need to receive Christ in the Blessed Sacrament. In a sense, we fast so as not "to spoil our appetite" but to increase it for the sharing of the Paschal Banquet. Jesus said in the Beatitudes, "Blest are they who hunger and thirst for holiness; they shall have their fill" (Matthew 5:6). In all, fasting is an exercise of humility, hope, and love – essential virtues in preparing ourselves to receive the Holy Eucharist.

This regulation, however, does not mean we have to be scrupulous and count-off seconds. I remember once I concelebrated Mass with a priest who had eaten one-half hour before Mass and was worried that he would not have a one-hour fast before receiving

Holy Communion. He literally set his watch for one-hour, dragged-out the prayers, and stood at the altar while I finished giving everyone else Holy Communion until the hour had ticked away. While we do not want to be lax, we do not need to be scrupulous. The goodness of receiving Holy Communion supersedes the precise "hour of fast" if there is a doubt.

However, note that one should also not be lax. Pope John Paul II lamented in *Dominicae Cenae* the problem of some people not being properly disposed to receive Holy Communion, even to the point of being in a state of serious mortal sin. He said, "In fact, what one finds most often is not so much a feeling of unworthiness as a certain lack of interior willingness, if one may use this expression, a lack of Eucharistic 'hunger' and 'thirst,' which is also a sign of lack of adequate sensitivity towards the great sacrament of love and a lack of understanding of its nature." We must make a good faith effort to prepare ourselves properly to receive the Lord.

Therefore, the Eucharistic fast assists us in preparing to receive Holy Communion wholly, body and soul. This physical mortification strengthens our spiritual focus on the Lord, so that we may humbly encounter the divine Savior who offers Himself to us.

WHAT IS THE PROPER USE OF THE LAITY AS EUCHARISTIC MINISTERS?

In answering this question, we will restrict our answer to the role of Eucharistic Ministers. Here we must keep in mind two premises: First, the most precious gift our Lord entrusted to His Church is the Most Holy Eucharist, the Sacrament of His Body and Blood. The Blessed Sacrament, as Vatican II stated, is the center and summit of our worship as Catholics. Second, the pastor of the parish is to insure that the Most Holy Eucharist is truly the center of parish life and that the faithful are nourished through a devout celebration of all the sacraments, especially through frequent reception of the sacraments of the Most Holy Eucharist and Penance (*Code of Canon Law*, #528.2).

Given this foundation, the Sacred Congregation for the Discipline of the Sacraments (now called the Sacred Congregation for the Sacraments and Divine Worship since 1975) issued on January 25, 1973 the *Instruction on Facilitating Sacramental Eucharistic Communion in Particular Circumstances*. The instruction addressed the appointment of "Extraordinary Ministers" of the Eucharist. (Note that the "Ordinary Ministers" of Holy Communion would be the Bishop, Priest, and Deacon (*Code of Canon Law*, #910.1).) Extraordinary Ministers may be used to assist the Ordinary Ministers in the following circumstances: (1) at Mass when the size of the congregation would "unduly" prolong the reception of Holy Communion (especially since the relaxation of the old "fasting laws"); (2) when the Ordinary Ministers would be prevented from distributing Holy Communion by ill health, advanced age, or other pastoral obligations; (3) when the number of sick or homebound in various places (hospitals, nursing homes, or private homes) requires assistance to provide for regular reception of Holy Communion. Therefore, the Vatican allowed Bishops to appoint a "suitable person" for a specific occasion or a period of time to assist the Ordinary Ministers to distribute Holy Communion.

The appointment of Extraordinary Ministers of the Eucharist and the privilege of distributing Holy Communion is granted for the good of the faithful and for cases of genuine necessity. These individuals should be properly instructed and should live an exemplary Christian life. They must show great devotion to the Holy Eucharist and be an example of piety and reverence. Except in rare occasions and for a particular circumstance, a lay person must first be appointed by the Bishop of the Diocese to act in this capacity. The *Instruction* also cautions, "Let no one be chosen whose selection may cause scandal among the faithful." In a sense, Extraordinary Eucharistic Ministers ought to have an extraordinary love for the Holy Eucharist and for the Church, the Body of Christ.

Each diocese sets its own regulations for the appointment of Extraordinary Ministers. Usually, a person must be mature and at least 21 years of age. The candidate must attend a workshop offered by the Office of Sacred Liturgy or be trained locally in the parish. Upon recommendation of the Pastor, the Bishop appoints Extraordinary Ministers of the Eucharist to a term, which may be renewed. The appointment, however, extends only to service within a particular parish.

A recent instruction entitled *Some Questions Regarding Collaboration of Nonordained Faithful in Priests' Sacred Ministry* issued on November 13, 1997 by eight Vatican offices warns against abusing this privilege so as to dilute the role of the ministerial, sacrificial priest. The instruction addressed the role of the faithful in the ministry of the Word, including preaching; in liturgical celebrations, including the distribution of Holy Communion and the conducting of a Communion Service when a priest is absent; and in caring for the sick. Frankly, the motivation for releasing this instruction was to counteract certain abuses that had arisen in these areas. Moreover, the Church wanted to present again the distinction between the roles of the ministerial, sacrificial priesthood of the ordained clergy and the roles of the common priesthood shared by all of the baptized faithful. We must keep in mind that extraordinary ministers are truly "extra-ordinary" not "ordinary." Extraordinary ministers may only distribute Holy Communion in accord with the guidelines as noted here. Moreover, certain practices are to be curtailed: Extraordinary ministers cannot give Holy Communion to themselves or apart from the faithful as though they were concelebrants at a Mass, and they cannot be used when there are sufficient ordained Ordinary Ministers for the distribution of Holy Communion.

In my own priestly ministry, I have seen the value of having laity as Extraordinary Ministers, especially in visiting the sick, the homebound, and those in institutions. Because of their assistance, the faithful can receive Holy Communion with greater regularity. However, the service of Extraordinary Ministers does not excuse the priest from visiting these people, especially to provide the Sacrament of Penance and Anointing of the Sick. Moreover, I have been edified by the devotion and love of several Extraordinary Ministers for the Most Blessed Sacrament. I have known several Eucharistic Ministers who at first refused when asked to perform this service because they felt "unworthy" – a sign of humility. And, I have seen many faithfully venture out in all kinds of inclement weather to visit those parishioners in their care.

On the other hand, I have seen abuses. Several years ago, I officiated at the wedding of my cousin, the groom. A priest, who was from a northern diocese and was also a friend of the bride's family, concelebrated. The priest thought it would be "meaningful" if the bride and groom gave each other Holy Communion. I refused. He said, "All the popular liturgical magazines suggest this." I said, "Too bad the Church doesn't." He wanted to abuse the privilege, and reduce a sacred privilege to something trite.

I was once assigned to a smaller parish that had three active priests and a deacon. There was no need for other assistance in distributing Holy Communion at Mass. Eucharistic Ministers did visit the local hospital and nursing home. After Mass, a lady from Massachusetts asked, "Why were there no lay people helping with Communion?" After I answered, she said, "Vatican II gave us that right," and walked away. Vatican II did not give anyone that right.

As an ordained priest, I have no right to distribute Holy Communion, but a privilege extended by the Bishop.

Therefore, while the laity may act as Extraordinary Ministers of the Eucharist and indeed provide valuable service to a parish, we must follow the norms of the Church. The norms as stated are to insure that due reverence and protection are given to the Most Blessed Sacrament.

WHY DOES THE CATHOLIC *"OUR FATHER"* HAVE A DIFFERENT ENDING THAN THE *PROTESTANT ONE?*

When discussing prayer with His disciples, our Lord said, "This is how you are to pray. 'Our Father in heaven, hallowed be your name, your kingdom come, your will be done on earth as it is in heaven. Give us today our daily bread and forgive us the wrong we have done as we forgive those who wrong us. Subject us not to the trial but deliver us from the evil one'" (Matthew 6:9-13). A similar version is found in Luke 11:2-4. Both versions do not include the ending sentence found in the Protestant version, "For thine is the Kingdom, the power, and the glory now and forever."

The "For thine ... " is technically termed a *doxology*. In the Bible, we find the practice of concluding prayers with a short, hymn-like verse which exalts the glory of God. An example similar to the doxology in question is found in David's prayer located in I Chronicles 29:10-13 of the Old Testament. The Jews frequently used these doxologies to conclude prayers at the time of our Lord.

In the early Church, the Christians living in the eastern half of the Roman Empire added the doxology "For thine ... " to the gospel text of the Our Father when reciting the prayer at Mass. Evidence of this practice is also found in the *Didache* (*Teaching of the Twelve Apostles*), a first century manual of morals, worship, and doctrine of the Church. Also when copying the scriptures, Greek scribes sometimes appended the doxology onto the original Gospel text of the Our Father; however, most texts today would omit this inclusion, relegate it to a footnote, or note that it was a later addition to the Gospel. Official "Catholic" Bibles including the Vulgate, the Douay-Rheims, the Confraternity Edition, and the New American have never included this doxology.

In the western half of the Roman Empire and in the Latin rite, we see the importance of the Our Father at Mass. St. Jerome (d. 420) attested to the usage of the Our Father in the Mass, and St. Gregory the Great (d. 604) placed the recitation of the Our Father after the Eucharistic Prayer and before the Fraction. In his *Commentary on the Sacraments*, St. Ambrose (d. 397) meditated on the meaning of "daily bread" in the context of the Holy Eucharist. In this same vein, St. Augustine (d. 430) saw the Our Father as a beautiful connection of the Holy Eucharist with the forgiveness of sins. In all instances, the Church saw this perfect prayer which our Lord gave to us as a proper means of preparing for Holy Communion. However, none of this evidence includes the use of the doxology.

Interestingly, the English wording of the Our Father that we use today reflects the version mandated for use by Henry VIII (while still in communion with the Catholic Church), which was based on the English version of the Bible produced by Tyndale (1525). Later in 1541 (after his official separation from the Holy Father), Henry VIII issued an edict saying, "His Grace perceiving now the great diversity of the translations (of the Pater Noster, etc.) hath willed them all to be taken up, and instead of them hath caused an uniform translation of the said Pater Noster, Ave, Creed, etc., to be set forth, willing all his loving subjects to learn and use the same and straitly [sic] commanding all parsons, vicars, and curates to read and teach the same to their parishioners." This English version without the doxology of the Our Father became accepted throughout the English speaking world, even though the later English translations of the Bible including the Catholic Douay-Rheims (1610) and Protestant King James versions (1611) had different renderings of prayers as found in the Gospel of St. Matthew. Later, the Catholic Church made slight modifications in the English: "who art" replaced "which art," and "on earth" replaced "in earth." During the reign of Edward VI, the *Book of Common Prayer* (1549 and 1552 editions) of the Church of England did not change the wording of the Our Father nor add the doxology. However, during the reign of Elizabeth I and a resurgence to rid the Church of England from any Catholic vestiges, the Lord's Prayer was changed to include the doxology, and this version became the standard for English-speaking Protestants.

The irony of this answer is that some Protestants sometimes accuse Catholics of not being "literally" faithful to Sacred Scripture and depending too much on Tradition. In this case, we see that the Catholic Church has been faithful to the Gospel text of the Our Father, while Protestant Churches have added something of Tradition to the words of Jesus.

WHAT DO WE MEAN BY "THE REAL PRESENCE OF CHRIST" IN THE HOLY EUCHARIST?

As Catholics, we firmly believe that the real presence of Christ is in the Holy Eucharist. The Second Vatican Council's *Decree on the Ministry and Life of Priests* asserts, "The other sacraments, and indeed all ecclesiastical ministries and works of the apostolate are bound up with the Eucharist and are directed towards it. For in the most blessed Eucharist is contained the whole spiritual good of the Church, namely Christ Himself, our Pasch and the living bread which gives life to men through His flesh'that flesh which is given life and gives life through the Holy Spirit" (#5). For this reason, the Council referred to the Holy Eucharist as the source and summit of the whole Christian life (*Dogmatic Constitution on the Church*, #11).

Our belief in the Holy Eucharist is rooted in Christ Himself. Recall the beautiful words of our Lord in the Bread of Life Discourse in the Gospel of St. John: "I myself am the living bread come down from heaven. If anyone eats this bread he shall live forever; the bread I will give is my flesh, for the life of the world. Let me solemnly assure you, if you do not eat the flesh of the Son of Man and drink His blood, you have no life in you. He who feeds on my flesh and drinks my blood has life eternal, and I will raise him up on the last day. For my flesh is real food and my blood real drink. The man who feeds on my flesh and drinks my blood remains in me, and I in him. Just as the Father who has life sent me and I have life because of the Father, so the man who feeds on me will have life because of me" (John 6:51, 53-57). Note that none of this language is symbolic – Jesus meant what He said. Moreover, even when there is grumbling and objections, and even after some disciples abandon our Lord because of this teaching, Jesus no where says, "Oh please, stop. I really meant this symbolically." Our Lord stood by His teaching.

The meaning of the Bread of Life Discourse becomes more clear at the Last Supper on the first Holy Thursday. There Jesus gathered His apostles around Himself. According to the Gospel of St. Matthew, Jesus took unleavened bread and wine, two sources of basic nourishment. He took the bread, blessed it, gave thanks, broke it, and gave it to the apostles, saying, "Take this and eat it; this is my body." He took the cup of wine, gave thanks, gave it to His apostles and said, "All of you must drink from it for this is my blood, the blood of the covenant, to be poured out in behalf of many for the forgiveness of sins." If we extracted the words of consecration recorded in the Last Supper accounts of the gospels and distilled them, we would have our words of consecration used at Mass. (Cf. Matthew 26:26-30; Mark 14:22-26; and Luke 22:14-20.)

Think of those words! Jesus was not just giving to the apostles blessed bread and wine. He was giving His whole life – Body, Blood, Soul, and Divinity. He was giving His very self. How true that was! The next day, Jesus' body hung upon the altar of the cross. His blood was spilled to wash away our sins. As priest, He offered the perfect sacrifice for the remission of sin. However, this sacrifice was not death rendering but life giving, for three days later our Lord rose from the dead conquering both sin and death. Yes, the perfect, everlasting covenant of life and love with God was made by our Lord Jesus Christ.

This whole mystery is preserved in the Most Holy Eucharist and the Sacrifice of the Mass. We too take unleavened bread and wine, two sources of nourishment. By the will of the Father, the work of the Holy Spirit, and the priesthood of Jesus entrusted to His ordained priests, and through the words of consecration, that bread and wine is transformed into the Body and Blood of Jesus. Yes, the bread and wine do not change in characteristics: they still look the same, taste the same, and hold the same shape. However, the reality, "the what it is," the substance does change. We do not receive bread and wine; we receive the Body and Blood of Christ. We call this *transubstantiation*, a term used at the Fourth Lateran Council (1215). Therefore, each time we celebrate Mass, we are plunged into the whole ever-present, everlasting mystery of Holy Thursday, Good Friday, and Easter, and share intimately in the life of our Lord through the Holy Eucharist.

The Catholic Church has always cherished this treasure. St. Paul wrote, "I received from the Lord what I handed on to you, namely, that the Lord Jesus on the night in which He was betrayed took bread, and after He had given thanks, broke it and said, 'This is my body, which is for you. Do this in remembrance of me.' In the same way, after the supper, He took the cup, saying, 'This cup is the new covenant in my blood. Do this, whenever you drink it, in remembrance of me.' Every time then you eat this bread and drink this cup, you proclaim the death of the Lord until he comes!" (I Corinthians 11:23-26).

During the days of Roman persecution, to clearly distinguish the Eucharist from the cultic rite of Mithra and to dispel Roman charges of cannibalism, St. Justin Martyr (d. 165) wrote in his *First Apology*,"We do not consume the Eucharistic bread and wine as if it were ordinary food and drink, for we have been taught that as Jesus Christ our Savior became a man of flesh and blood by the power of the Word of God, so also the food that our flesh and blood assimilate of its nourishment becomes the flesh and blood of the incarnate Jesus by the power of His own words contained in the prayer of thanksgiving."

Later, the Council of Trent in 1551 addressed the heretical views of the Reformers. Remember Zwingli and Calvin believed that Christ was present only "in sign"; Luther believed in *consubstantiation* whereby the Eucharist is both body and blood, and bread and wine; and Melancthon believed that the Eucharist reverts back to just bread and wine after communion.

Trent's *Decree on the Most Holy Eucharist* specified, "In the Blessed Sacrament of the Holy Eucharist, after the consecration of the bread and wine, our Lord Jesus Christ, true God and man, is truly, really, and substantially contained under the appearances of those perceptible realities. For there is no contradiction in the fact that our Savior always sits at the right hand of the Father in Heaven according to His natural way of existing and that, nevertheless, in His substance He is sacramentally present to us in many other places."

Therefore, no faithful, knowledgeable Catholic would say that the Holy Eucharist "symbolizes" the Body and Blood of Christ. Yes, we pray for grace that we may believe more strongly each day in this precious gift of Christ Himself. Perhaps we should dwell on the words of Thomas Aquinas in *Adoro Te Devote* "Godhead here in hiding, whom I do adore; masked by these bare shadows, shape and nothing more. See, Lord, at thy service low lies here a heart: Lost, all lost in wonder at the God thou art."

WHY DO WE OFFER MASSES FOR THE DEAD?

The offering of Masses for the repose of the soul of the faithful departed is linked with our belief in Purgatory. We believe that if a person has died fundamentally believing in God but with venial sins and the hurt caused by sin, then God in His divine love and mercy will first purify the soul. After this purification has been completed, the soul will have the holiness and purity needed to share in the beatific vision in heaven.

While each individual stands in judgment before the Lord upon death and must render an account of his life, the communion of the Church shared on this earth continues, except for those souls damned to Hell. Vatican Council II affirmed, "This sacred council accepts loyally the venerable faith of our ancestors in the living communion which exists between us and our brothers who are in the glory of heaven or who are yet being purified after their death ... " (*Dogmatic Constitution on the Church*, #51). Therefore, just as we now pray for each other, share each other's burdens, and help each other on the path of salvation, the faithful on earth can offer prayers and sacrifices to help the departed souls undergoing purification, and no better prayer could be offered than that of the Holy Sacrifice of the Mass.

In 1902, Pope Leo XIII in his encyclical *Mirae caritatis* beautifully elaborated this point and emphasized the connection between the communion of saints with the Mass: "The grace of mutual love among the living, strengthened and increased by the Sacrament of the Eucharist, flows, especially by virtue of the Sacrifice [of the Mass], to all who belong to the communion of saints. For the communion of saints is simply ... the mutual sharing of help, atonement, prayers, and benefits among the faithful, those already in the heavenly fatherland, those consigned to the purifying fire, and those still making their pilgrim way here on earth. These all form one city, whose head is Christ, and whose vital principle is love. Faith teaches that although the august Sacrifice can be offered to

God alone, it can nevertheless be celebrated in honor of the saints now reigning in Heaven with God, who has crowned them, to obtain their intercession for us, and also, according to apostolic tradition, to wash away the stains of those brethren who died in the Lord but without yet being wholly purified." Think of this point: The Holy Mass transcends time and space, uniting the faithful in heaven, on earth, and in purgatory into a Holy Communion, and the Holy Eucharist Itself augments our union with Christ, wipes away venial sins, and preserves us from future mortal sins (cf. *Catechism*, #1391-1396). Therefore, the offering of the Mass and other prayers or sacrifices for the intentions of the faithful departed are good and holy acts.

This practice is not new. The *Catechism* asserts, "From the beginning the Church has honored the memory of the dead and offered prayers in suffrage for them, above all the Eucharistic Sacrifice, so that, thus purified, they may attain the beatific vision of God" (#1032). Actually, this "beginning" has roots even in the Old Testament. Judas Maccabees offered prayers and sacrifices for the Jewish soldiers who had died wearing pagan amulets, which were forbidden by the Law; II Maccabees reads, "Turning to supplication, they prayed that the sinful deed might be fully blotted out" (12:43) and "Thus, [Judas Maccabees] made atonement for the dead that they might be freed from sin" (12:46).

In the early history of the Church, we also see evidence of prayers for the dead. Inscriptions uncovered on tombs in the Roman catacombs of the second century evidence this practice. For example, the epitaph on the tomb of Abercius (d. 180), Bishop of Hieropolis in Phrygia begs for prayers for the repose of his soul. Tertullian in 211 attested to observing the anniversary of death with prayers. Moreover, the *Canons* of Hippolytus (c. 235) explicitly mention the offering of prayers for the dead during the Mass.

The testimony of the Church Fathers beautifully supports this belief: St. Cyril of Jerusalem (d. 386), in one of his many catechetical discourses, explained how at Mass both the living and dead are remembered, and how the Eucharistic Sacrifice of our Lord is of benefit to sinners, living and dead. St. Ambrose (d. 397) preached, "We have loved them during life; let us not abandon them in death, until we have conducted them by our prayers into the house of the Lord." St. John Chrysostom (d. 407) stated, "Let us help and commemorate them. If Job's sons were purified by their father's sacrifice, why would we doubt that our offerings for the dead bring them some consolation? Let us not hesitate to help those who have died and to offer our prayers for them." Finally, Pope St. Gregory (d. 604) said, "Let us not hesitate to help those who have died and to offer our prayers for them."

One may wonder, "What if the person's soul has already been purified and gone to heaven?" We on earth know neither the judgment of God nor the divine time frame; so, there is always goodness in remembering our departed and commending them to God through prayer and sacrifice. However, if indeed the departed soul has been purified and now rests in God's presence in heaven, then those prayers and sacrifices offered benefit the other souls in purgatory through the love and mercy of God.

Therefore, we find not only the origins of this practice dating to the early Church but we also clearly recognize its importance. When we face the death of someone, even a person who is not Catholic, to have a Mass offered for the repose of his soul and to offer our prayers are more beneficial and comforting than any other sympathy card or bouquet of flowers. Most importantly, we should always remember our own dearly departed loved ones in the Holy Mass and through our own prayers and sacrifices help them in their gaining eternal rest.

WHAT IS THE LITURGICAL YEAR?

Quite simply, the liturgical year is the celebration of a series of religious feasts and seasons. In so doing, we make sacred the ordinary time of a twelve-month calendar. Actually, we inherited this notion from our Jewish ancestors of the Old Testament. In the Book of Leviticus, Chapter 23, we find the Jewish calendar which speaks of a week of seven days, with six for work and the seventh day, the Sabbath, for rest and for "sacred assembly." This Sabbath Day belongs to the Lord. Leviticus then continues to speak of the dates of Passover, Yom Kippur, and other special feast days.

For Roman Catholics, we too have a liturgical calendar, which has evolved during the history of the Church. The purpose of such a calendar was to trace the mystery of salvation and the course of salvation history. Again, the idea is to sanctify time. Pope Pius XII wrote, "By commemorating the mysteries of the Savior, the sacred liturgy strives to bring all believers to participate in them in such a way that the divine Head of the Mystical Body may live in each of His members with the fullness of His holiness" (*Mediator Dei*, #152).

We see the beginnings of the calendar in the early Church. The Christians changed the Lord's day to Sunday, in honor of the resurrection. In Acts, we read, "On the first day of the week when we gathered for the breaking of the bread ... " (20:7). Fridays were designated as days of penance and sacrifice, in honor of our Lord's sacrifice of Himself for our sins on Good Friday; to this day, Friday should be a day of penance when we abstain from meat or make some other sacrifice. In the early Church, the *Didache* (AD 80) also marked Wednesdays as a day of penance and prayer, which is perhaps why many parishes still have novenas or Holy Hours on Wednesday evenings. By the 10th century, especially in the Western Church, our Blessed Mother was honored on Saturdays.

Over the centuries, the Church has punctuated the course of the year with feast days or holy days. In the midst of our normal routine, these days help focus our attention on Christ and the mystery of salvation. Several feast days are dedicated to our Blessed Mother, the exemplar of our faith, who participated intimately in the mystery of salvation, such as the Solemnity of Mary, Mother of God (January 1), the Annunciation (March 25), the Visitation (May 31), the Assumption (August 15), the Nativity of Mary (September 8), the Presentation of Mary (September 22) and the Immaculate Conception (December 8).

Many feast days commemorate the saints who glorified Christ in their lives on earth and now share His glory in the Kingdom of Heaven. Their feast days usually correspond to the date of death, the birth of the saint into eternal life. Many of the dates were established over time and sometimes varied according to locale. However, in 1568, Pope Pius V promulgated the universal calendar setting the feast days and their dates which would be celebrated throughout the whole Church. To date, various Popes have increased or decreased the number of feast days of saints honored by the whole church. The purpose is clear: "For the feasts of the saints proclaim the wonderful works of Christ in His servants and offer to the faithful fitting examples for their imitation" (*Constitution on the Sacred Liturgy*, #111).

Finally, the calendar follows a series of seasons: The calendar begins with Advent, which focuses on the preparation for the birth of the Messiah. Christmas Season then follows, beginning with the birth of the our Lord, celebrates the Epiphany, and concludes with the Baptism of the Lord. The Feast of the Baptism of the Lord also commences the season of Ordinary Time, which traces the public ministry of Jesus. Lent interrupts Ordinary Time, and lasts for 40 days (not including Sundays) and prepares us for Easter. Easter Season begins with the Easter Vigil Mass, is followed by the 40 days leading to the Ascension and then concludes 10 days later with Pentecost. After Pentecost, Ordinary time resumes and concludes with the Solemnity of Christ the King, the last Sunday of the liturgical year.

WHAT IS THE DIFFERENCE BETWEEN A SOLEMNITY, A FEAST, AND A MEMORIAL?

The Church punctuates the liturgical year by celebrating various events important to the mystery of our salvation. During the course of the liturgical year, the Church celebrates the whole mystery of Christ, from His incarnation and birth to His ascension, to Pentecost and the founding of the Church, and finally to the second coming of Christ in judgment on the Solemnity of Christ the King. On Sundays in particular, we commemorate the Resurrection, when our Lord triumphed over sin and death. In a special way, the Church also honors our Blessed Mother, marking those special events of her participation in the mystery of salvation. Finally, the Church also commemorates the memorial days of saints, who through their lives bring to the minds of the faithful the call to holiness. Saints' days are celebrated with few exceptions on the date of the saint's death – their birth into eternal life.

Technically, the divisions are as follows:

Solemnities are the celebrations of greatest importance. Each Solemnity begins on the prior evening with first vespers (evening prayer) and several of the solemnities have their own Vigil Mass. On these days, both the Gloria and the Creed are recited. Sundays and Holy Days of Obligation (which in the United States are the Solemnity of Mary Mother of God, Ascension, Assumption, All Saints, Immaculate Conception, and Christmas) are always considered solemnities. Other examples of solemnities include the Solemnity of St. Joseph (March 19), the Solemnity of the Sacred Heart of Jesus (Friday after the Feast of Corpus Christi), and the Solemnity of St. Peter and St. Paul (June 29).

Feasts are of second importance in our liturgical calendar and are celebrated on a particular day. These feasts do not have a first vespers or Vigil Mass the prior evening. An exception would be the feasts of the Lord which occur on Sundays in Ordinary Time and Sundays in the Christmas season. For example, the Feast of the

Presentation of the Lord (February 2) has its own first vespers. On these days, the Gloria is recited but not the Creed.

Next in line are memorials, which are classified as either obligatory or optional. Memorials commemorate a saint or saints. Obligatory memorials must be observed whereas optional memorials do not have to be observed. For example, the memorial of St. John Bosco (January 31) is obligatory while the memorial of St. Blase (February 3) is optional. Only the memorials of those saints who are of "universal significance" are observed by the whole Church and marked in the general liturgical calendar.

Particular churches, countries, or religious communities may also celebrate the memorials of other saints of "special significance" in accord with their special devotions. For example, the memorial in honor of the patron saint of a diocese is raised to a "feast."

The celebration of memorials is also governed by the liturgical season. For instance, obligatory memorials occurring in Lent are only celebrated as optional memorials. During "Privileged Seasons" (December 17-31 and Lent) the prayer of the Saint may be substituted for the regular collect (opening prayer) of the Mass. During weekday Masses during Advent (prior to December 17), Christmas Season, Easter Season, and Ordinary Time, the priest may offer the Mass of the saint, or the Mass of any saint of the Roman Martyrology, or a Mass such as one for "Various Occasions" (e.g. Masses for the Spread of the Gospel or for Religious Vocations) or a Votive Mass (e.g. the Mass of St. Joseph or the Mass of the Angels). Also on Saturdays, when there is no obligatory memorial, it is most appropriate to offer the Mass of the Blessed Mother.

For complete details on the order of precedence, please consult the *General Norms for the Liturgical Year* and the *New General Roman Calendar* issued by Pope Paul VI in 1969. Nevertheless, the basic rule of thumb is this: Sundays, other Solemnities, Holy Week, and the Octave of Easter always take precedence. These are followed by Feasts, weekdays of Advent (December 17-24), days within the Octave of Christmas, weekdays of Lent, obligatory memorials, optional memorials, weekdays of Advent (through December 16), other weekdays of the Christmas Season, other weekdays of the Easter Season, and weekdays in Ordinary Time.

If reading this sequence seems a bit confusing, perhaps that is why the Bishop's Committee on the Liturgy of the National Conference of Catholic Bishops publishes an annual *Ordo* which outlines the proper celebrations and their particulars throughout the liturgical year.

WHAT ARE THE HOLY DAYS OF OBLIGATION?

According to the *Code of Canon Law*, Sunday, the day we celebrate the resurrection of our Lord, is always observed as the foremost holy day of obligation for the universal Church. (The obligation involved is simply the duty to attend Mass on that day.) The *Code* also lists ten other holy days of obligation: Christmas; the Epiphany; the Ascension of our Lord; the Solemnity of Corpus Christi (the Most Holy Body and Blood of Christ); the Solemnity of Mary, Mother of God; Mary's Immaculate Conception; her Assumption; the Solemnity of St. Joseph; the Solemnity of St. Peter and St. Paul; and All Saints Day. The Code notes that the conference of bishops can reduce the number of holy days of obligation or transfer them to Sunday with the approval of the Holy Father. (cf. the *Code of Canon Law*, #1246.)

In the United States, the Epiphany is transferred to the Sunday after January 1, and Corpus Christi is transferred to the second Sunday after Pentecost. At their November, 1991 meeting, the National Conference of Catholic Bishops in the United States decided to retain as holy days of obligation the Solemnity of Mary, Mother of God (January 1), Ascension Thursday (40 days after Easter), the Assumption of Mary (August 15), All Saints Day (November 1), the Immaculate Conception (December 8), and Christmas (December 25). However, whenever the Solemnity of Mary, Mother of God; the Assumption; or All Saints Day falls on a Saturday or on a Monday, the obligation to attend Mass is dispensed, meaning that the day is still a "holy day" but a person is not required to attend Mass. For example, if Christmas falls on a Saturday, the obligation remains to attend Mass; on the other hand, if the Solemnity of Mary, Mother of God (January 1) also falls on a Saturday, it remains a holy day but without the obligation to attend Mass. The Vatican confirmed this decision on July 4, 1992, and it became effective on January 1, 1993.

Nevertheless, we should not forget the importance of these holy days, whether or not there is the "legal" obligation to attend Mass. The *Constitution on the Sacred Liturgy* of the Second Vatican Council stated, "Thus recalling the mysteries of the redemption, [the Church] opens up to the faithful the riches of her Lord's powers and merits, so that these are in some way made present for all time; the faithful lay hold of them and are filled with saving grace" (#102). Therefore, the importance of attending Mass on Sunday or any other holy day is not simply because of an obligation, but why it is an obligation. Our lives are so busy, and we face so many distractions. We could lose sight of God or become numb to His presence. Maybe we do have to sacrifice to attend Mass by rearranging our schedule or suffering some inconvenience to the normal course of life. So what? Our cherishing the mysteries of our salvation should take precedence over the exigencies of living in this world. Remember at the Last Supper, Jesus reminded the apostles that while they live in the world, they are not of this world (John 17:13-19). The holy days help us to remember the same. Therefore, we must pause to ponder, celebrate, and live the mystery of salvation by marking each Sunday, these special holy events, and the lives of those who are exemplars of faith with the offering of the Holy Mass.

WHY DO WE GENUFLECT BEFORE THE TABERNACLE AND KNEEL DURING MASS?

The 1985 Extraordinary Synod of Bishops asserted "that the liturgy must favor the sense of the sacred and make it shine forth. It must be permeated by the spirit of reverence, adoration, and the glory of God." To foster such a spirit, the Church has prescribed certain gestures and actions, especially toward the Blessed Sacrament.

The practice of genuflecting before the Blessed Sacrament, whether enclosed in the tabernacle or exposed in a monstrance, is a beautiful sign of adoration. This physical act of genuflection symbolizes our heart bowing before the Lord who is substantially and really present in the Eucharist. St. Ambrose (d. 397) said, "The knee is made flexible by which the offense of the Lord is mitigated, wrath appeased, grace called forth," and Alcuin (d. 804) later added, "By such a posture of the body we show forth our humbleness of heart."

Following the same line of thought, kneeling also holds a special place in fostering a proper reverence. Going back to our Lord's time, the Jewish people often stood while praying; however, when the occasion was solemn, the petition urgent, or the prayer was offered with great fervor, then the person humbly knelt before his God to pray. For instance, when Jesus prayed in the Garden of Gethsemane, the gospel reads, He "went down on His knees and prayed ... " (Luke 22:41).

Concerning the Eucharistic Prayer of the Mass, the *General Instruction on the Roman Missal* stipulated that the congregation stand during the Eucharistic Prayer except for the consecration. As a matter of fact, the *General Instruction* only specified kneeling during the consecration (#21), which accounts for the observed difference in some other countries. However, the Holy See extended permission to local Bishops' Conferences to adapt gestures and postures to meet the sensibilities of their own people as long as the meaning and purpose of the part of the Mass were not diminished. Therefore, in 1969, the National Conference of Catholic Bishops decided to retain for parishes in America the practice of the congregation kneeling through the entire Eucharistic Prayer, after the recitation of the Sanctus until after the Amen. Moreover, we kneel after the Agnus Dei until the time to receive Holy Communion, and most people kneel out of reverence while they make an act of thanksgiving after receiving Holy Communion. This practice of kneeling seems most appropriate during the Eucharistic Prayer of the Mass, for "in this divine sacrifice which is celebrated in the Mass, the same Christ who offered Himself once in a bloody manner on the altar of the cross is contained and is offered in an unbloody manner" (Council of Trent).

Concerning the reception of Holy Communion, the Sacred Congregation for Sacraments and Divine Worship in *Inaestimabile donum* (1980) permitted the faithful to receive Holy Communion either kneeling or standing according to the norms established by the local Bishops' Conference. In each diocese, kneeling or standing to receive Holy Communion is established by parish custom.

Some confusion arises concerning whether it is proper to genuflect before receiving Holy Communion. The Sacred Congregation for Sacraments and Divine Worship did state, "When the faithful communicate kneeling, no other sign of reverence towards the Blessed Sacrament is required, since kneeling is itself a sign of adoration. When they receive Communion standing, it is strongly recommended that, coming up in procession, they should make a sign of reverence before receiving the Sacrament. This should be done at the right time and place, so that the order of people going to and from Communion is not disrupted" (*General Instruction*, #11). This "strong recommendation" seems most appropriate for those places that do not kneel during Mass except for the consecration; in those cases, the faithful would practice a common gesture of genuflection or bowing. However, given that in the United States Catholics kneel during the entire Eucharistic Prayer and also after the Lamb of God until the time of receiving Holy Communion, this practice of genuflection or bowing has not been mandated.

These regulations help unify the worship of a congregation as well as foster in the individual both a proper reverence while participating at Mass and devotion toward the Blessed Sacrament. The *General Instruction* asserted, "A bodily posture common to all who are present is a sign of their unity with each other as a congregation; it expresses the mental attitude and dispositions of those taking part and enhances them" (#20).

WHERE SHOULD THE TABERNACLE BE PLACED IN A CHURCH?

To approach this question fairly and adequately, we need to understand some of the liturgical laws through history surrounding tabernacles. Actually the first norms governing tabernacles were promulgated in the Middle Ages. Until this time, no uniform custom regarding where tabernacles were located in churches existed. The Fourth Lateran Council (1215) decreed that the Blessed Sacrament be kept in a secure receptacle and placed in a clean, conspicuous place. The Synods of Cologne (1281) and Munster (1279) stipulated that the Blessed Sacrament be kept above the altar, sometimes in tabernacles shaped like doves and suspended by chains. Overall, during these times, the Blessed Sacrament was reserved in four possible ways: in a locked cabinet in the sacristy, a custom originating in the early church; in a cabinet in the wall of the choir area, or in a cabinet called the "Sacrament House" which was constructed like a tower and attached to a wall near the altar; in a "dove" receptacle suspended from the baldachino above the altar; and in a tabernacle on the altar itself or in the reredos of the altar.

In the sixteenth century, the Blessed Sacrament became customarily reserved in a tabernacle that was placed on the altar or part of the reredos. However, only in 1863, did the Sacred Congregation of Rites prohibit the use of suspended doves and sacrament houses.

The liturgical reforms of the Second Vatican Council prompted a "rethinking" of the location of the tabernacle in the Church. Two important points must always be kept in mind: First, reverence for the Holy Eucharist must be preserved and promoted. The *Constitution on the Sacred Liturgy* reminded us that the Holy Eucharist is "a sacrament of love, a sign of unity, a bond of charity, a paschal banquet in which Christ is consumed, the mind is filled with grace, and a pledge of future glory is given to us" (#46). We must not forget that being in the presence of the Blessed Sacrament is being in the divine presence of our Lord and Savior.

Second, the significance of the offering of the Mass itself where the Holy Eucharist is confected must be preserved and promoted. The *Dogmatic Constitution on the Church* asserted, "Taking part in the eucharistic sacrifice, the source and summit of the Christian life, they offer the divine victim to God and themselves along with it" (#11).

Accordingly, the *Instruction on the Worship of the Eucharistic Mystery* (1967) issued regulations (later incorporated into the *Code of Canon Law*) concerning tabernacles (cf. #52-57 and Canons 934-944): The Holy Eucharist may be reserved only on one altar or one place in any Church, and a vigil lamp must burn at all times to indicate and honor the presence of our Lord in the Blessed Sacrament. This tabernacle must be immovable, made of solid and opaque material, and locked to prevent theft or desecration of the Blessed Sacrament. The tabernacle "should be placed in a part of the Church that is prominent, conspicuous, beautifully decorated, and suitable for prayer" (Canon 938).

Here is where some confusion emerges. To promote prayer and devotion, the *Instruction* stated, "It is therefore recommended that, as far as possible, the tabernacle be placed in a chapel distinct from the middle or central part of the church, above all in those churches where marriages and funerals take place frequently, and in places which are much visited for their artistic or historical treasures" (#53). For example, at St. Patrick's Cathedral in New York City, which has a constant flow of tourists, the Blessed Sacrament is reserved in Our Lady's Chapel located behind the main altar; this beautiful chapel provides a quiet place for the faithful to pray without the distraction of the comings and goings of people. A similar situation exists at the Basilica of the Immaculate Conception in Washington, D.C.

However, this recommendation does not necessitate the interiors of "old" churches be destroyed to move the tabernacle: The *Instruction* stated, "In adapting churches, care will be taken not to destroy treasures of sacred art" (#24). Moreover, any renovation should be done with "prudence." I hate to think of how many beautiful churches have been whitewashed and their beautiful artwork thrown out or sent to the antique dealers because of someone who wanted to do liturgical renewal. I also wonder how many hearts have been broken because of imprudent renovations. Sadly, I have visited some churches – new ones and renovated ones – where it looks like the position of the tabernacle was more of an afterthought than an attempt to provide a prominent, conspicuous place.

Moreover, the *Instruction*'s recommendation does not prohibit having the tabernacle in the center of the Church, stating, "The Blessed Sacrament should be reserved in a solid, inviolable tabernacle in the middle of the main altar or on a side altar, but in a truly prominent place" (#54). The tabernacle can be located in the "center of the church," perhaps on an elevated area behind the altar so as not to diminish the attention to the Eucharistic sacrifice. Actually, the visual alignment of the tabernacle and altar emphasizes best both the reverence for the Holy Eucharist and the significance of the sacrifice of the Mass.

From a purely educational perspective, the goodness of having the tabernacle in the body of the Church either in the center, or at least to the side, is that it fosters devotion to the Blessed Sacrament. For instance, people genuflect in reverence to the Blessed Sacrament. Since the one day most parishioners visit their Church is on Sunday, having the tabernacle visible in a prominent and conspicuous location makes them aware of the Eucharistic presence of our Lord. The people are more mindful that the church itself is the "House of God" and a sacred space, not just a meeting house. In an age of doubt and disbelief, we need to do all we can to promote and foster devotion to our Lord in the Blessed Sacrament, and one clear way to accomplish this is by highlighting the tabernacle.

HOW SHOULD WE KEEP THE SABBATH HOLY?

The Third Commandment given by God to Moses clearly stated, "Remember to keep holy the Sabbath day. Six days you may labor and do all your work, but the seventh day is the Sabbath of the Lord, your God. No work may be done then either by you, or your son or daughter, or your male or female slave, or your beast, or by the alien who lives with you. In six days the Lord made the heavens and the earth, the sea and all that is in them; but on the seventh day He rested. That is why the Lord has blessed the Sabbath day and made it holy" (Exodus 20:8-11). While the Sabbath commemorated God's day of rest during the seven-day creation account of Genesis, it was also sacred because of what God had done for His people when He liberated them from slavery in Egypt: "For remember that you too were once slaves in Egypt, and the Lord your God, brought you from there with his strong hand and outstretched arm. That is why the Lord, your God, has commanded you to observe the Sabbath day" (Deuteronomy 5:15). Therefore, the Sabbath was not only a day of rest and refreshment for everyone, being mindful of the many blessings received through creation, but also a day of remembering the covenant He had made with His people through the Passover sacrifice and the giving of the Law at Mount Sinai. The Sabbath was indeed the Day of the Lord.

For Christians the "Sabbath" rest was transferred to the first day of the week – Sunday, the day our Lord Jesus Christ rose from the dead. For us, Sunday marks the day of the new creation, when Christ conquered sin, darkness, and death. Sunday marks the day of the new covenant when Christ, the High Priest who had offered Himself as the Unblemished Passover Lamb of Sacrifice on the altar of the cross, gave the promise of everlasting life. Therefore, Sunday is the fulfillment of the Sabbath of the Old Testament. St. Justin Martyr (d. 165) wrote, "Sunday, indeed, is the day on which we hold our common assembly because it is the first day on which God, transforming the darkness and matter, created the world; and our Savior, Jesus Christ, arose from the dead on the same day."

Despite our very complex and busy modern times, we must strive to keep the "Sabbath Day" – Sunday – holy. Our first priority is to worship God publicly by participating at Holy Mass. Since the days of the apostles, the Church community has gathered together on Sunday to attend Mass. The *Code of Canon* Law logically mandates, "On Sundays and other holy days of obligation the faithful are bound to participate in the Mass" (#1247). This obligation makes perfect sense: Following St. Thomas Aquinas' thought, we have a moral obligation to give visible, public, and regular worship to the God who created all things, including ourselves, who has blessed us in many ways, and who has saved us from sin. Just as we attend to our material and physical concerns, such as getting proper sleep, food, exercise, and hygiene, we must attend to the well-being of our souls through prayer and public worship.

While this is a precept of our Church, we should consider it a privilege to attend Mass. We gather as a Body of Christ sharing a common unity of faith and baptism which overrides any ethnic, cultural, or other difference. At Mass, we affirm our identity as a Roman Catholic Christian. We are nourished through the Word of God proclaimed in Sacred Scripture and explicated by the priest. We are then plunged into the mystery of Christ's passion, death, and resurrection, and nourished again through a sharing in His sacred Body and Blood in the Holy Eucharist. When "the Mass has ended" and we have given thanks, we then go on to our regular routine and our busy world, but we take Jesus with us. The ending really marks a beginning. The Mass becomes the launchpad for the rest of the week.

Those that disregard the obligation of attending Sunday Mass for some frivolous reason or lame excuse either do not understand what they are missing or have their priorities out of order. God must come first, not soccer or baseball, the shopping mall, or bed. We cannot play games with God and say, "Oh, God will understand. I can pray in my heart." God is God, and we are His creatures: unless we are sick, facing an emergency, or have some other serious reason, we owe God His due worship. If we consider ourselves part of the Church, it is only right to worship as part of a Church. To fail in this obligation is to commit a grave sin (*Catechism*, #2181). I often think of so many people who lived under communism and risked the loss of freedom, job opportunities, and education just to attend Mass. What good excuse do we have to skip Mass? How blessed we are in this country to be able to worship freely and easily!

If Mass seems "boring" and not as exciting as some other activity, maybe the problem is the person is just not putting enough effort into it. We ought to arrive ahead of time to collect our thoughts and focus on God, to pay attention to the readings and sermon, to pray the Eucharistic Prayer with the priest in the quiet of our hearts, to receive Holy Communion with a hunger for the Lord, and to give thanks for what we have received. I fear too many people are like "pew potatoes" instead of active worshippers. In an anonymous sermon of the very early Church, the faithful were admonished, "Tradition preserves the memory of an ever-timely exhortation: Come to Church early, approach the Lord, and confess your sins, repent in prayer ... . Be present at the sacred and divine liturgy, conclude its prayer and do not leave before the dismissal ... . We have often said, 'This day is given to you for prayer and rest. This is the day that the Lord has made, let us rejoice and be glad in it.'"

The second priority is to take time for personal rest and for those that we love. In our fast paced world, sometimes Sunday becomes "catch-up" day of running to the store, doing laundry, and the like. Granted, sometimes we have no choice in the matter, and surely we cannot neglect our responsibilities. However, we should reflect on the structure of our lives and strive to accomplish those routine tasks sometime during the week.

By doing so, we can take good leisurely time for ourselves. All of us need some time to read, think, meditate, and talk with God in the quiet of our hearts. We need to enjoy hobbies, visit museums, or even browse in shops for pleasure. For some people, cooking the special dinner is not only relaxing but also an act of love for the family.

Sunday should be a family oriented day. Unfortunately, many families lead fragmented lives, with people running in different directions. Some families seem more like a bunch of people living under the same roof rather than a real family living in a home. We need to enjoy our loved ones' company and take time to share our lives with them. We should also think of our "extended family": Sunday should also be a day for charitable activities, such as visiting the sick or elderly, especially elderly relatives who know the burden of being alone.

In our very complex and busy modern times, we need to make Sunday the Lord's Day. Voltaire (d. 1791), the great critic and attacker of the Church, said, "If you want to kill Christianity, you must abolish Sunday." Sadly, many have abolished Sunday on their own by how they live their lives, and in so doing, have abolished the presence of God in their lives. We would all be much better off if we were mindful of Sunday as a day for worshipping God as a Church, praying to Him, and sharing ourselves and our love with our families.

WHAT IS THE ROSARY
AND HOW DID IT ORIGINATE?

The Rosary is one of the most cherished prayers of our Catholic Church. Introduced by the Creed, the Our Father, three Hail Mary's and the Doxology ("Glory Be"), and concluded with the Salve Regina, the Rosary involves the recitation of five decades, each consisting of the Our Father, 10 Hail Mary's, and the Doxology. During this recitation, the individual meditates on the saving mysteries of our Lord's life and the faithful witness of our Blessed Mother. Journeying through the Joyful, Sorrowful, and Glorious mysteries of the Rosary, the individual brings to mind our Lord's incarnation, His passion and death, His resurrection from the dead, and His ascension into glory. In so doing, the Rosary assists us in growing in a deeper appreciation of these mysteries, in uniting our life more closely to our Lord, and in imploring His graced assistance to live the faith. We also ask for the prayers of our Blessed Mother, the exemplar of faith, who leads all believers to her Son.

The origins of the Rosary are "sketchy" at best. The use of "prayer beads" and the repeated recitation of prayers to aid in meditation stem from the earliest days of the Church and have roots even in pre-Christian times. Evidence exists from the Middle Ages that strings of beads were used to help a person count the number of Our Fathers or Hail Marys recited. Actually, these strings of beads became known as "Paternosters," the Latin for "Our Father."

The structure of the Rosary gradually evolved between the 12th and 15th centuries. Eventually 50 Hail Marys were recited and were linked with verses of psalms or other phrases evoking the lives of Jesus and Mary. During this time, this prayer form became known as the *rosarium* ("rose garden"), actually a common term used to designate a collection of similar material, such as an anthology of stories on the same subject or theme. Finally, during the 16th century, the structure of the five decade Rosary based on the three sets of mysteries prevailed.

Tradition does hold that St. Dominic (d. 1221) devised the Rosary as we know it. Moved by a vision of our Blessed Mother, he preached the use of the Rosary in his missionary work among the Albigensians, who had denied the mystery of Christ's incarnation. Some scholars take exception to St. Dominic's actual role in forming the Rosary since the earliest accounts of his life do not mention it, the Dominican constitutions do not link him with it, and contemporaneous paintings of St. Dominic do not include it as an identifying symbol of the saint.

In 1922, Dom Louis Gougaud stated, "The various elements which enter into the composition of that Catholic devotion commonly called the Rosary are the product of a long and gradual development which began before St. Dominic's time, which continued without his having any share in it, and which only attained its final shape several centuries after his death." However, other scholars would rebut that St. Dominic not so much "invented" the Rosary as he preached its use to convert sinners and those who had strayed from the faith. Moreover, at least a dozen popes have mentioned St. Dominic's connection with the Rosary in various papal pronouncements, sanctioning his role as at least a "pious belief."

The Rosary gained greater popularity in the 1500s. At this time, the Moslem Turks were ravaging eastern Europe. Recall that in 1453, Constantinople had fallen to the Moslems, leaving the Balkans and Hungary open to conquest. With Moslems raiding even the coast of Italy, the control of the Mediterranean was now at stake. In 1571, Pope Pius V organized a fleet under the command of Don Juan of Austria, the half-brother of King Philip II of Spain. While preparations were underway, the Holy Father asked all of the faithful to say the Rosary and implore our blessed Mother's prayers, under the title Our Lady of Victory, that our Lord would grant victory to the Christians. Although the Moslem fleet outnumbered that of the Christians in both vessels and sailors, the forces were ready to meet in battle. The Christian flagship flew a blue banner depicting Christ crucified. On October 7, 1571, the Moslems were defeated at the Battle of Lepanto. The following year, Pope St. Pius V in thanksgiving established the Feast of the Holy Rosary on October 7 where the faithful would not only remember this victory, but also continue to give thanks to the Lord for all of His benefits and to remember the powerful intercession of our Blessed Mother.

Mindful of the action of Pope Pius V, our Holy Father, Pope John Paul II, in an Angelus address given in October, 1983, stated, "The Rosary also takes ón fresh perspectives and is charged with stronger and vaster intentions than in the past. It is not a question now of asking for great victories, as at Lepanto and Vienna; rather it is a question of asking Mary to provide us with valorous fighters against the spirit of error and evil, with the arms of the Gospel, that is, the Cross and God's Word. The Rosary prayer is man's prayer for man. It is the prayer of human solidarity, the collegial prayer of the redeemed, reflecting the spirit and intent of the first of the redeemed, Mary, Mother and Image of the Church. It is a prayer for all the people of the world and of history, living and dead, called to be the Body of Christ with us and to become heirs together with Him of the glory of the Father."

The fact that our Church continues to include the Feast of the Holy Rosary on the liturgical calendar testifies to the importance and goodness of this form of prayer. Archbishop Fulton Sheen said, "The Rosary is the book of the blind, where souls see and there enact the greatest drama of love the world has ever known; it is the book of the simple, which initiates them into mysteries and knowledge more satisfying than the education of other men; it is the book of the aged, whose eyes close upon the shadow of this world, and open on the substance of the next. The power of the Rosary is beyond description."

WHAT IS A NOVENA?

Succinctly, a novena is a nine day period of private or public prayer to obtain special graces, to implore special favors, or make special petitions. (Novena is derived from the Latin *novem*, meaning nine.) As the definition suggests, the novena has always had more of a sense of urgency and neediness.

In our liturgical usage, the novena differs from an octave which has a more festive character, and either precedes or follows an important feast. For example, in our Church calendar we celebrate the Octave before Christmas, where the recitation of the "O" Antiphons during vespers help us prepare for the birth of our Savior, e.g. "O Sacred Lord" or "O Flower of Jesse's stem." We also celebrate the Octaves of Christmas and Easter, which include the feast days themselves and the seven days that follow, to highlight the joy of these mysteries.

The origin of the novena in our Church's spiritual treasury is hard to pinpoint. The Old Testament does not indicate any nine-days celebration among the Jewish people. On the other hand, in the New Testament at the Ascension scene, our Lord gives the apostles the Great Commission, and then tells them to return to Jerusalem and to await the coming of the Holy Spirit. Acts of the Apostles recounts, "After that they returned to Jerusalem from the mount called Olivet near Jerusalem'a mere Sabbath's journey away. Together they devoted themselves to constant prayer" (Acts 1:12,14). Nine days later, the Holy Spirit descended upon the Apostles at Pentecost. Perhaps, this "nine-day period of prayer" of the apostles is the basis for the novena.

Long before Christianity, the ancient Romans celebrated nine days of prayers for various reasons. The author Livy recorded how nine days of prayers were celebrated at Mount Alban to avert some evil or wrath of the gods as predicted by the soothsayers. Similarly, nine days of prayers were offered when some "wonder" had been predicted. Families also held a nine-day mourning period upon the death of a loved one with a special feast after the burial on the ninth day. The Romans also celebrated the *parentalia novendialia*, a yearly novena (February 13-22) remembering all departed family members. Since novenas were already part of Roman culture, it is possible that Christianity "baptized" this pagan practice.

Whatever the exact origins may be, the early Christians did have a nine-day mourning period upon the death of a loved one. Eventually, a novena of Masses for the repose of the soul was offered. To this day, there is the *novendialia* or Pope's Novena, observed upon the death of the Holy Father. Similarly, many parishes have novenas beginning on All Souls Day to pray for the faithful departed.

In the Middles Ages, particularly in Spain and France, novenas of prayers were offered nine days before Christmas, signifying the 9 months our Lord spent in the womb of our blessed Mother. These special novenas helped the faithful prepare for the festive, yet solemn, celebration of the birth of our Lord. Eventually, various novenas were composed to help the faithful prepare for a special feast or to invoke the aid of a saint for a particular reason. Some of the popular novenas still widely used in our Church include those of the Miraculous Medal, Sacred Heart of Jesus, St. Joseph, and St. Jude, to name a few.

It is difficult to say why we do not find novenas as much a part of public worship now as before Vatican II. I remember asking this question to an elderly priest, who basically said that he remembered people who would skip Mass yet attend the weekly novena. As Catholics, the primary focus of our spirituality and public worship should be the Holy Eucharist and the Mass. With the advent of the liturgical renewal and the increased participation of the congregation at Mass, perhaps this is why novenas fell by the wayside.

Also, some people I think have hurt the cause of novenas because of superstition. In every parish I have been assigned, I have found copies of a St. Jude novena which basically states that if a person goes to Church for nine days and leaves a copy of the novena to St. Jude, then the prayer will be granted – sort of like a spiritual chain letter. This is dispensing machine Catholicism: just as a person puts the coin in the vending machine and presses the button to get the desired soda, here a person says the prayers, goes to church, and is supposedly guaranteed that the request will be granted. So much for God's will. What is really sad these days is that the person simply Xeroxes the letter; one would think they could at least hand-write it. Worse yet, I usually have to pick up these letters which are left all over the Church.

Nevertheless, novenas still hold a legitimate place in our Catholic spirituality. The *Enchiridion of Indulgences* notes, "A partial indulgence is granted to the faithful, who devoutly take part in the pious exercise of a public novena before the feast of Christmas or Pentecost or the Immaculate Conception of the Blessed Virgin Mary" (#34). Here the Church is again emphasizing that the novena is a pious, spiritual exercise to bolster the faith of the individual, and that the individual should be truly devout, always remembering the goodness of the Lord who answers all of our prayers according to His divine will.

WHAT IS EXPOSITION AND BENEDICTION OF THE BLESSED SACRAMENT?

Exposition and benediction of the Blessed Sacrament is not only a very old devotion in our Church, but one that highlights the fundamental mystery of the Holy Eucharist – that our Lord is truly present, body and blood, soul and divinity in the Blessed Sacrament. In his 1980 Holy Thursday letter to priests, *Dominicae cenae*, Pope John Paul II wrote, "Since the Eucharistic mystery was instituted out of love, and makes Christ sacramentally present, it is worthy of thanksgiving and worship. And this worship must be prominent in all our encounters with the Blessed Sacrament ... " (#3). While emphasizing the importance of the Mass, the Holy Father then recommends various forms of Eucharistic devotion: personal prayer and periods of adoration before the Blessed Sacrament, exposition and benediction, Forty Hours devotion, Eucharistic processions, Eucharistic Congresses, and a special observance of the Solemnity of Corpus Christi. All of these devotions which focus on the Blessed Sacrament aid in our spiritual union with our Lord. As Jesus said, "I myself am the Bread of Life. No one who comes to me shall ever be hungry, no one who believes in me shall ever thirst" (John 6:35).

The ritual for exposition and benediction as presented in 1973 by the Sacred Congregation for Divine Worship basically follows this sequence: The priest places the Blessed Sacrament in a monstrance or *ostensorium* on the altar for adoration. (A ciborium containing the Blessed Sacrament may also be used, but the monstrance allows one to view the Holy Eucharist.) At this time, a hymn of praise (such as *O Salutaris Hostia*) is sung as the priest incenses the Blessed Sacrament. During the period of adoration, the faithful may pray in quiet and foster a deeper spiritual communion with the Lord. However, the adoration period should also include prayers, such as a novena or Liturgy of the Hours, and readings from Sacred Scripture accompanied perhaps by a homily or exhortation to increase the understanding of the Eucharistic mystery. At the end of the period of adoration, the priest again incenses the Blessed Sacrament as a hymn of praise is sung (such as *Tantum Ergo*), and then blesses the congregation with the Blessed Sacrament, making the sign of the cross. After the blessing, the priest reposes the Blessed Sacrament in the tabernacle.

This ritual seems to arise around the institution of the Feast of Corpus Christi by Pope Urban IV in 1264. On this feast day, the Holy Eucharist was carried in procession in vessels similar to our present day monstrances which allowed the faithful to view the Blessed Sacrament. Eventually a custom arose, especially in Germany, of keeping the Blessed Sacrament continually exposed to view in all of the Churches.

At the same time, members of guilds began to gather to sing canticles in the evening after work in honor of the Blessed Mother. In particular, the singing of the Salve Regina, composed in the 11th century, became popular in these devotions. These evening services were called *Salut* in France.

Over the next two or three centuries, these two services seem to have merged. The faithful would gather, usually in the evening for chanted prayers, particularly in honor of our Blessed Mother. The Blessed Sacrament would be exposed, more prayers would be chanted or recited, and the service would end with benediction. Interestingly, benediction is still known in France as *Le Salut Tres Saint Sacrement*.

WHY DO SOME GROUPS ATTACK THE USAGE OF RELIGIOUS STATUES AND PICTURES? WHY DO CATHOLICS HAVE STATUES AND ICONS?

The attack against the Church's use of religious statues or pictures arises from a misinterpretation of the clauses following the First Commandment: "I, the Lord, am your God ... . You shall not have other gods besides me. *You shall not carve idols for yourselves in the shape of anything in the sky above or on the earth below or in the waters beneath the earth; you shall not bow down before them or worship them*" (Exodus 20:2-5). (Actually, some Protestant denominations list the italicized clause as the second commandment and then combine our Ninth and Tenth Commandments.)

In understanding the context of the First Commandment, we must remember that at the time the 10 Commandments were given, no one had ever looked upon the face of God. Even Moses who was in the presence of God on Mount Sinai did not see the face of God: God said to Moses, "I will make all my beauty pass before you and in your presence I will pronounce my name, 'Lord ... .' But my face you cannot see, for no man sees me and still lives" (Exodus 33:19-20). So no one could ever possibly capture God in a statue or a picture; to do so would be simply a conjuring of the imagination.

However, Christ – true God and true man – entered this world and took on our own human flesh. The Word of God became flesh and dwelt among us. In the gospel Prologue, St. John wrote, " ... We have seen His glory: The glory of an only Son coming from the Father filled with enduring love" (John 1:14); therefore, "no one has ever seen God. It is God the only Son, ever at the Father's side, who has revealed Him" (John 1:18).

Precisely because of the incarnation of the Lord, St. John Damascene (d. 749) asserted in his *Apologetic Sermons Against Those Who Reject Sacred Images*, "Previously God, who has neither a body nor a face, absolutely could not be represented by an image. But now that He has made Himself visible in the flesh and has lived with men, I can make an image of what I have seen of God ... and contemplate the glory of the Lord, His face unveiled." Since the earliest days of the Church we have evidence of depictions of our Lord, of scenes from Sacred Scripture, or of the Saints; examples of such depictions can be found today in the catacombs.

However, in no way does a statue or picture depicting a religious subject – such as Christ, the Blessed Mother, or a saint – become an object of worship. Simply stated, Christ is not a statue. To think of a statue or picture as the actual person or to worship that statue or object would be idolatry.

The purpose of these sacred images is clearly to help us human beings in our contemplation of our Lord, of His deeds, and of the saints, so that we may draw closer to Him and be more fully joined to the Communion of Saints. For example, all of us have pictures of our own loved ones, living and deceased. I remember being shown pictures of my great grandparents and even three of my grandparents whom I never personally knew or saw because they had died before I was born. These loved ones whom I know through their pictures and stories are living realities for me. My family ties are strengthened with these people. I am able to be mindful of the history that is a part of my life. How much more true this is when I look at the picture of my dear maternal Grandmother that I did know but who has now gone home to our Lord. Granted the actual picture is not the person. The picture, though, reminds me of that person, and the life I still share with the person retains its focus.

The same is exactly true with a religious statue or image. Again, St. John Damascene stated, "The beauty of the images moves me to contemplation, as a meadow delights the eyes and subtly infuses the soul with the glory of God."

In her history, the Church has battled the misinterpretation of the First Commandment prohibition against graven images. In 730, Emperor Leo III, who ruled what remained of the Roman Empire in the East, ordered the destruction of icons, which are part of the Eastern liturgical tradition. The motive for the action was due to an exaggerated emphasis on the divinity of Christ and unfortunately an abuse of genuine devotion to these images. The destruction of these icons or any other sacred image became known as *iconoclasm* and was condemned by the Holy Father in Rome. Later in 787, the Second Council of Nicea, defending the use of sacred images, declared, "For, the more frequently one contemplates these pictorial representations, the more gladly will he be led to remember the original subject whom they represent, the more too will he be drawn to it and inclined to give it ... a respectful veneration ... . For 'the honor given to an image goes to the original model' [St. Basil]; and he who venerates an image, venerates in it the person represented by it."

A new iconoclasm emerged in the Protestant movement. The "reformation" fervor resulted in the stripping of altars, the destruction of religious artwork, and the whitewashing of interiors in many former Catholic Churches. Calvin in particular declared the honoring of the saints as the devil's invention and the veneration of sacred images as idolatry; Calvin's hostility overflowed into the Presbyterian, Dutch Reformed, Huguenot, Baptist, and Puritan traditions. (The Amish today even consider photographs of loved ones graven images.) The Council of Trent in 1563 reacted, stating, "The Images of Christ, of the Virgin Mother of God, and of other saints are to be kept and preserved, in places of worship especially; and to them due honor and veneration is to be given, not because it is believed that there is in them anything divine or any power for which they are revered, nor in the sense that something is sought from them or that a blind trust is put in images as once was done by the Gentiles who placed their hope in idols; but because the honor which is shown to them is referred to the original subjects which they represent. Thus through these images which we kiss and before which we kneel and uncover our heads, we are adoring Christ and venerating the saints whose likeness these images bear."

The Second Vatican Council affirmed the use of sacred images in its *Constitution on the Sacred Liturgy*: "The practice of placing sacred images in churches so that they be venerated by the faithful is to be maintained. Nevertheless, their number should be moderate and their relative positions should reflect right order" (#125). These sacred images help create a sense of the transcendent. Therefore, whether in our Churches or in our homes, sacred images are a visible reminder of our Lord, the Blessed Mother, and the Saints. Conscious of their living yet invisible presence in our lives, we join our prayers with our Blessed Mother and the Saints to our Lord, looking forward to the time when we will see Him face to face.

WHAT IS A BLESSING?

Blessings come under the category of sacramentals. A sacramental is a special prayer, action, or object which, through the prayers of the Church, prepares a person to receive grace and to better cooperate with it. For example, we make the sign of the cross using Holy Water when entering a Church: That pious action and the Holy Water itself, which together remind us of our Baptism, awaken us to the presence of God and dispose us to receiving God's grace. Unlike a sacrament, a sacramental does not itself confer the grace of the Holy Spirit. Nevertheless, like a sacrament, a sacramental helps the faithful to sanctify each moment of life and to live in the Paschal mystery of our Lord.

Among the sacramentals, blessings would be foremost. In the decree publishing the *Book of Blessings*, Cardinal Mayer, then prefect of the Congregation for Divine Worship, wrote, "The celebration of blessings holds a privileged place among all the sacramentals created by the Church for the pastoral benefit of the people of God. As a liturgical action, the celebration leads the faithful to praise God and prepares them for the principal effect of the sacraments. By celebrating a blessing, the faithful can also sanctify various situations and events in their lives." Blessings are signs to the faithful of the spiritual benefits achieved through the Church's intercession.

Throughout Sacred Scripture, we find how God issued various blessings: In the Genesis account of creation, God blessed all the living creatures and especially Adam and Eve, telling them to be fertile, to multiply, and to fill the earth and subdue it (cf. Genesis 1:22, 28). After the flood, God blessed Noah and his sons (Genesis 9:1ff). The patriarchs administered blessings, particularly to the eldest son, signifying a bestowing of God's benevolence, peace, and protection. In a similar vein, the Lord spoke to Moses and commanded the following blessing for all the Israelites: "The Lord bless you and keep you! The Lord let His face shine upon you, and be gracious to you! The Lord look upon you kindly and give you peace!" (Numbers 6:22-27). The people also blessed God, praising His goodness shown through creation, as illustrated in the beautiful hymn of praise in the Book of Daniel (3:52-90). The Preface for Eucharistic Prayer IV captures well this understanding of a blessing: "Father in Heaven ... , source of life and goodness, you have created all things, to fill your creatures with every blessing and lead all men to the joyful vision of your light."

For us Christians, blessings have taken on an even greater meaning through Christ who perfectly revealed to us the goodness and love of God. St. Paul wrote, "Praised be the God and Father of our Lord Jesus Christ, who has bestowed on us in Christ every spiritual blessing." Jesus blessed those He encountered: the little children (Mark 10:13-16) and the apostles at the ascension (Luke 24:50-53). He blessed objects: the loaves used to feed the 5000 (Mark 6:34ff) and the bread at the Last Supper (Matthew 26:26-30). Since Christ entrusted His saving ministry to the Church, it has instituted various blessings for people as well as objects to prompt the faithful to implore God's protection, divine assistance, mercy, faithfulness, and favor.

Who can do a blessing? The *Catechism* states, "Every baptized person is called to be a 'blessing,' and to bless. Hence lay people may preside at certain blessings; the more a blessing concerns ecclesial and sacramental life, the more is its administration reserved to the ordained ministry (bishops, priests, or deacons)" (#1669). Priests are the ordinary ministers of blessings, asking God's help for those people being blessed or dedicating something to a sacred service; the priest's blessing is imparted with the weight of the Church and therefore has great value in the eyes of God. The blessing of a layperson upon another, such as a parent blessing a child, is an act of goodwill whereby the person implores God's aid for the person; the value of this blessing in the eyes of God depends upon the person's individual sincerity and sanctity.

Blessings are categorized into two types: invocative and constitutive. In an invocative blessing, the minister implores the divine favor of God to grant some spiritual or temporal good without any change of condition, such as when a parent blesses a child. This blessing is also a recognition of God's goodness in bestowing this "blessing" upon us, such as when we offer a blessing for our food at meal time. In blessing objects or places, a view is also taken toward those who will use the objects or visit the places.

A constitutive blessing, invoked by a bishop, priest, or deacon, signifies the permanent sanctification and dedication of a person or thing for some sacred purpose. Here the person or object takes on a sacred character and would not be returned to non-sacred or profane use. For example, when religious sisters or brothers profess final vows, they are blessed, indicating a permanent change in their lives. Or, when a chalice is blessed, it becomes a sacred vessel dedicated solely to sacred usage.

In all, in bestowing His own blessing, God declares His goodness. We in turn bless God by praising Him, thanking Him for all of His benefits, and offering to Him our service, adoration, and worship. When we invoke God's blessing, we implore His divine beneficence, trusting that He will respond to our needs.

WHY DO PRIESTS USE INCENSE AT MASS?

Incense is an aromatic substance which is the resin from certain trees. When burned over charcoal, the incense produces a sweet smelling aroma. To make the smoke thicker and to enhance the fragrance, sometimes other perfumes are blended with the incense.

The use of incense in the ancient world was common, especially in religious rites where it was used to keep demons away. Herodotus (c. 500 BC), the Greek historian, recorded that it was popular among the Assyrians, Babylonians, and Egyptians. In Judaism, incense was included in the thanksgiving offerings of oil, grain, fruits, and wine (cf. Numbers 7:13-17). The Lord instructed Moses to build a golden altar for the burning of incense (cf. Exodus 30:1-10), which was placed in front of the veil to the entrance of the meeting tent where the Ark of the Covenant was kept.

We do not know exactly when the use of incense was introduced into our Mass or other liturgical rites. At the time of the early Church, the Jews continued to use incense in their own Temple rituals, so it would be safe to conclude that the Christians would have adapted its usage for their own rituals.

In the liturgies of Sts. James and Mark, which in their present form originate in the fifth century, the use of incense was prescribed. A Roman Ritual of the seventh century marked its usage in the procession of a Bishop to the altar and on Good Friday. Moreover, in the Mass, an incensation at the Gospel appeared very early; at the offertory, in the eleventh century; and at the Introit, in the twelfth century. About the thirteenth century, incense was also used at the Benedictus during Lauds and at the Magnificat during Vespers, and for the exposition and benediction of the Blessed Sacrament about the fourteenth century. Gradually, its usage was extended to the incensing of the celebrant and assisting clergy.

The purpose of incensing and the symbolic value of the smoke is that of purification and sanctification. For example, in the Eastern Rites at the beginning of Mass, the altar and sanctuary area are incensed while Psalm 50, the "Miserere," was chanted invoking the mercy of God. The smoke symbolizes the prayers of the faithful drifting up to heaven: The Psalmist prays, "Let my prayer come like incense before you; the lifting up of my hands, like the evening sacrifice" (Psalm 141).

Incense also creates the ambiance of heaven: The Book of Revelation describes the heavenly worship as follows: "Another angel came in holding a censer of gold. He took his place at the altar of incense and was given large amounts of incense to deposit on the altar of gold in front of the throne, together with the prayers of all God's holy ones. From the angel's hand, the smoke of the incense went up before God, and with it the prayers of God's people" (Revelation 8:3-4).

In the *General Instruction of the Roman Missal* incense may be used during the entrance procession; at the beginning of Mass, to incense the altar; at the procession and proclamation of the gospel; at the offertory, to incense the offerings, altar, priest, and people; and at the elevation of the Sacred Host and chalice of Precious Blood after the consecration. The priest may also incense the Crucifix and the Paschal Candle. During funeral Masses, the priest at the final commendation may incense the coffin, both as a sign of honor to the body of the deceased which became the temple of the Holy Spirit at Baptism and as a sign of the people's prayers for the deceased rising to God.

The usage of incense adds a sense of solemnity and mystery to the Mass. The visual imagery of the smoke and the smell remind us of the transcendence of the Mass which links heaven with earth, and allows us to enter into the presence of God.

WHAT ARE THE DIFFERENT COLORS USED FOR THE VESTMENTS AT MASS?

The Church's liturgical norms prescribe specific vestment colors for various celebrations. The purpose of utilizing different colors for vestments is twofold: First, the colors highlight the particular liturgical season and the faithful's journey through these seasons. Second, the colors punctuate the liturgical season by highlighting a particular event or particular mystery of faith. The following explanation is based on the norms of the *General Instruction on the Roman Missal*, #307-10.

White or gold, a color symbolizing rejoicing and purity of soul, is worn during the liturgical seasons of Christmas and Easter. White vestments are also used for feasts of our Lord (except those pertaining to His passion), the Blessed Virgin Mary, the angels, and the saints who were not martyrs. White vestments are also worn on the Solemnity of St. Joseph, and the Feasts of All Saints, St. John the Baptist, St. John the Evangelist, the Chair of St. Peter, and the Conversion of St. Paul. White may also be used for the Feast of All Souls, Masses of Christian Burial, and Masses for the Dead to signify our sharing in the resurrection of our Lord, when He triumphed over sin and death, sorrow and darkness.

Red has a dual imagery: On one hand, red symbolizes the shedding of blood and is therefore used on Palm Sunday (when Christ entered Jerusalem to prepare for His death), Good Friday, any other commemoration of the Lord's passion, the votive Mass of the Precious Blood, the days marking the martyrdom of the apostles (including St. John even though he survived the means of execution), and the feasts of other martyrs who offered their lives for the faith.

On the other hand, red also signifies the burning fire of God's love. For this reason, red vestments are worn on Pentecost when the Holy Spirit descended on the apostles and tongues of fire rested on their heads; for the celebration of the Sacrament of Confirmation; and for the votive Masses of the Holy Spirit.

Green is used during the liturgical season called Ordinary Time. This season focuses on the three-year period of our Lord's public ministry, and the gospel passages, particularly on Sundays, recount His teachings, miracles, exorcisms, and other deeds during this time. All of these teachings and events engender great hope in the mystery of salvation. We focus on the life He shared with mankind during His time on this earth, the life we share now with Him in the community of the Church and through His sacraments, and the everlasting life we look forward to sharing with Him perfectly in Heaven. Green appropriately symbolizes this hope and life, just as the hint of green on trees in early Spring arouses the hope of new life.

Violet or purple is used during Advent and Lent as a sign of penance, sacrifice, and preparation. At the midpoint of both of these seasons – Gaudete Sunday (the third Sunday of Advent) and Laetare Sunday (the fourth Sunday of Lent) – rose vestments are traditionally worn as a sign of joy: we rejoice at the midpoint because we are half-way through the season and anticipate the coming joy of Christmas or Easter. Some liturgists in other Christian denominations have tried to introduce the use of blue vestments during Advent as a way of distinguishing this season from Lent; however, no approval for blue vestments has been given for the Catholic Church. Purple vestments may also be used for the Feast of All Souls, Masses of Christian Burial, and Masses for the Dead.

Although not seen very frequently in the United States today, black vestments may be worn for Masses of Christian Burial as a sign of death and mourning. Black may also be used on the Feast of All Souls or for any Mass of the Dead, such as on the anniversary of the death of a loved one.

In all, the colors of the vestments awaken us to the sense of sacred time. They are another visible way to make present the sacred mysteries we celebrate.

WHY DO WE USE VOTIVE CANDLES?

Before addressing the use of votive candles in particular, we have to appreciate the symbolism of light and the general usage of candles in religious practice. In Judaism, a perpetual light was kept burning in the Temple and the synagogues not only to insure the ability to light other candles or oil lamps in the evening but also to show the presence of God (cf. Exodus 27:20-21 and Leviticus 24:2-4). Later, the Talmud prescribed a lit lamp at the Ark, where the Torah and other writings of Sacred Scripture were kept, to show reverence to the Word of God. (This practice probably influenced our own one of having a lit candle near the Tabernacle to indicate the presence of and to show reverence for the Blessed Sacrament.)

Roman pagan culture also used candles in religious practice. Lit candles were used in religious and military processions, showing the divine presence, aid, or favor of the gods. With the development of emperor worship, candles were also lit near his image as a sign of respect and reverence. Remember that by the time of Jesus, the emperor was considered divine and even given the titles, *Pontifex Maximus* (High Priest) and *Dominus et Deus* (Lord and God).

Christians adapted the use of lit candles (and oil lamps in the Eastern Roman Empire) for Mass, liturgical processions, evening prayer ceremonies, funeral processions, and, again, to show reverence to the reserved Blessed Sacrament. Moreover, there is evidence that lit candles or oil lamps were burned at the tombs of saints, particularly martyrs, by the 200s, and before sacred images and relics by the 300s. St. Jerome (d. 420) in his *Contra Vigilantium* attested to this practice. Note, however, that this practice probably existed well before our available written evidence.

In our Catholic tradition, in early times as well as today, light has a special significance – Christ. Recall Jesus said, "I am the light of the world. No follower of mine shall ever walk in darkness; no, he shall possess the light of life" (John 8:12) and "I have come to the world as its light, to keep anyone who believes in me from remaining in the dark" (John 12:46). Moreover, the Prologue of St.

John's Gospel connects Christ and true life with the imagery of light: "Whatever came to be in Him, found life, life for the light of men" and "The real light which gives light to every man was coming into the world" (John 1:4, 9). For this reason, in our liturgy for the Sacrament of Baptism, the priest presents a candle lit from the Paschal candle, which in turn symbolizes the Paschal mystery, and says to the newly baptized, "You have been enlightened by Christ. Walk always as children of the light and keep the flame of faith alive in your hearts. When the Lord comes, may you go out to meet Him with all the saints in the heavenly kingdom" (*Rite of Christian Initiation of Adults*). The light then is a symbol of faith, truth, wisdom, virtue, grace, the divine life, charity, the ardor of prayer, and the sacred presence which flow from Christ Himself.

With this background, we can appreciate the usage of votive candles. Here, as in early Christian times, we light a candle before a statue or sacred image of our Lord or of a saint. Of course, we do not honor the statue or the image itself, but whom that statue or image represents. The light signifies our prayer offered in faith coming into the light of God. With the light of faith, we petition our Lord in prayer, or petition the saint to pray with us and for us to the Lord. The light also shows a special reverence and our desire to remain present to the Lord in prayer even though we may depart and go about our daily business.

Interestingly, in the Middle Ages, the symbolism of the votive candles was elaborated. St. Radegund (d. 587) described a practice whereby a person would light a candle or several candles which equaled his own height; this was called "measuring to" such a saint. Although it may seem peculiar to us, this "measuring" actually reflects the idea of the candle representing the person in faith who has come into the light to offer his prayer.

Also, some Medieval spiritual writers expanded the imagery of the candle itself: beeswax symbolized the purity of Christ; the wick, the human soul of Christ; and the light, His divinity. Also, the burning candle symbolized a sacrifice, which is made in both the offering of the prayer and the acceptance of the Lord's will.

In all, the usage of votive candles is a pious practice which continues today in many Churches. The symbolism does remind us that prayer is a "coming into" the light of Christ, allowing our souls to be filled with His light, and letting that light burn on in our souls even though we may return to other activities.

WAS CHRIST REALLY BORN ON DECEMBER 25TH?

One would think that if anyone's date of birth were remembered exactly, it would be that of our Savior, Jesus Christ. Unfortunately, the gospels do not pinpoint the date of Christ's birth. The reason is probably that the focus of the gospels is on the kerygma or mystery of redemption – the passion, death, and resurrection of Christ. This focus is also probably why St. Mark's Gospel does not even include the Christmas story but begins with the Baptism of the Lord at the River Jordan. Easter, on the other hand, can be better dated because of its linkage with Passover.

Prior to the legalization of Christianity by the Emperor Constantine in the year 313, no universal date or even formal celebration of Christmas is found. For instance, Origen (d. 255), St. Irenaeus (d. 202), and Tertullian (d. 220) do not include Christmas or its date on their lists of feasts and celebrations.

After legalization, the Church was better able to establish universal dates for feasts and to organize their public celebration. Moreover, we now see the Church addressing controversies concerning Jesus as true God and true man, and how He entered this world. Such concern about the mystery of the incarnation would focus more attention on the importance of celebrating Christmas, the birth of our Lord.

On the more "practical" side of this issue, Roman pagans used to gather at the hill where the Vatican is presently located to commemorate the "Birth of the Unconquered Sun." This pagan feast was celebrated throughout the Empire either on December 25th (according to the Julian Calendar) or on January 6th (according to the Egyptian calendar). Although not proven with certainty, some historians credit Constantine, who declared Sunday as a day of rest in the Empire, with replacing the pagan festival with that of Christmas. Interestingly, since the 200s, Jesus was honored with the title, "Sun of Justice."

Somehow all of these elements converged to the formal celebration of Christmas on December 25th. For instance, Christmas was celebrated in Rome by Pope Liberius (352-66) on December 25th. On December 25, 379, St. Gregory Nazianzus (d. 389) preached a Christmas sermon in Constantinople. In the Cathedral of Milan, St. Ambrose (d. 397) celebrated Christmas on December 25. Therefore, by the year 400, generally, the birth of Christ was set on December 25th with the exception of Palestine, where it was celebrated on January 6th until the mid-600s when it was then transferred to December 25th.

As an aside, the Feast of the Epiphany also emerged in Gaul (the Roman province of present day France) about the year 361. This feast was moved to January 6th which remains the official date.

While the concern for exact dating may preoccupy us at times, the most important point is celebrating the birth of our Lord and meditating on His incarnation. Remember that the title Christmas is derived from the Old English title *Cristes Maesse* which means "The Mass of Christ." Each time we celebrate Mass and receive the Body and Blood of our Lord in the Holy Eucharist, we celebrate Christmas, when He, true God, was born as true man.

WHAT IS THE ORIGIN OF
THE NATIVITY SCENE (CRECHE)?

In the year 1223, St. Francis, a deacon, joined his fellow Franciscans at the town of Grecio to celebrate Christmas. Grecio was a small town built on a mountainside overlooking a beautiful valley. The people had cultivated the fertile area with vineyards. St. Francis realized that the chapel of the Franciscan hermitage would be too small to hold the congregation for Midnight Mass. So he found a niche in the rock near the town square and set up the altar. However, this Midnight Mass would be very special, unlike any other Midnight Mass.

St. Bonaventure (d. 1274) in his *The Life of St. Francis of Assisi* recorded the story:

"It happened in the third year before his death, that in order to excite the inhabitants of Grecio to commemorate the nativity of the Infant Jesus with great devotion, [St. Francis] determined to keep it with all possible solemnity; and lest he should be accused of lightness or novelty, he asked and obtained the permission of the sovereign Pontiff. Then he prepared a manger, and brought hay, and an ox and an ass to the place appointed. The brethren were summoned, the people ran together, the forest resounded with their voices, and that venerable night was made glorious by many and brilliant lights and sonorous psalms of praise. The man of God [St. Francis] stood before the manger, full of devotion and piety, bathed in tears and radiant with joy; the Holy Gospel was chanted by Francis, the Levite of Christ. Then he preached to the people around the nativity of the poor King; and being unable to utter His Name for the tenderness of His love, He called Him the Babe of Bethlehem. A certain valiant and veracious soldier, Master John of Grecio, who, for the love of Christ, had left the warfare of this world, and become a dear friend of this holy man, affirmed that he beheld an Infant marvelously beautiful, sleeping in the manger, Whom the blessed Father Francis embraced with both his arms, as if he would awake Him from sleep. This vision of the devout soldier is credible, not only by reason of the sanctity of him that saw it, but by reason of the miracles which afterwards confirmed its truth. For the example of Francis, if it be considered by the world, is doubtless sufficient to excite all hearts which are negligent in the faith of Christ; and the hay of that manger, being preserved by the people, miraculously cured all diseases of cattle, and many other pestilences; God thus in all things glorifying his servant, and witnessing to the great efficacy of his holy prayers by manifest prodigies and miracles."

Although the story is long old, the message is clear for us. Our own Nativity scenes which rest under our Christmas trees are a visible reminder of that night when our Savior was born. May we never forget to see in our hearts the little Babe of Bethlehem, who came to save us from sin. Moreover, we must never forget that the wood of the manger that held Him so securely would one day give way to the wood of the cross. May we too embrace Him with all of our love as did St. Francis.

WHAT IS THE ORIGIN OF THE CHRISTMAS TREE?

The story of the Christmas tree is part of the story of the life of St. Boniface, whose name was originally Winfrid. St. Boniface was born about the year 680 in Devonshire, England. At the age of five, he wanted to become a monk, and entered the monastery school near Exeter two years later. When he was fourteen, he entered the abbey of Nursling, in the Diocese of Winchester. Very studious himself, St. Boniface was the pupil of the learned abbot, Winbert. Later Boniface became the director of the school.

At this time, much of northern and central Europe still had not been evangelized. St. Boniface decided he wanted to be a missionary to these people. After one brief attempt, he sought the official approval of Pope St. Gregory II. The Pope charged him with preaching the gospel to the German people. (Also at this time, St. Boniface changed his name from Winfrid to Boniface.) St. Boniface travelled to Germany through the Alps into Bavaria and then into Hesse and Thuringia. In 722, the Pope consecrated St. Boniface as a bishop with jurisdiction over all of Germany. He knew that his greatest challenge was to eradicate pagan superstitions which hindered the acceptance of the gospel and the conversion of the people. Known as "the Apostle to Germany," he would continue to preach the gospel until he was martyred in 754. At this point we can begin our story about the Christmas tree.

With his band of faithful followers, St. Boniface was traveling through the woods along an old Roman road one Christmas Eve. Snow covered the ground, muffling their footsteps. Their breath could be seen in the crisp, cold air. Although several suggested that they camp for the night, St. Boniface encouraged them to push forward, saying, "Courage, brothers, and forward yet a little. God's moon will light us presently, and the path is plain. Well know I that you are weary; and my own heart wearies also for the home in England, where those I love so dearly are keeping feast this Christmas Eve. Oh, that I might escape from this wild, storm-tossed sea of Germany into the peaceful haven of my fatherland! But we have work to do before we feast tonight. For this is the Yule-tide, and the heathen people of the forest have gathered at the Oak of Geismar to worship their god, Thor; and strange things will be seen there, and deeds which make the soul black. But we are sent to lighten their darkness; and we will teach our kinsmen to keep a Christmas with us such as the woodland has never known. Forward, then, in God's name!"

They pushed ahead, reinvigorated by St. Boniface's plea. After a while, the road opened to a clearing. They could see houses, but dark and seemingly vacant. No human was in sight. Only the noise of hounds and horses broke the quiet. Continuing on, they came to a glade in the forest, and there appeared the sacred Thunder Oak of Geismar. "Here," St. Boniface proclaimed as he held his bishop's crozier high with its cross on top, "here is the Thunder-oak; and here the cross of Christ shall break the hammer of the false god Thor."

In front of the tree was a huge bonfire. Sparks danced in the air. The townspeople surrounded the fire facing the sacred oak. St. Boniface interrupted their meeting, "Hail, sons of the forest! A stranger claims the warmth of your fire in the winter night." As St. Boniface and his companions approached the fire, the eyes of the townspeople were on these strangers. St. Boniface continued, "Your kinsman am I, of the German brotherhood and from Wessex, beyond the sea, have I come to bring you a greeting from that land, and a message from the All-Father, whose servant I am."

Hunrad, the old priest of Thor, welcomed St. Boniface and his companions. Hunrad then said to them, "Stand still, common man, and behold what the gods have called us hither to do! This night is the death-night of the sun-god, Baldur the Beautiful, beloved of gods and men. This night is the hour of darkness and the power of winter, of sacrifice and mighty fear. This night the great Thor, the god of thunder and war, to whom this oak is sacred, is grieved for the death of Baldur, and angry with this people because they have forsaken his worship. Long is it since an offering has been laid upon his altar, long since the roots of his holy tree have been fed with blood. Therefore its leaves have withered before the time, and its boughs are heavy with death. Therefore, the Slavs and the Saxons have beaten us in battle. Therefore, the harvests have failed, and the wolf-hordes have ravaged the folds, and the strength has departed from the bow, and the wood of the spear has broken, and the wild boar has slain the huntsman. Therefore, the plague has fallen on your dwellings, and the dead are more than the living in all your villages. Answer me, you people, are not these things true?" The people sounded their approval and then began a chant of praise to Thor.

When the last sounds faded, Hunrad pronounced, "None of these things will please the god. More costly is the offering that shall cleanse your sin, more precious the crimson dew that shall send new life into this holy tree of blood. Thor claims your dearest and your noblest gift."

With that, Hunrad approached the children, grouped together around the fire. He selected the fairest boy, Asulf, the son of Duke Alvold and his wife, Thekla, and declared that he would be sacrificed to travel to Valhalla and bear the people's message to Thor. Asulf's parents were deeply shaken. Yet, no one spoke.

Hunrad led the boy to a large stone altar between the oak and the fire. He blindfolded the child, and had him kneel down placing his head on the stone altar. The people moved closer, and St. Boniface positioned himself near the priest. Hunrad then lifted his sacred black-stone hammer of the god Thor high into the air, ready to have it crush little Asulf's skull. As the hammer fell, St. Boniface thrust his crozier against the hammer, and it fell from Hunrad's hand, splitting in two against the stone altar. Sounds of awe and joy filled the air. Thekla ran to her child spared of this bloody sacrifice and embraced him tightly.

St. Boniface, his face radiant, then spoke to the people, "Hearken, sons of the forest! No blood shall flow this night save that which pity has drawn from a mother's breast. For this is the birth-night of the white Christ, the son of the All-Father, the Savior of mankind.

Fairer is He than Baldur the Beautiful, greater than Odin the Wise, kinder than Freya the Good. Since He has come sacrifice is ended. The dark, Thor, on whom you have vainly called, is dead. Deep in the shades of Niffelheim he is lost forever. And now on this Christ-night you shall begin to live. This blood-tree shall darken your land no more. In the name of the Lord, I will destroy it." St. Boniface then took his broad ax and began striking the tree. A mighty wind suddenly arose and the tree fell, wrenching its roots from the earth and splitting into four pieces.

Behind the mighty oak stood a young fir tree, pointing like a cathedral spire toward heaven. St. Boniface again spoke to the people, "This little tree, a young child of the forest, shall be your holy tree tonight. It is the wood of peace, for your houses are built of the fir. It is the sign of an endless life, for its leaves are ever green. See how it points upward to heaven. Let this be called the tree of the Christ-child; gather about it, not in the wild wood, but in your own homes; there it will shelter no deeds of blood, but loving gifts and rites of kindness."

So they took the fir tree and carried it to the village. Duke Alvold set the tree in the middle of his great hall. They placed candles on its branches, and it seemed filled with stars. Then St. Boniface, with Hunrad sitting at his feet, told the story of Bethlehem, the Baby Jesus in the manger, the shepherds, and the angels. All listened intently. Little Asulf, sitting on his mother's lap, said, "Mother, listen now, for I hear those angels singing again behind the tree." Some say it is true; some say it was St. Boniface's companions singing, "All glory be to God on high, and to the earth be peace; goodwill, henceforth, from heaven to men begin and never cease."

When we gather around our Christmas trees in our own homes, may we give thanks for the gift of our faith, hold the story of our Savior's birth in our hearts, and listen for the song of the angels.

IS THERE A SANTA CLAUS?

Yes, there is a Santa Claus. However, we know him more as St. Nicholas. Unfortunately, we have little historical evidence about this popular saint. Tradition holds that he was born in Patara in Lycia, a province in Asia Minor, in the mid-200s. He was born to a rather wealthy Christian family, and benefited from a solid Christian upbringing. Some say that at age five he began to study the teachings of the Church. He practiced virtue and piety.

His parents died when he was young and left him with a substantial inheritance, which he used for many good works. One popular story tells of a widower who had three daughters. He was going to sell them into prostitution since he could not afford to provide the necessary dowries for their marriages. St. Nicholas heard of the plight of the daughters and decided to help. In the dark of the night, he went to their home and tossed a bag of gold through an open window of the man's house, thereby supplying the money for a proper dowry for the oldest daughter. The next two nights, he did the same. St. Nicholas' generosity spared the girls from a sad fate.

St. Nicholas' reputation as a holy man spread. When the Bishop of Myra died, St. Nicholas was chosen to succeed him as Bishop. Several accounts agree that St. Nicholas suffered imprisonment and torture for the faith during the persecution waged by Emperor Diocletian about the year 300. Some sources attest that after the legalization of Christianity, he was present at the Council of Nicea (325) and joined in the condemnation of the heresy of Arianism, which denied the divinity of Christ. A later story tells of how St. Nicholas intervened to spare three innocent men sentenced to death by a corrupt governor named Eustathius, whom St. Nicholas confronted and moved to do penance. He died in the fourth century between the years 345 and 352 on December 6th, and was buried at his cathedral.

St. Nicholas has been continually venerated as a great saint. In the sixth century, Emperor Justinian I built a church in honor of St.

Nicholas at Constantinople, and St. John Chrysostom included his name in the liturgy. In the tenth century, an anonymous Greek author wrote, "The West as well as the East acclaims and glorifies him. Wherever there are people, in the country and the town, in the villages, in isles, in the furthest parts of the earth, his name is revered and churches are built in his honor. All Christians, young and old, men and women, boys and girls, reverence the memory and call upon his protection." After the Moslem invasion and persecution of Christianity, his body was taken by Italian merchants in 1087 and entombed in a new church in Bari, Italy.

The devotion to St. Nicholas was distorted by the Dutch Protestants, who wanted to erase his "Catholic trappings." For instance, St. Nicholas was rendered Sint Klaes and later Santa Claus. They also stripped him of his Bishop's regalia and made him a more Nordic looking Father Christmas with a red suit.

Nevertheless, is there a Santa Claus? I remember reading once the response of the editor of *The New York Sun* in 1897 to an eight-year-old girl named Virginia who asked the same question. Part of the answer, which still applies, was this: "Yes, Virginia, there is a Santa Claus. He exists as certainly as love and generosity and devotion exist, and you know that they abound and give to your life its highest beauty and joy. Alas! How dreary would be the world if there were no Santa Claus! It would be as dreary as if there were no Virginias. There would be no childlike faith then, no poetry, no romance to make tolerable this existence. We should have no enjoyment, except in sense and sight. The external light with which childhood fills the world would be extinguished ... . Nobody sees Santa Claus but that is no sign that there is no Santa Claus. The most real things in the world are those that neither children nor men can see ... . Thank God! He lives, and he lives forever." This is a pretty good testimonial of St. Nicholas and the joy he brings to our Christmas celebration. May we invoke St. Nicholas' prayers and be inspired by his example, so that we may always live in the spirit of Christmas.

WHAT ARE THE ORIGINS OF ASH WEDNESDAY AND THE USE OF ASHES?

The liturgical use of ashes originated in the Old Testament times. Ashes symbolized mourning, mortality, and penance. For instance, in the Book of Esther, Mordecai put on sackcloth and ashes when he heard of the decree of King Ahasuerus (or Xerxes, 485-464 BC) of Persia to kill all of the Jewish people in the Persian Empire (Esther 4:1). Job (whose story was written between the 7th and 5th centuries BC) repented in sackcloth and ashes (Job 42:6). Prophesying the Babylonian captivity of Jerusalem, Daniel (c. 550 BC) wrote, "I turned to the Lord God, pleading in earnest prayer, with fasting, sackcloth, and ashes" (Daniel 9:3). In the 5th century BC, after Jonah's preaching of conversion and repentance, the town of Nineveh proclaimed a fast and put on sackcloth, and the king covered himself with sackcloth and sat in the ashes (Jonah 3:5-6). These Old Testament examples evidence both a recognized practice of using ashes and a common understanding of their symbolism.

Jesus Himself also made reference to ashes: Referring to towns that refused to repent of sin although they had witnessed the miracles and heard the gospel, our Lord said, "If the miracles worked in you had taken place in Tyre and Sidon, they would have reformed in sackcloth and ashes long ago" (Matthew 11:21).

The early Church continued the usage of ashes for the same symbolic reasons. In his book, *De Poenitentia*, Tertullian (c. 160-220) prescribed that the penitent must "live without joy in the roughness of sackcloth and the squalor of ashes." Eusebius (260-340), the famous early Church historian, recounted in his *The History of the Church* how an apostate named Natalis came to Pope Zephyrinus clothed in sackcloth and ashes begging forgiveness. Also during this time, for those who were required to do public penance, the priest sprinkled ashes on the head of the person leaving confession.

In the Middle Ages (at least by the time of the eighth century), those who were about to die were laid on the ground on top of sackcloth sprinkled with ashes. The priest would bless the dying person with holy water, saying, "Remember that thou art dust and to dust thou shalt return." After the sprinkling, the priest asked, "Art thou content with sackcloth and ashes in testimony of thy penance before the Lord in the day of judgment?" To which the dying person replied, "I am content." In all of these examples, the symbolism of mourning, mortality, and penance is clear.

Eventually, the use of ashes was adapted to mark the beginning of Lent, the 40-day preparation period (not including Sundays) for Easter. The ritual for the "Day of Ashes" is found in the earliest editions of the *Gregorian Sacramentary* which dates at least to the 8th century. About the year 1000, an Anglo-Saxon priest named Aelfric preached, "We read in the books both in the Old Law and in the New that the men who repented of their sins bestrewed themselves with ashes and clothed their bodies with sackcloth. Now let us do this little at the beginning of our Lent that we strew ashes upon our heads to signify that we ought to repent of our sins during the Lenten fast." As an aside, Aelfric reinforced his point by then telling of a man who refused to go to Church on Ash Wednesday and receive ashes; the man was killed a few days later in a boar hunt. Since the Middle Ages, the Church has used ashes to mark the beginning of the penitential season of Lent, when we remember our mortality and mourn for our sins.

In our present liturgy for Ash Wednesday, we use ashes made from the burned palm branches distributed on the Palm Sunday of the previous year. The priest blesses the ashes and imposes them on the foreheads of the faithful, making the sign of the cross and saying, "Remember, man you are dust and to dust you shall return," or "Turn away from sin and be faithful to the Gospel." When we begin the holy season of Lent in preparation for Easter, we must remember the significance of the ashes we have received: We mourn and do penance for our sins. We again convert our hearts to the Lord, who suffered, died, and rose for our salvation. We renew the promises made at our baptism, when we died to an old life and rose to a new life with Christ. Finally, mindful that the kingdom of this world passes away, we strive to live the kingdom of God now and look forward to its fulfillment in heaven.

WHAT ARE THE ORIGINS OF THE STATIONS OF THE CROSS?

The Stations of the Cross which follow the path of Christ from Pontius Pilate's praetorium to Christ's tomb have been a popular devotion in parishes, especially during Lent and the preparation for Easter. In the 16th century, this pathway was officially entitled the *Via Dolorosa* (Sorrowful Way), or simply the *Way of the Cross* or *Stations of the Cross*.

This devotion has evolved over time. Tradition holds that our Blessed Mother visited daily the scenes of our Lord's passion. After Constantine legalized Christianity in the year AD 313, this pathway was marked with its important stations. St. Jerome (342-420), living in Bethlehem during the latter part of his life, attested to the crowds of pilgrims from various countries who visited these holy places and followed the Way of the Cross. Interestingly, St. Sylvia in her *Peregrinatio ad loca sancta* (380) in which she described in great detail various religious practices, does not mention a particular practice or set of prayers for following the stations; however, this omission does not entail that pilgrims did not in fact follow the Way of the Cross.

Actually, the devotion continued to grow in popularity. In the fifth century, an interest developed in the Church to "reproduce" the holy places in other areas so pilgrims who could not actually travel to the Holy Land could do so in a devotional, spiritual way in their hearts. For instance, St. Petronius, Bishop of Bologna, constructed a group of chapels at the monastery of San Stefano which depicted the more important shrines of the Holy Land, including several of the stations. (The same notion inspired the building of the Franciscan Monastery in Washington, where one can visit and see reproductions of the Bethlehem Chapel, the tomb of our Lord, and other important shrines of the Holy Land.)

In 1342, the Franciscans were appointed as guardians of the shrines of the Holy Land. The faithful received indulgences for praying at the following stations: At Pilate's house, where Christ met His mother, where He spoke to the women, where He met Simon of Cyrene, where the soldiers stripped Him of His garments, where He was nailed to the cross, and at His tomb.

William Wey, an English pilgrim, visited the Holy Land in 1458 and again in 1462, and is credited with the term *stations*. He described the manner in which a pilgrim followed the steps of Christ. Prior to this time, the path usually followed the reverse course of ours today – moving from Mount Calvary to Pilate's house. At this time, the reverse – going from Pilate's house to Calvary – seems to have taken hold.

When the Moslem Turks blocked the access to the Holy Land, reproductions of the stations were erected at popular spiritual centers, including the Dominican Friary at Cordova and the Poor Clare Convent of Messina (early 1400s); Nuremberg (1468); Louvain (1505); Bamberg, Freiborg and Rhodes (1507); and Antwerp (1520). Many of these stations were produced by renown artists and are considered masterpieces today. By 1587, Zuallardo reported that the Moslems forbade anyone "to make any halt, nor to pay veneration to [the stations] with uncovered head, nor to make any other demonstration," basically suppressing this devotion in the Holy Land. Nevertheless, the devotion continued to grow in popularity in Europe.

At this time, the number of stations varied. William Wey's account has 14 stations, but only 5 correspond to our own. Some versions included the house of Dives (the rich man in the Lazarus story), the city gate through which Christ passed, and the houses of Herod and Simon the Pharisee. In 1584, a book written by Adrichomius entitled *Jerusalem sicut Christi Tempore floruit* gives 12 stations which match those in our present version. This book was translated into several languages and circulated widely. In the 16th century, devotional books appeared especially in the Low Countries which had 14 stations with prayers for each one.

At the end of the 17th century, the erection of stations in churches became more popular. In 1686, Pope Innocent XI, realizing that few people could travel to the Holy Land due to the Moslem oppression, granted the Franciscans the right to erect stations in all of their churches and that the same indulgences would be given to the faithful for practicing the devotion as if on an actual pilgrimage. Pope Benedict XIII extended these indulgences to all of the faithful in 1726. Five years later, Pope Clement XII permitted stations to be erected in all churches and fixed the number at 14. In 1742, Pope Benedict XIV exhorted all priests to enrich their churches with the Way of the Cross, which must include 14 crosses and are usually accompanied with pictures or images of each particular station. The popularity of the devotion was also encouraged by preachers like St. Leonard Casanova (1676-1751) of Porto Maurizio, Italy, who reportedly erected over 600 sets of stations throughout Italy.

To date, there are 14 traditional stations: Pilate condemns Christ to death; Jesus carries the cross; the first fall; Jesus meets his blessed Mother; Simon of Cyrene helps carry the cross; Veronica wipes the face of Jesus; the second fall; Jesus speaks to the women of Jerusalem; the third fall; Jesus is stripped of His garments; Jesus is nailed to the cross; Jesus dies on the cross; Jesus is taken down from the cross; and Jesus is laid in the tomb. Because of the intrinsic relationship between the passion and death of our Lord with his resurrection, several of the devotional booklets now include a "fifteenth" station which commemorates the resurrection. A plenary indulgence is granted for those who piously exercise the Way of the Cross, actually moving from station to station where they are legitimately erected and while mediating on the passion and death of our Lord (*Enchiridion of Indulgences*, #63). Those who are impeded from visiting a church may gain the same indulgence by piously reading and meditating on the passion and death of our Lord for one-half hour. The continued importance of the stations in the devotional life of Catholics is attested by both Pope Paul VI who approved a gospel based version of the stations in 1975 and Pope John Paul II who has also written his own version.

WHY DOES THE DATE FOR EASTER CHANGE AND WHAT ARE THE ORIGINS OF THE WORD EASTER?

In accord with the gospels, Easter is the solemn feast celebrating the resurrection of Christ. In the Western tradition of the Church, Easter has been celebrated on the first Sunday following the new full moon which occurs on or immediately after the vernal or Spring equinox. This dating was established by the Council of Nicea in 325 A.D. As such, the dates for Easter may range from March 22 to April 25. (The Orthodox Churches follow a different dating system and will thereby celebrate Easter one, four, or five weeks later.)

The word *Easter* is more difficult to explain. In the original language of the gospels, the Greek word *pascha* is used for the Aramaic form of the Hebrew word *pesach*, which means Passover. During the first three centuries of the Church, Pasch referred specifically to the celebration of Christ's passion and death; by the end of the fourth century, it also included the Easter Vigil; and by the end of the fifth century, it referred to Easter itself. In all, the term signified Christ as the new Passover Lamb. Together, the mystery of the Last Supper, the sacrifice of Good Friday, and the resurrection of Easter form the new Passover – the new Pasch.

Latin used the Greek-Hebrew root for its word *Pascha* and other derivatives to signify Easter or the Easter mysteries: For instance, the Easter Vigil in Latin is *Sabbato Sancto de Vigilia Paschali* and in the First Preface of Easter, the priest prays, "*... Cum Pascha nostrum immolatus est Christus*" ("When Christ our Pasch was sacrificed"). The Romance languages later used the Hebrew-Greek-Latin root for their words denoting Easter: Italian, *Pasqua*; Spanish, *Pascua*; and French, *Paques*. Even some non-Romance languages employ the Hebrew-Greek-Latin root: Scottish, *Pask*; Dutch, *Paschen*; Swedish, *Pask*; and the German dialect along the lower Rhine, *Paisken*.

However, according to St. Bede (d. 735), the great historian of the Middle Ages, the title *Easter* seems to originate in English around the eighth century A.D. The word Easter is derived from the word *Eoster*, the name of the Teutonic goddess of the rising light of day and Spring, and the annual sacrifices associated with her. If this is the origin of our word *Easter*, then the Church "baptized" the name to denote that first Easter Sunday morning when Christ, our Light, rose from the grave and when the women found the tomb empty just as dawn was breaking.

Another possibility which arises from more recent research suggests the early Church referred to Easter week as *hebdomada alba* ("white week"), from the white garments worn by the newly baptized. Some mistranslated the word to mean "the shining light of day" or "the shining dawn," and therefore used the Teutonic root *eostarun*, the Old German plural for dawn, as the basis for the German *Ostern* and for the English equivalent Easter. In early English translations of the Bible made by Tyndale and Coverdale, the word *Easter* was substituted for the word *Passover*, in some verses.

Even though the etymological root of Easter may be linked to the name of a pagan goddess or pagan ceremonies, the feast which the word describes is Christian without question. Exactly why the English language did not utilize to the Hebrew-Greek-Latin root remains a mystery.

WHY CAN ONLY MEN BE ORDAINED AS PRIESTS?

In our politically charged world, the debate over the restriction of ordination to men alone too often focuses on the political rather than the theological. Moreover, how some people receive the Church's teaching also seems to focus on a political framework rather than a theological. Concerning the political sphere, we must remember that because of our theological foundation, the Church has condemned discrimination based on sex: "Forms of social or cultural discrimination in basic personal rights on the grounds of sex, race, color, social conditions, language or religion must be curbed and eradicated as incompatible with God's design" (Vatican II, *Pastoral Constitution on the Church in the Modern World*, #29).

Therefore, to understand the Church's position for reserving the Sacrament of Holy Orders and thereby the ordination of deacons, priests, and bishops to men only (cf. *Code of Canon Law*, #1024), we must leave politics and turn to our theological foundation. Here we remember that by definition a sacrament is an outward sign instituted by Christ to give grace. First, Christ instituted the Sacrament of Holy Orders. According to His plan, He called 12 men as His apostles. Nowhere in the gospel do we find evidence of Jesus giving "orders" to women to baptize, to anoint the sick, to confect the Holy Eucharist, or to forgive sins as He did to the apostles.

Some might respond, "But in Jewish society at that time, women were not considered equal to men. Women were seen in a second class way, and that is why Jesus only chose men as apostles." To some extent, this statement is true. However, Jesus was not constricted by such social custom. Even His adversaries stated, "Teacher, we know you are a truthful man and teach God's way sincerely. You court no one's favor and do not act out of human respect" (Matthew 22:16). Actually, our Lord went against the grain of society and not only associated with women but clearly showed a respect for them equal to males. While Jewish law allowed men to divorce their wives but not vice versa, Jesus spoke of marriage as a covenant between a man and a woman as two equals made in God's image and likeness (Matthew 319:3ff). He spoke with the Samaritan woman, a public sinner, whom "good" rabbis would have avoided (John 4:4ff). He acknowledged the presence of Mary Magdalene and forgave her sins although she was considered "untouchable" by other religious leaders (Luke 7:36ff). Many women did follow our Lord during His public ministry, and witnessed His crucifixion and burial. On Easter, women were the first to discover the empty tomb, and Mary Magdalene was the first to see the risen Lord. Moreover, Jesus clearly honored His blessed Mother, Mary, for whom He even performed the first miracle at the wedding feast at Cana even though His time had not come. Clearly, Jesus did not omit calling woman as apostles because of some social or political convention. Pope John Paul II in his apostolic letter *Mulieris Dignitatem* stated, "In calling only men as his apostles, Christ acted in a completely free and sovereign manner. In doing so, He exercised the same freedom with which, in all His behavior, He emphasized the dignity and the vocation of women, without conforming to the prevailing customs and to the traditions sanctioned by the legislation of the time" (#26).

Moreover, there is no indication in the history of the Church of women being called to Holy Orders. For instance, although women, including our Blessed Mother, were with the apostles in the "upper room" after the ascension (Acts 1:14), St. Peter addressed the "brothers," concerning the selection of a replacement for Judas, and the Eleven apostles chose Matthias, one of two men nominated (Acts 1:15ff). If we examine the *Didache* (the first manual of doctrine, morality, and spirituality of the Church written about AD 80 and attributed to the apostles) or survey the writings of the Church Fathers, such as St. Clement (d. 101) or St. Ignatius of Antioch (d. 110) to name just two, we find a clear testimony that men were chosen as bishops, priests, and deacons. I remember Archbishop Fulton Sheen once said, "If our Lord would have ordained women, He would have definitely ordained His own Blessed Mother, free of sin, but He did not" (Preached at a Priests'

Retreat, 1974). Therefore, the Church remains faithful to the type of ordained ministry willed by Christ and maintained by the apostles.

Second, the Church must also be faithful to the sign value or the substance of the sacrament. Pope Pius XII, echoing the teachings of the Council of Trent, stated, "The Church has no power over the substance of the sacraments, that is to say, over what Christ the Lord, as the sources of Revelation bear witness, determined should be maintained in the sacramental sign" (*Sacramentum Ordinis*, #5). These sacramental signs are symbolic of actions and things, such as water in baptism symbolizes life and cleansing, and reminds us of the parting of the waters to bring life at Genesis, the flood waters which destroyed evil in Noah's time, the parting of the Red Sea to bring the people out of slavery, and the water which flowed from the heart of Christ on the cross. These signs also unite a person to the everlasting, eternal ministry of Christ Himself. For example, the Mass is not just a ritual meal or pious remembrance of the Last Supper; the Mass participates in and makes present now the everlasting, eternal sacrifice of our Lord on the cross and His resurrection.

In the same way, through Holy Orders, a priest is called to represent Christ Himself, to be an *alter Christus*. For instance, at Mass, the priest acts *in persona Christi* – "the priest enacts the image of Christ, in whose person and by whose power he pronounces the words of consecration" (St. Thomas Aquinas, *Summa Theologiae*, III, 83, 1, 3). In this sense, an intrinsic part of the sacramental sign of Holy Orders is the manhood of Christ.

Using St. Paul's analogy on Christ's relationship to the Church as the groom with His bride, Pope John Paul II (as did Pope Paul VI) reflected that our Lord's sacrifice on the cross with the offering of His body and blood "gives definitive prominence to the spousal meaning of God's love" (*Mulieris Dignitatem*, #26). Christ is the bridegroom who has offered Himself completely as Redeemer to His bride, the Church, which He has created. The Holy Eucharist continues to make present the redemptive act of our

Lord, and continues to nourish the Church. Thereupon, Christ, the bridegroom, is united with His bride, the Church, through the Eucharist. The Holy Father concluded, "Since Christ, in instituting the Eucharist linked it in such an explicit way to the priestly service of the Apostles, it is legitimate to conclude that He thereby wished to express the relationship between man and woman, between what is 'feminine' and what is 'masculine.' It is a relationship willed by God both in the mystery of creation and in the mystery of Redemption. It is the Eucharist above all that expresses the redemptive act of Christ, the Bridegroom, toward the Church, the Bride. This is clear and unambiguous when the sacramental ministry of the Eucharist, in which the priest acts 'in persona Christi,' is performed by man" (#26). For a fuller discussion of this point, please confer Pope Paul VI's *Declaration on the Admission of Women to the Ministerial Priesthood* (*Inter Insigniores*) and Pope John Paul II's *Mulieris Dignitatem*, #26.

Pope Paul VI echoed these points when he wrote to Archbishop Coggan, Archbishop of Canterbury and spiritual leader of the Anglican Church, concerning the ordination of women to the priesthood (November 30, 1975): "[The Catholic Church] holds that it is not admissible to ordain women to the priesthood, for very fundamental reasons. These reasons include: the example recorded in the Sacred Scriptures of Christ choosing His apostles only from among men; the constant practice of the Church, which has imitated Christ in choosing only men; and her living teaching authority which has consistently held that the exclusion of women from the priesthood is in accordance with God's plan for His Church."

The *Catechism* also addressed someone's "right" to be a priest: "No one has a right to receive the sacrament of Holy Orders. Indeed, no one claims this office for himself; he is called to it by God. Anyone who thinks he recognizes the signs of God's call to the ordained ministry must humbly submit his desire to the authority of the Church, who has the responsibility and right to call someone to receive orders. Like every grace this sacrament can be received only as an unmerited gift" (#1578).

Despite the consistent teaching of the Church concerning this matter, Pope John Paul II deemed it necessary to reiterate it once again in his apostolic letter *Ordinatio Sacerdotalis* (May 22, 1994): "Wherefore, in order that all doubt may be removed regarding a matter of great importance, a matter which pertains to the Church's divine constitution itself, in virtue of my ministry of confirming the brethren, I declare that the Church has no authority whatsoever to confer priestly ordination on women and that this judgment is to be definitively held by all the Church's faithful" (#4). The Holy Father's answer is clear and definitive.

The restriction of Holy Orders to men alone does not denigrate the role of women in the Church. Think of some of the great female saints like St. Clare, St. Teresa of Avila, and St. Catherine of Siena whose spiritual writings and example are still honored today. Think of the remarkable work of Mother Teresa (God rest her soul) or Mother Angelica and how many lives they touch. Think of famous women in our American Church: St. Elizabeth Ann Seton (a wife, mother, and religious), Blessed Katherine Drexel, St. Frances Cabrini, and Blessed Kateri Tekawitha. Our country in America has a beautiful legacy of women religious who have served in schools, hospitals, and orphanages. Each parish benefits greatly from the services of lay women who offer their time and talent in numerous capacities. Pope John Paul II emphasized in his apostolic letter, "The presence and the role of women in the life and the mission of the Church, although not linked to the ministerial priesthood, remain absolutely necessary and irreplaceable" (#3).

In all, I remember how our Holy Father addressed this question when he visited Philadelphia in 1979, while I was still in the seminary. He reminded us that Christ calls each of us to share in His mission. Some people are called to be priests, some religious brothers and sisters, some as spouses, some as parents, some as single laity. A vocation a not a "right" but a call from Christ through the Church as He has established it. The distinction is not based on superiority, but on a difference in the levels of function and service. Everyone shares in the mission of Christ according to His plan and design, and by His grace helps build up the Kingdom of God. As counseled by Vatican II's *Dogmatic Constitution on the Church*, may we faithfully, humbly, and respectfully submit to the teachings of our Church as guided by the Holy Spirit. In pondering this politically charged question, we are mindful that we must strive to live in the Kingdom of God and faithfully and humbly submit to the teaching of our Church guided by the Holy Spirit.

WHY DOES THE CHURCH MANDATE THAT PRIESTS BE CELIBATE?

In examining the issue of celibacy, we should first address its historical development in the life of the Church and then its spiritual basis and relevance for today's clergy.

Our Lord presented celibacy as a legitimate lifestyle not only by His very life since He never married but also in His teaching. When our Lord emphasized that marriage was a covenant between husband and wife and thereby prohibited divorce and re-marriage (cf. Matthew 19:3-12), He concluded, "Some men are incapable of sexual activity from birth; some have been deliberately made so; and some there are who have freely renounced sex for the sake of God's reign." Traditionally, our Church, as evidenced in the *Catechism* (#1579), points to this "free renunciation of sex for the sake of God's reign" as a basis for celibacy.

Nevertheless, in the early Church, clerical celibacy was not mandated. St. Paul in his First Letter to St. Timothy wrote, "A bishop must be irreproachable, married only once, of even temper, self-controlled, modest, and hospitable" (3:2) and "Deacons may be married but once and must be good managers of their children and their households" (3:12). However, one should not erroneously construe this teaching to mean that a bishop, priest, or deacon had to be married; St. Paul admitted that he himself was not married (I Corinthians 7:8).

Clement of Alexandria (d. 215) echoed St. Paul's teaching: "All the same, the Church fully receives the husband of one wife whether he be priest or deacon or layman, supposing always that he uses his marriage blamelessly, and such a one shall be saved in the begetting of children."

Nevertheless, the move to clerical celibacy began to grow in areas of the Church. St. Epiphanius of Salamis (d. 403) stated, "Holy Church respects the dignity of the priesthood to such a point that she does not admit to the diaconate, the priesthood, or the episcopate, nor even to the subdiaconate, anyone still living in marriage and begetting children. She accepts only him who if married gives up his wife or has lost her by death, especially in those places where the ecclesiastical canons are strictly attended to." The local, Spanish Council of Elvira (306) imposed celibacy on the clergy: "We decree that all bishops, priests, deacons, and all clerics engaged in the ministry are forbidden entirely to live with their wives and to beget children: whoever shall do so will be deposed from the clerical dignity." Later the Council of Carthage extended the celibacy requirement to the subdiaconate.

After the legalization of Christianity in 313, greater discussion regarding clerical celibacy emerged. At the ecumenical Council of Nicea I (325), Bishop Hosius of Cordova proposed a decree mandating clerical celibacy, including for those clergy already married. Egyptian Bishop Paphnutius, unmarried himself, rose in protest, asserting that such a requirement would be too rigorous and imprudent. Rather, he proposed that those members of the clergy already married should continue to be faithful to their wives, and those who were unmarried should personally decide whether or not to be celibate.

Actually, during this time, the new spiritual fervor of "white martyrdom" arose. During the persecution, many suffered "red martyrdom," the shedding of their blood for the faith. With white martyrdom, men and women chose to renounce the things of this world and to die to their old selves so as to rise to live a life totally dedicated to Christ. This notion of a white martyrdom was the thrust behind monasticism and vows of poverty, celibacy, and obedience.

At this point, the tradition of clerical celibacy differed between the Western and Eastern traditions of the Church. For the Western Church several popes decreed celibacy: Damasus I (384), Siricius (385), Innocent I (404), and Leo I (458). Local councils issued edicts imposing celibacy on the clergy: in Africa, Carthage (390, 401-19); in France, Orange (441) and Tours (461); and in Italy, Turin (398). By the time of Pope Leo I (d. 461), no bishop, priest, deacon, or subdeacon could be married.

In the Eastern Church, Emperor Justinian's Code of Civil Law forbade anyone who had children or even nephews to be consecrated a bishop. The Council of Trullo (692) mandated that a bishop be celibate, and if he was married, he would have to separate from his wife before his consecration. Priests, deacons, and subdeacons were forbidden to marry after ordination, although they were to continue to fulfill their marital vows if married before ordination. These regulations still stand for most of the Eastern Churches.

Sadly, in the Middle Ages, we find abuses of clerical celibacy, which incited a strong reaction from the Church. The Synod of Augsburg (952), and the local Councils of Anse (994) and Poitiers (1000) all affirmed the rule of celibacy. Pope Gregory VII in 1075 forbade married priests or those who had concubines from saying Mass or performing other ecclesiastical functions, and forbade the laity from hearing these Masses or participating in other liturgical functions offered by such priests. Finally, the First Lateran Council (1123), an ecumenical council of the Church, mandated celibacy for the Western clergy. The Second Lateran Council (1139) subsequently decreed Holy Orders as an impediment to marriage, making any attempt at marriage by an ordained cleric invalid. Finally, the regulations concerning celibacy seemed clear and consistent throughout the Catholic Church.

Protestant leaders later ridiculed and attacked the discipline of clerical celibacy. In response, the Council of Trent in its *Doctrine on the Sacrament of Orders* (1563) admitted that celibacy was not a divine law, but stipulated that the Church had the authority to impose celibacy as a discipline. While holding celibacy in high regard, the Church did not diminish the sanctity of marriage or marital love. Moreover, the Council asserted that celibacy was not impossible to live but at the same time recognized that celibates needed the grace of God to do so.

The Catholic Church has continued to affirm the discipline of clerical celibacy, most recently in the Second Vatican Council's decree *Presbyterorum ordinis* (1965), Pope Paul VI's encyclical *Sacerdotalis Caelibatus* (1967), and in the *Code of Canon Law* (1983).

Given the history of how celibacy came to be required for clergy in the Roman Catholic Church (except in several of the Eastern Rites), we can now examine the spirituality which undergirds the regulation. The Second Vatican Council's *Decree on the Ministry and Life of Priests (Presbyteroum ordinis)* (1965) asserted, "Perfect and perpetual continence for the sake of the Kingdom of Heaven was recommended by Christ the Lord. It has been freely accepted and laudably observed by many Christians down through the centuries as well as in our own time, and has always been highly esteemed in a special way by the Church as a feature of priestly life. For it is at once a sign of pastoral charity and an incentive to it as well as being in a special way a source of spiritual fruitfulness in the world" (#16). While recognizing that celibacy is not demanded by the very nature of the priesthood, the Council affirmed ways celibacy is in harmony with the priesthood: Through celibacy, a priest, identifying himself with Christ, dedicates his whole life to the service of his Lord and the church. Celibacy enables the priest to focus entirely on building up the kingdom of God here and now. Priests can "cling to Christ with undivided hearts and dedicate themselves more freely in Him and through Him to the service of God and of men" (#16). They are a sign in this world of the union of the Church to her spouse, Christ, and of the life in the world to come "in which the children of the resurrection shall neither be married nor take wives" (Luke 20:35-367).

Pope Paul VI highlighted these same themes in his encyclical *Sacerdotalis Caelibatus* (1967), which actually was written at a time when some people questioned the need for mandatory celibacy. The Holy Father pinpointed three "significances" or senses to celibacy: the Christological, the ecclesiological, and the eschatological. In the Christological sense, a priest must look to Christ as the ideal, eternal priest. This identification permeates his whole being. Just as Christ remained celibate and dedicated His life to the service of His Father and all people, a priest accepts celibacy and consecrates himself totally to serve the mission of the Lord. This total giving and commitment to Christ is a sign of the Kingdom present here and now.

In the ecclesiological sense, just as Christ was totally united to the Church, the priest through his celibacy bonds his life to the Church. He is better able to be a Minister of the Word of God – listening to that Word, pondering its depth, living it, and preaching it with whole hearted conviction. He is the Minister of Sacraments, and, especially through the Mass, acts in the person of Christ, offering himself totally to the Lord. Celibacy allows the priest greater freedom and flexibility in fulfilling his pastoral work: "[Celibacy] gives to the priest, even in the practical field, the maximum efficiency and the best disposition of mind, psychologically and affectively, for the continuous exercise of a perfect charity. This charity will permit him to spend himself wholly for the welfare of all, in a fuller and more concrete way" (*Sacerdotalis Caelibatus*, #32).

Finally, in the eschatological sense, the celibate life foreshadows the freedom we will have in heaven when perfectly united with God as His child.

The *Code of Canon Law* reflects these three "significances" in Canon 277, which mandates clerical celibacy: "Clerics are obliged to observe perfect and perpetual continence for the sake of the Kingdom of Heaven and therefore are obliged to observe celibacy, which is a special gift of God, by which sacred ministers can adhere more easily to Christ with an undivided heart and can more freely dedicate themselves to the service of God and mankind."

Throughout the Church's teaching on celibacy, three important dimensions must be kept in mind: First, celibacy involves freedom. A man when called to Holy Orders freely accepts the obligation of celibacy, after prayerful reflection and consideration. Having made that decision, celibacy does grant the bishop, priest, or deacon the freedom to identify with Christ and to serve Him and the Church without reservation, condition, or hesitation.

Secondly, celibacy involves sacrifice, and a sacrifice is an act of love. For instance, when a man and a woman marry, they make a sacrifice to live "in good times and in bad, in sickness and in health until death." They sacrifice to live a faithful love, no longer dating others or giving into selfish pleasures. When they become parents, they sacrifice to support the raising of children. Decisions of love always entail sacrifice.

And so it is with the clergy. To be a priest means to make a sacrifice of oneself to Christ for the good of His Church. The priest sacrifices being married to a woman and having his own family to being "wedded" to Christ and His Church and serving their needs as "father."

Finally, celibacy requires the grace of God to be lived. Repeatedly, celibacy is seen as a gift of the Holy Spirit. However, this gift is not just to keep one's physical desires under control or to live as a bachelor; this gift is being able to say "yes" to our Lord each day and live His life.

Sadly, in our world, many people cannot appreciate the discipline of celibacy, whether for the clergy or anyone else. We live in a society where the media bombards us with uncontrolled sexual imagery. If some people cannot appreciate the values of virginity before marriage, fidelity in marriage, or sacrifice for children, they cannot begin to appreciate anyone – man or woman – who lives a celibate lifestyle in dedication to a vocation. As a Church, we should be thankful to the clergy, and the men and women religious, who have made the total sacrifice of themselves out of love to serve our Lord and the Church.

WHY DO WE CALL PRIESTS "FATHER" WHEN JESUS SAID NOT TO CALL ANYONE ON EARTH "FATHER"?

This question refers to Jesus' teaching found in the gospel of St. Matthew, when He said, "Do not call anyone on earth your father. Only one is your father, the One in heaven" (Matthew 23:9). Taken literally, we would have to wonder why we do use this title "Father" when Jesus seems to forbid it. First, we must remember the context of the passage. Jesus was addressing the hypocrisy of the scribes and the Pharisees – the learned religious leaders of Judaism. Our Lord castigated them for not providing good example; for creating onerous spiritual burdens for others with their various rules and regulations; for being haughty in exercising their office; and for promoting themselves by looking for places of honor, seeking marks of respect, and wearing ostentatious symbols. Basically, the scribes and the Pharisees had forgotten that they were called to serve the Lord and those entrusted to their care with humility and a generous spirit.

Given that context, Jesus said not to call anyone on earth by the title "Rabbi," "Father," or "Teacher," in the sense of arrogating to oneself an authority which rests with God and of forgetting the responsibility of the title. Yes, as Jesus said, only the heavenly Father is the true Father, and the Messiah, the true teacher and rabbi. Nevertheless, we do use these titles in our common parlance: We call those who instruct us and others "teacher"; our male parent, "father"; and Jewish religious leaders, "rabbi." Especially in a religious sense, those who serve the Lord and represent His authority, as a teacher, parent, and especially a priest, must be mindful of exercising it diligently, humbly, and courageously. To use this authority for self-aggrandizement is pure hypocrisy. Jesus said at the end of this passage, "Whoever exalts himself shall be humbled, but whoever humbles himself shall be exalted."

Since the earliest times of our Church, we have used the title "Father" for religious leaders. Bishops, who are the shepherds of the local Church community and the authentic teachers of the faith, were given the title "Father." Actually, until about the year 400, a bishop was called "papa" for Father; this title was then restricted solely to addressing the Bishop of Rome, the successor of St. Peter, and in English was rendered "Pope." In an early form of his rule, St. Benedict (d. c. 547) designated the title to spiritual confessors, since they were the guardians of souls. Moreover, the word *abbot*, denoting the leader in faith of the monastic community, is derived from the word *abba*, the Aramaic Hebrew word for *father*, but in the very familiar sense of "daddy." Later, in the Middle Ages, the term "father" was used to address the mendicant friars – like the Franciscans and Dominicans – since by their preaching, teaching, and charitable works they cared for the spiritual and physical needs of all of God's children. In more modern times, the heads of male religious communities or even those who participate in ecumenical councils, such as Vatican II, are given the title "father." In the English speaking world, addressing all priests as "Father" has become customary.

On a more personal note, the title for me is very humbling. As a priest, "Father" reminds me that I am entrusted with a grave responsibility by our Lord to His faithful people. Just as a father must nourish, instruct, challenge, correct, forgive, listen, and sustain his children, so must a priest do the same for his spiritual children. The priest must meet the spiritual needs of those entrusted to his care, providing them with the nourishment of our Lord through the sacraments. He must preach the gospel with fervor and conviction in accord with the mind of the Church, challenging all to continue on that path of conversion which leads to holiness. He must correct those who have erred but with mercy and compassion. In the same spirit as the father with his prodigal son, the priest must reconcile sinners who have gone astray but seek a way back to God. As a father listens to his child, so must a priest listen to his spiritual children, providing counsel and consolation. A priest must also be mindful of the "physical" needs of his flock – food, housing, clothing, and education. While priests may be celibate, the words of our Lord to His apostles ring true: "I give you my word, there is not one who has given up home, brothers or sisters, mother or father, children or property, for me and for the gospel who will not receive in this present age a hundred times as many homes, brothers and sisters, mothers, children and property – and persecution besides – and in the age to come, everlasting life" (Mark 10:29-30). All of us must pray for our priests, especially those that serve in our own parishes, that by God's grace they may strive to fulfill the responsibility of being "Father."

WHY GO TO CONFESSION?

Jesus entered this world to forgive sins. Recall the words of our Lord: "God so loved the world that He gave His only Son, that whoever believes in Him may not die but may have eternal life" (John 3:16). During His public ministry, Jesus preached about the forgiveness of sins: remember the parables of the Prodigal Son (Luke 15:11ff) or the Lost Sheep (Luke 15:1ff), and His teaching that "there will likewise be more joy in heaven over one repentant sinner than over ninety-nine righteous people who have no need to repent" (Luke 15:7). Jesus Himself forgave sins: remember the story of the woman caught in adultery (John 8:1ff) or the woman who washed His feet with her tears (Luke 7:36ff). He also taught us to pray for forgiveness in the "Our Father": "Forgive us our trespasses as we forgive those who trespass against us" (cf. Matthew 5:9ff). His mission of reconciliation would climax in His passion, death, and resurrection: Jesus suffered, died, and rose to free us from sin and death.

However, Jesus never trivialized sin nor rationalized it. No, for Jesus, sin is sin, a violation of love against God, self, and neighbor. However, in His divine mercy, Jesus called the sinner to realize the sin, to repent of it, and to be reconciled with God, self, and neighbor.

Jesus wanted this ministry of reconciliation to continue. On that first Easter Sunday evening, Jesus appeared to His apostles, "breathed on them," and said, "Receive the Holy Spirit. If you forgive men's sins, they are forgiven them; if you hold them bound, they are held bound" (John 20:21-23). Only twice in Sacred Scripture do we find God breathing into human beings. First, in the Genesis account of creation, God breathes the life of a soul into the man He has created (Genesis 2:7). Now, Jesus, the Son, breathes His life into His apostles, His priests, so that through them He will "breathe" life into the souls of contrite sinners. In this scene, Christ instituted the Sacrament of Penance and made His apostles the ministers of it.

At the ascension, Jesus again charged His apostles with this ministry: "Thus it is written that the Messiah must suffer and rise from the dead on the third day. In His name, penance for the remission of sins is to be preached to all the nations, beginning at Jerusalem. You are witnesses of this" (Luke 24:46ff). Clearly, Jesus came to forgive sins, He wanted that reconciliation to continue, and He gave the Church a sacrament through which priests would continue to act as the ministers of this reconciliation.

We see this ministry of reconciliation lived-out in the early Church. St. Paul wrote, "God has reconciled us to Himself through Christ and has given us the ministry of reconciliation" (II Cor 5:18). The *Didache* (or *Teachings of the Twelve Apostles*), written about AD 80, stated, "In the congregation you shall confess your transgressions" and "On the Lord's Day, come together and break bread ... having confessed your transgressions that your sacrifice may be pure." St. Cyprian in his *De lapsis* (c. 251) concerning the reconciliation of Christians who had succumbed to offering pagan worship rather than face martyrdom, wrote, "Let each confess his sin while he is still in this world, while his confession can be received, while satisfaction and the forgiveness granted by the priests is acceptable to God." At this time of persecution, when local "parishes" were small, individuals publicly confessed their sins at the beginning of Mass (as mentioned in the *Didache*) and received absolution from the bishop or priest.

After the legalization of the Church by Constantine, the Church Fathers continued to emphasize the importance of confession. St. Ambrose (d. 397) wrote, "It seemed impossible that sins should be forgiven through penance; Christ granted this power to the Apostles and from the Apostles it has been transmitted to the office of priests" (*De poenitentia*). Similarly, St. Athanasius (d. 373) asserted, "As the man whom the priest baptizes is enlightened by the grace of the Holy Ghost, so does he who in penance confesses his sins, receive through the priest forgiveness in virtue of the grace of Christ" (*Contra Novatus*). By the mid-400s and the pontificate of Leo I, private confession under the seal of secrecy became the norm to safeguard the reputation of the penitent and to attract others to the sacrament.

Therefore, we go to confession because it is a sacrament given to us by Christ, and it has always been a practice of the Church. This sacrament reconciles us first with God: "The whole power of the Sacrament of Penance consists in restoring us to God's grace and joining us with Him in an intimate friendship" (*Catechism*, #1468). Secondly, the sacrament reconciles us with the Church: "It must be recalled that ... this reconciliation with God leads, as it were, to other reconciliations, which repair the other breaches caused by sin. The forgiven penitent is reconciled with himself in his inmost being, where he regains his innermost truth. He is reconciled with his brethren whom he has in some way offended and wounded. He is reconciled with the Church. He is reconciled with all creation" (John Paul II, *Reconciliatio et paenitentia*).

This sacrament is so important in our sharing in the life of Christ that the Church has even mandated its practice. To prevent laxity, the Fourth Lateran Council (1215) required that "every faithful of either sex who has reached the age of discretion should at least once a year faithfully confess all his sins to his own priest. He should strive as far as possible to fulfill the penance imposed on him, and with reverence receive at least during Easter time the sacrament of the Eucharist": This rule is still a precept of the Church, commonly called the "Easter Duty." The Council of Trent in 1551 in its *Doctrine on the Sacrament of Penance* asserted that since mortal sin "kills" the life of God in our souls, these sins must be confessed and absolved through the Sacrament of Penance (a principle repeated by Pope John Paul II in *The Splendor of Truth*). Trent also said "it is right and profitable" to confess venial sins.

We could end the answer here. However, regular confession is a healthy spiritual practice. Each sincere Catholic needs to periodically – every month or two – do a good examination of conscience holding himself to the standard of Christ. Each person should reflect on how well he has lived a "Christ like life" by following the commandments and the teachings of the Church. Perhaps one's failures are not so much commissions as they are omissions. For all of these, we bring our soul to the Lord and receive forgiveness. The healing grace of the Sacrament of Penance washes away sin and gives us the strength to avoid that sin again. The more we love the Lord, the more we are aware of the smallest sins and the more we want to say, "Lord, I am sorry. Please forgive me." I am sure this is why Pope John Paul II goes to confession weekly, as did Mother Teresa during her life. We too ought to take full advantage of this beautiful sacrament which draws us closer to the Lord.

HOW DO YOU GO TO CONFESSION?

Some of the faithful are inhibited from going to confession because they fear that they do not know how to go, especially with the various changes initiated since Vatican Council II. The Council did decree that "the rite and formulas of penance are to be revised in such a way that they may more clearly express the nature and effects of this sacrament" (*Constitution on the Sacred Liturgy*, #72). Accordingly the Sacred Congregation for Divine Worship issued *The Rite of Penance* in 1973. The new rite did add options for prayers, provide for a reading of Sacred Scripture, and introduce "penance services" with private confessions. Nevertheless, the norms stipulated, "It is for priests, and especially parish priests in reconciling individuals or the community, to adapt the rite to the concrete circumstances of the penitents" (#40). Therefore, on a Saturday afternoon with a line of penitents waiting for confession, the parish priest may follow a more "streamlined" version of the rite, which would include by custom the traditional format for confession.

With that in mind, a person begins with a good examination of conscience. We need to hold up our life to the pattern of life God has revealed for us to live. For instance, we take time to reflect on the 10 Commandments, the Beatitudes, the precepts of the Church, and the virtues of prudence, fortitude, temperance, and justice. (Several clear, simple pamphlets with an examination of conscience may be purchased at local religious book and gift stores.)

The examination of our conscience is like stepping back and looking at the picture of our life in comparison to the masterpiece of life revealed by God. Remember when we were children, we used to trace pictures. Tracing helped us learn to draw. We would take a piece of plain paper, hold it over the original picture, and then put it up to the window. The light would enable us to trace the original picture onto our blank sheet of paper. Periodically, we had to stop and step back to see if our paper had slipped and was out of kilter with the original or if we had deviated from the lines.

In a similar way, as we live our lives, we are tracing them in accord with God's pattern of life. In examining our consciences, we step back and honestly assess how well we fit God's pattern and have stayed within His boundaries. At this time, we reflect on the progress we have made since our last confession in dealing with weaknesses, faults, temptations, and past sins. Hopefully, we see improvement in our spiritual well-being. However, when we have gone out of kilter or gone out of bounds with God's masterpiece, we have sinned. We must recognize the venial sins – those lighter sins which weaken our relationship with the Lord – from the mortal sins – those sins which sever our relationship with the Lord and "kill" the presence of sanctifying grace in our souls. Here we remember the words of Jesus, "Everyone who practices evil hates the light; he does not come near it for fear his deeds will be exposed. But he who acts in truth comes into the light, to make clear that his deeds are done in God" (John 3:20-21).

Given this examination of conscience, we have contrition for our sins. While we are sorry for sin because we do fear the fires of Hell and the loss of Heaven, and the just punishments of God, we are sorry most of all because our sins offend God whom we should love above all things. The love for God moves us to repent of sin and seek reconciliation. Pope John Paul II goes to confession once a week. One must ask, "Why? What sins does he possibly commit?" They love the Lord so much that even the slightest omission or commission moves them to confession. They do not want even the slightest sin to separate them from the love of God. For love of God, we too are sorry for our sins.

Sorrow for sin moves us to have a firm amendment not to sin again. We probably will sin again, but we try not to do so. We do not plan on leaving the confessional and committing the same sins again.

We then confess our sins. In the parish setting, we stand in line which is a humbling experience. Three weeks ago I was at St. Dominic's for confession, and I ran into two parishioners from St. John, one from our Lady of Lourdes, and one from Queen of Apostles – that is a humbling experience. Even so, we remember we are all sinners striving to do better and to get to heaven.

When we enter the confessional in most Churches, we have the option of remaining anonymous or facing the priest. Whichever option a person chooses, always remember that whatever is said during the confession is held in secret by the priest.

Remember also that we confess to the priest for three reasons: First, the priest has the authority of the apostles by virtue of his ordination. On the night of the resurrection, Jesus said, "Receive the Holy Spirit. If you forgive men's sins, they are forgiven them; if you hold them bound, they are held bound" (John 20:22-23). The priest is the minister of the sacrament acting in the person of Christ.

Second, he is the spiritual father. Just as we see a doctor for healing when we are physically sick, we see a priest when our soul is sick and needs healing.

Third, the priest represents the Church and the people we have sinned against. In the early days of the Church, people publicly confessed sin at the beginning of Mass and were absolved. Much to our relief, for centuries now we have had private confession.

We proceed by making the sign of the cross and saying, "Bless me Father for I have sinned." One could also simply begin, "In the name of the Father ... ." We should then state when we made our last confession: "It has been (so long) since my last confession."

We then confess our sins. We must be specific. Sometimes people say, "I broke the sixth commandment," which covers everything from a lustful thought to rape and adultery. We do not need to provide the full-blown story, just the basics to enable the priest to help. We need to give some quantification – missing Mass once is different from several times which is different from all of the time. When we are finished confessing our sins, we state, "I am sorry for these and all of my sins." With this information, the priest may counsel us. He also assigns a penance for the healing of the hurt caused by sin and the strengthening of our soul against future temptation. He then asks us to say an act of contrition, which is generally the traditional prayer: "Oh my God, I am heartily sorry for having offended Thee. I detest all of my sins because of Thy just punishments, but most of all because they offend Thee, my God, who are all good and deserving of all of my love. I firmly resolve with the help of Thy grace to sin no more and to avoid the near occasions of sin. Amen."

Finally, the priest imparts absolution. Ponder the beautiful words: "God the Father of mercies, through the death and resurrection of His son, has reconciled the world to Himself and sent the Holy Spirit among us for the forgiveness of sins; through the ministry of the Church may God give you pardon and peace, and I absolve you from your sins, in the name of the Father, and of the Son, and of the Holy Spirit."

The priest dismisses us, saying, "Give thanks to the Lord, for He is good," to which we respond, "His mercy endures forever." (Many priests may simply say, "May God bless you.") We then leave the confessional to do the assigned penance.

The Sacrament of Penance is a beautiful sacrament through which we are reconciled to God, ourselves, and our neighbors. A good spiritual discipline is to make a good confession every month or two months. We never want any sin to weaken our relationship with our Lord. Remember the words of St. Paul, "God is rich in mercy; because of His great love for us, He brought us to life with Christ when we were dead in sin" (Ephesians 2:4).

CAN THE SEAL OF CONFESSION BE BROKEN OR THE SECRETS EVER BE REVEALED BY PRIESTS?

The secrecy surrounding a confession outweighs that involving any kind of professional secret or confidentiality. Concerning "professional secrets," the information a client shares with a lawyer, physician, or some other professional is considered confidential. Here the seal of secrecy or confidentiality must be maintained, except in some extreme cases: If the professional perceives that grave harm could come either to the person who shared the information, such as through committing suicide, or to a third party, such as through murder, then the information may be divulged to protect the parties at risk. However, such disclosure should occur only in exceptional circumstances and for a proportionate reason. (Cf. *Catechism*, #2491.)

However, when a person unburdens his soul and confesses his sins to a priest in the Sacrament of Penance, a very sacred trust is formed, greater than any professional secret or confidentiality. The priest must maintain absolute secrecy about anything that a person confesses. For this reason, confessionals were developed with screens to protect the anonymity of the penitent. This secrecy is called "the sacramental seal," "the seal of the confessional," or "the seal of confession."

The sacramental seal is inviolable. Quoting Canon 983 of the *Code of Canon Law*, the *Catechism* states, " ... It is a crime for a confessor in any way to betray a penitent by word or in any other manner or for any reason" (#2490). A priest, therefore, cannot break the seal to save his own life, to protect his good name, to refute a false accusation, to save the life of another, to aid the course of justice (like reporting a crime), or to avert a public calamity. He cannot be compelled by law to disclose a person's confession or be bound by any oath he takes, e.g. as a witness in a court trial. A priest cannot reveal the contents of a confession either directly, by repeating the substance of what has been said, or indirectly, by some sign, suggestion, or action. A Decree from the Holy Office (November 18, 1682) mandated that confessors are forbidden, even where there would be no revelation direct or indirect, to make any use of the knowledge obtained in the confession that would "displease" the penitent or reveal his identity.

(Just as an aside, a great movie which deals with this very topic is Alfred Hitchcock's *I Confess*, which is about a priest who hears a murder confession and then is framed for the murder. As a priest, I was in agony during much of the movie.)

However, a priest may ask the penitent for a release from the sacramental seal to discuss the confession with him or others. For instance, if the penitent wants to discuss the subject matter of a previous confession – a particular sin, fault, temptation, circumstance – in a counseling session or in a conversation with the same priest, that priest will need the permission of the penitent to do so. For instance, especially with the advent of "face-to-face confession," I have had individuals come up to me and say, "Father, remember that problem I spoke to you about in confession?" I have to say, "Please refresh my memory," or "Do you give me permission to discuss this with you now?"

Or if a priest needs guidance from a more experienced confessor to deal with a difficult case of conscience, he first must ask the permission of the penitent to discuss the matter. Even in this case, the priest should still keep the identity of the person secret.

What happens if a priest violates the seal of confession? The *Catechism* (#1467) cites the *Code of Canon Law* (#1388) in addressing this issue, which states, "A confessor who directly violates the seal of confession incurs an automatic excommunication reserved to the Apostolic See; if he does so only indirectly, he is to be punished in accord with the seriousness of the offense." From the severity of the punishment, we can clearly see how sacred the sacramental seal of confession is in the eyes of the Church.

Actually, the Church's position in this matter has long-standing credibility. The Fourth Lateran Council (1215) produced one of the first comprehensive teachings concerning the Sacrament of

Penance. Addressing various problems ranging from abuses to heretical stands against the sacrament, the council defended the sacrament itself, stipulated the need for the yearly sacramental confession of sins and reception of the Holy Eucharist, and imposed disciplinary measures upon priest confessors. The council decreed, "Let the confessor take absolute care not to betray the sinner through word or sign, or in any other way whatsoever. In case he needs expert advice he may seek it without, however, in any way indicating the person. For we decree that he who presumes to reveal a sin which has been manifested to him in the tribunal of penance is not only to be deposed from the priestly office, but also to be consigned to a closed monastery for perpetual penance."

A beautiful story (perhaps embellished over time) which captures the reality of this topic is the life of St. John Nepomucene (1340-93), the vicar general to the Archbishop of Prague. King Wenceslaus IV, described as a vicious, young man who easily succumbed to rage and caprice, was highly suspicious of his wife, the Queen. St. John happened to be the Queen's confessor. Although the king himself was unfaithful, he became increasingly jealous and suspicious of his wife, who was irreproachable in her conduct. Although Wencelaus tortured St. John to force him to reveal the Queen's confessions, he would not. In the end, St. John was thrown into the River Moldau and drowned on March 20, 1393. He died rather than break the seal of confession.

Each priest realizes that he is the ordained mediator of a very sacred and precious sacrament. He knows that in the confessional, the penitent speaks not so much to him, but through him to the Lord. Therefore, humbled by his position, the priest knows that whatever is said in confession must remain secret at all costs.

WHY IS BLASPHEMY AGAINST THE HOLY SPIRIT AN UNFORGIVABLE SIN? ARE NOT ALL SINS FORGIVABLE?

The gospels clearly attest that our Lord came to forgive our sins and all sins. When the angel of the Lord appeared to St. Joseph in a dream to inform him of Mary's conception by the power of the Holy Spirit, he said, " ... You are to name him Jesus because He will save His people from their sins" (Luke 1:21). We easily call to mind powerful stories of Jesus reconciling sinners, such as the Samaritan woman or the woman caught in adultery. Oftentimes His miracles of curing a physical ailment were preceded by the spiritual cure of forgiveness, such as the story of the paralytic man. We also remember the parables of the Prodigal Son or the Merciless Official, which exhort us to forgive as well as to seek forgiveness. Our Lord was accused of being a friend of sinners and tax collectors. Even from the cross our Lord said, "Father, forgive them; they do not know what they are doing" (Luke 23:34). Finally, on the night of the resurrection, Jesus said, "Receive the Holy Spirit. If you forgive men's sins, they are forgiven them; if you hold them bound, they are held bound" (John 20:23), clearly establishing the Sacrament of Penance and indicating the Holy Spirit's role in channeling God's forgiveness.

Therefore, we do believe that our Lord forgives any sin if we are truly sorry for that sin, repent of that sin, confess it, and make a firm amendment to strive not to commit that sin again. The *Dogmatic Constitution on the Church* of Vatican II stated, "Those who approach the Sacrament of Penance obtain pardon from the mercy of God for their offenses committed against Him. They are, at the same time, reconciled with the Church whom they have wounded by their sin ... " (#11).

So what about blasphemy against the Holy Spirit as an unforgivable sin? First, remember what Jesus said about the Holy Spirit. He identified the Holy Spirit as "the Paraclete," meaning advocate, comforter, and guide, who instructs us and reminds us of all that our Lord taught. The Holy Spirit is also the Spirit of Truth, God's eternal, immutable truth to which we pattern our own lives. (Cf. John 14:16-27; 16:7-14.)

As Paraclete and Spirit of Truth, the Holy Spirit conveys the grace to enlighten our consciences to judge what is right versus what is wrong, and strengthens our wills to do good and avoid evil. The Holy Spirit also moves us to examine our conscience, and reflect on what we have done or what we have failed to do. In this task, the Holy Spirit also moves us to conversion, helping us to recognize when we have turned away from the Lord through sin, and moving us to turn back to Him with a contrite and humble heart. Through the Holy Spirit, forgiveness is conveyed, and the truth and love of the Lord is restored in our souls. Pope John Paul II captured this spiritual dynamic well: "The hidden giver of this saving power is the Holy Spirit: He, whom the Church calls 'the light of consciences,' penetrates and fills the depths of the human heart. Through just such a conversion in the Holy Spirit a person becomes open to forgiveness, to the remission of sins" (*Dominum et Vivificantem*, #45).

To blaspheme the Holy Spirit, according to our Holy Father, "does not properly consist in offending against the Holy Spirit in words; it consists rather in the refusal to accept the salvation which God offers to man through the Holy Spirit, working through the power of the cross" (#46). Such blasphemy is to reject the Holy Spirit, to refuse radically to recognize sin and repent of it, and to block the healing and forgiveness offered by the Lord. So the sin is not unforgivable because of its seriousness, but because the sinner lacks the proper disposition to seek forgiveness and thereby to be forgiven. As St. Thomas Aquinas said, " ... It excludes the elements through which the forgiveness of sin takes place." How can the Lord forgive us and reconcile us to a sharing in His life if we refuse to recognize the sin as a sin and to say, "Please forgive me, Lord, for I have sinned against you and my neighbor"? This "hardness of heart" leads to a sustained and firm rejection of the love and mercy of God, which in turn leads to damnation.

WHAT ARE INDULGENCES?

For some reason these days, we do not hear much about indulgences. Although I can remember learning about them in my early education at St. Bernadette's grade school. Unfortunately, I think the word sometimes sparks to mind Martin Luther, the Protestant movement, and certain abuses of indulgences that existed. Therefore, for some people indulgences are one of those "Catholic things" we have put to rest on the shelf.

Nevertheless, we do hold to the doctrine of indulgences and to the practice of granting them. Perhaps motivated by doubts and confusion over indulgences after Vatican Council II, Pope Paul VI in his *Apostolic Constitution on the Revision of Indulgences* (1967) stated, "They would appear to be solidly founded on divine Revelation, handed down from the Apostles." Even the *Catechism* has a section on indulgences.

Strictly speaking, "An indulgence is the remission before God of the temporal punishment due to sins whose guilt has been forgiven, which the faithful Christian who is duly disposed gains under certain defined conditions through the Church's help when, as minister of Redemption, she dispenses and applies with authority the treasury of the satisfaction won by Christ and the saints" (Norm #1). Now, what does this mean?

We believe that when we sin, we commit a free-willed offense against God, ourselves, and our neighbor. God in His love and mercy forgives the guilt of any sin for which we are truly sorry. However, God in His justice requires that we expiate sin, or heal the hurt caused by sin. We call this the temporal punishment for sin. For example, if I damage my neighbor's car, I can sincerely plead for forgiveness and my neighbor can genuinely forgive me; yet, I will also in justice have to pay for the repair of the car. Well, during our life we perform penances here to expiate sin and purify our souls. If we die with venial sins, we will expiate these sins in Purgatory.

Since sin has a communal dimension, i.e. sin affects the whole body of the Church, salvation also has a communal dimension. This is why we pray for each other's intentions at Mass or privately. From the earliest days of the Church, individuals have offered prayers and good works for the salvation of sinners. In those times when reconciliation was not complete until both confession and penance had been performed, martyrs facing death were asked by penitents for aid so that full reconciliation with the Church and re-admission to the sacraments could be obtained more speedily.

The communion of the Church, though, includes the faithful in Purgatory and the saints in Heaven. These saints intercede on our behalf and pray for us. The Treasury of the Church includes the infinite, inexhaustible value of the merits of our Lord's death and resurrection, and the prayers and good works of the Blessed Mother and all of the saints. Just as they aided those in the journey of salvation while living on this earth, they continue to do so now. As the Minister of Redemption, the Church invokes their aid to help reconcile fully penitents and alleviate the temporal punishment due to sin.

Also, in the early Church, bishops allowed penances, which were oftentimes severe, to be substituted with other works (indulgences) which may have been easier to fulfill but which promoted piety and strengthened the person spiritually. Eventually, Popes decreed that certain practices could replace imposed penances. These practices must be performed by faithful individuals who have confessed their sins and are truly contrite; if so, then they will have totally alleviated punishment due to sin. Note the Church has continually condemned any abuse of indulgences, and the person performing the indulgence must have a sincere, contrite, and humble heart.

An indulgence is considered plenary or partial according to whether it expiates all or part of the temporal punishment due for sin. To gain a plenary indulgence, one must perform the work attached to the indulgence and make a sacramental confession, receive Holy Communion, and pray for the intentions of the Holy Father (reciting one Our Father and one Hail Mary, or any other suitable prayer). The conditions may be met several days before or after performing the work of the indulgence. A partial indulgence is gained by doing the particular work sincerely. The *Enchiridion of Indulgences* (1968) lists the norms and grants.

Nevertheless, we must not forget that, as Pope Paul VI asserted, the Church grants indulgences so that the faithful will expiate sins and also encourage them to do works of penance, charity, and piety, which lead to a spiritual growth and strengthening of the Church.

WHAT IS AN ANNULMENT?

Before addressing the issue of an annulment, we must first have a clear understanding of marriage. When the Pharisees questioned our Lord about divorce, He replied, "Have you not read that at the beginning the Creator made them male and female, and declared, 'For this reason a man shall leave his father and mother and cling to his wife, and the two shall become as one'? Thus, they are no longer two but one flesh. Therefore, let no man separate what God has joined" (Matthew 19:3-6). Given this teaching, we as Catholics believe that when a baptized, Christian man freely marries a baptized, Christian woman, they form an indissoluble, sacramental bond. This union is evidenced in the vows they exchange: "I take you, to be my wife/husband. I promise to be true to you in good times and in bad, in sickness and in health. I will love you and honor you all the days of my life," or "I take you for my lawful wife/husband, to have and to hold, from this day forward, for better, for worse, for richer, for poorer, in sickness and in health, until death do us part" (*Rite of Marriage*). These vows express a love that is permanent, exclusive, faithful, self-giving, and life-giving.

Moreover, we must never forget that marriage is indeed a sacrament. The Lord Himself gives the couple the grace to live the marriage. By turning to the Lord each day and imploring His assistance, by rejoicing in the countless blessings they share as well as sharing their crosses with Him, the husband and wife will have a strong marriage. Recently, a dear friend's father died who had been married to his wife for 66 years. Imagine sixty-six years of marriage to the same person! This couple faced the regular routine of life – war and peace, economic depression and abundance, good health and medical problems; they faced burying one of their own children; they faced their own personal and family difficulties. Yet, they had a strong faith in God and in each other. They never stopped believing in their vows. That faith and the grace of God kept their marriage strong. One could honestly see that "the two had become one."

Sadly though, divorce does occur. The state court considers marriage as a contract, not as a sacrament. The divorce decree establishes the rights of both parties, and now legally, the former spouses can again marry civilly. However, in the eyes of God and the Church, a indissoluble sacramental marriage is presumed to have occurred: "Marriage enjoys the favor of the law; consequently, when a doubt exists, the validity of a marriage is to be upheld until the contrary is proven" (*Code of Canon Law*, #1060). One cannot deny that the couple exchanged those vows before God, their family and their friends, and indeed the whole Church, and those witnesses presume the vows were freely exchanged and sincere "until death do us part." Therefore, no one can just pretend that the marriage never took place and remarry.

The Church sincerely tries to help those individuals who have suffered the tragedy of divorce as well as to hold true to the teachings of our Lord. A person who is divorced may petition the Church to review the marriage and investigate whether a full, free-willed consent (as much as any person can give) was exchanged at the time of the wedding. The *Code of Canon Law* specifies that "matrimonial consent is an act of the will by which a man and a woman, through an irrevocable covenant, mutually give and accept each other to establish marriage" (#1057.2). If the Church determines that a defect in the consent existed at the time of marriage, then a Declaration of Nullity (an annulment) would be granted. Such a declaration proclaims that one or both parties did not (or could not) give a full, free-willed consent, and therefore no indissoluble, sacramental bond was established. Yes, a ceremony took place, but no sacrament occurred.

In investigating these cases, the Tribunal of the Diocese carefully examines the circumstances of the couple at the time of the marriage: Such circumstances include their age and maturity; a pattern of alcohol, drug, or any substance abuse; any physical or emotional abuse in their personal history and in their relationship; any deviant sexual practices; any conditions placed upon the marriage; their openness to children; any history of serious psychological problems or mental illness; any previous marriages or attempts to marry; and the ability to enter a permanent, faithful, exclusive union. In examining these circumstances and how they impact upon the couple's ability to make a full, free-willed consent, the Tribunal looks at the couple's relationship during the courtship, the time of marriage, and their lived-life in marriage. The Tribunal will also ask for witnesses, who knew the couple during this time frame, and contact them to answer specific questions. In all, the Tribunal strives to be compassionate and just. Moreover, the proceedings are done under strict confidentiality.

Sometimes people ask, "If a marriage is annulled, does this make the children illegitimate?" The Declaration of Nullity simply states that a sacramental marriage did not take place and therefore both parties are now free to marry. The declaration has no civil bearing on the legitimacy of the children. After all, the children are the innocent victims.

Another question arises concerning the status of a divorced person in the Church. Since divorce involves a civil decree by the state and is not recognized by the Church, a divorced person remains in good standing and may receive the sacraments. However, if a divorced person remarries without a Declaration of Nullity, then strictly speaking, an act of adultery is committed, since the first marriage still is presumed valid. Remarriage without an annulment places the person in a state of mortal sin. Therefore, the Church encourages a divorced person who may think he may one day remarry to see his parish priest and pursue the annulment process.

The Church must be very careful in administering this annulment process. In 1968, 338 annulments were granted in the United States; in 1990, 62,824 were granted. (79,067 Declarations of Nullity were granted for the entire Church throughout the world, revealing the disproportionate number in the United States.) Never should the Church give the impression that the annulment process is merely a burdensome, rubber stamping, hoop-jumping game which eventually leads to a guaranteed annulment. No such guarantee exists. Never should a couple enter marriage thinking, "Well, if it doesn't work out, I can always get it annulled." Rather, we must teach and uphold that marriage is for life. Couples should be encouraged to prepare spiritually for entering the Sacrament of Marriage and for making a Christ-centered marriage for the rest of their lives.

IS BAPTISM NECESSARY FOR SALVATION?

Jesus said, "I solemnly assure you, no one can enter into God's kingdom without being begotten of water and Spirit" (John 3:5). At the ascension, our Lord commanded the apostles, "Go, therefore, and make disciples of all the nations. Baptize them in the name 'of the Father, and of the Son, and of the Holy Spirit.' Teach them to carry out everything I have commanded you" (Matthew 28:19-20). In another account of the ascension, Jesus added, "The man who believes in the good news and accepts Baptism will be saved; the man who refuses to believe in it will be condemned" (John 16:16).

Given these teachings of our Lord, the Second Vatican Council in the *Dogmatic Constitution on the Church* stated, "[Jesus] Himself explicitly asserted the necessity of faith and baptism, and thereby affirmed at the same time the necessity of the Church which men enter through baptism as through a door. Hence they could not be saved who, knowing that the Catholic Church was founded as necessary by God through Christ, would refuse either to enter it, or to remain in it" (#14). Therefore, sacramental baptism is the only means given by our Lord which assures salvation. The Church must never neglect the duty to proclaim the gospel, and by the grace of God, call people in faith to baptism.

The *Catechism*, however, adds an italicized caution: *"God has bound salvation to the Sacrament of Baptism, but He Himself is not bound by His sacraments"* (#1257). Besides the normal ritual baptism of water and the invocation of the Holy Trinity, the Church has also accepted two other forms of Baptism – a baptism of blood and a baptism of desire. While these two forms are not the Sacrament of Baptism *per se*, they do render the same graces and effects (*Catechism*, #1258).

First, consider baptism by blood. During the age of Roman persecution, catechumens – those individuals who were preparing for Baptism and entrance into the Church – oftentimes were arrested, tried as Christians, and condemned to death. The Church considered them to be martyrs since they died for the faith and with Christ. In his treatise on baptism, Tertullian (d. c. 220) coined the phrase "laver of blood," to distinguish the baptism of these cate- chumen martyrs from that of those baptized with the "laver of wa- ter": He wrote in his treatise *On Baptism*, "We have a second laver which is one and the same, namely the laver of blood." St. Augus- tine (d. 430) (writing after the persecution) stated, "When any die for the confession of Christ without having received the laver of re- generation, it avails as much for the remission of their sins as if they had been washed in the sacred font of Baptism" (*City of God*, XIII, 7). This belief in the efficacy of a baptism by blood is based again on the teachings of Christ: "Whoever acknowledges me be- fore men I will acknowledge before my Father in heaven" (Matthew 10:32) and "Whoever wishes to be my follower must deny his very self, take up his cross each day, and follow in my steps. Whoever would save his life will lose it, and whoever loses his life for my sake will save it" (Luke 9:23-24).

The baptism of desire is based on the belief that Christ desired all people to be saved. The saving action of our Lord's passion, death, and resurrection eternally radiates touching even those peo- ple who may not explicitly ever have the benefit of missionary ac- tivity, come to know the gospel, or to receive the Lord through the Sacrament of Baptism. The Second Vatican Council stated, "Since Christ died for all, and since all men are in fact called to one and the same destiny, which is divine, we must hold that the Holy Spir- it offers to all the possibility of being made partakers, in a way known to God, of the Paschal mystery" (*Pastoral Constitution of the Church in the Modern World*, #1260).

In speaking of the "People of God," and affirming that the full- ness of the means of salvation subsists within the confines of the Catholic Church, the Council clearly expressed that other Chris- tians, who share with Catholics Baptism, the Sacred Scriptures, and perhaps even apostolic succession (as with the Orthodox), can also be saved (*Dogmatic Constitution on the Church*, #15). The Council then addressed non-Christians – the Jews, the Moslems, and those who "seek the unknown God": "Those who, through no fault of their own, do not know the Gospel of Christ or His Church, but who nevertheless seek God with a sincere heart, and moved by grace, try in their actions to do His will as they know it through the dictates of their conscience – those too may achieve eternal salvation" (#16). In this sense, these people have a sincere desire for God and would have desired Baptism explicitly if they had the opportunity to receive it or if they had known its necessity (*Catechism*, #1260).

However, such a statement should not seduce us into an indifferentism where one thinks that Baptism is either not important or optional: Baptism is the sacrament which infuses the divine life of the Holy Trinity into our soul and opens to us fully the mystery of Christ's passion, death, and resurrection. Through the nourishment of grace from the reception of other sacraments, the study of the faith, and our life within the Church, we live our Baptism looking forward to its fulfillment in the Kingdom of Heaven.

What then about infants who die without baptism? Here, we trust in the infinite mercy of God, who desires all people to be saved. We cherish the beautiful story of the gospel where Jesus said, "Let the children come to me and do not hinder them. It is to just such as these that the Kingdom of God belongs" (Mark 10:14). Therefore, we hope that these children who die without the benefit of sacramental Baptism will have eternal salvation – that is the desire of the whole Church, the family of the child, the innocent child himself who naturally longs for God, and – we trust – the desire of God. Just think of the Holy Innocents who died because of Herod's wrath: we consider them saints. Nevertheless, we must not again be seduced into thinking Baptism does not matter – Baptism is the definite means that opens the path of salvation. The *Catechism* rightly cautions, "As regards children who have died without Baptism, the Church can only entrust them to the mercy of God, as she does in her funeral rites for them ... . All the more urgent is the Church's call not to prevent little children coming to Christ through the gift of holy Baptism" (#1261).

Baptism is indeed a precious gift. In examining this question, we see the need to be vigilant in insuring the Baptism of our own loved ones. Here grandparents should encourage their children, who may have become lax, to return to Church, to have their own children baptized, and to live the faith with them. Faithful family members should do their best to share their faith with those children who are neglected spiritually by their own parents. Moreover, we also see the responsibility of bearing witness to the faith in word and action, so as to lead others to Baptism and to a full life in Christ.

WHAT IS THE ROLE OF A GODPARENT AND WHO CAN BE ONE?

The role of the godparent for baptism is rooted in the role of the sponsor in the catechumenate, which originated in the early Church. Recall that until the year 313, the Church was under the persecution of the Roman Empire and had to be cautious in conducting its affairs so as to prevent pagan infiltration and persecution. Also, until the Middle Ages, the Sacraments of Initiation – Baptism, Holy Eucharist, and Confirmation – were administered at once. The role of the sponsor then was to attest to the integrity of the person, oftentimes an adult, seeking admission into the Church as well as to assist him during the catechumenate in preparing for these sacraments and in living a Christian life. For infants, these sponsors would also make the Profession of Faith in the child's name, and accept the responsibility of instructing the child in the faith, especially if the parents failed in this duty. About the year 800 when infant baptism was truly the norm, these sponsors were called *"patrinus,"* or "godfather." Traditionally, we identify the sponsor of a child for baptism as the godparent – godmother or godfather – but the technical term remains "sponsor."

According to the *Code of Canon Law*, "Insofar as possible, one to be baptized is to be given a sponsor who is to assist an adult in Christian initiation, or, together with the parents, to present an infant at the baptism, and who will help the baptized to lead a Christian life in harmony with baptism, and to fulfill faithfully the obligations connected with it" (#872). This statement clearly reflects the historical roots of the role of sponsor.

To be a sponsor, a person must be chosen by the person to be baptized, or by the parents or guardians of a child, or, in their absence, by the pastor or minister of the sacrament. The sponsor must not only have the intention of being a sponsor but also meet proper qualifications. The sponsor must have completed his sixteenth year unless the Bishop has established another age for sponsorship, or the pastor or minister judges that a just cause warrants an exception to the rule. He must be a Catholic who has received the Sacraments of Holy Eucharist and Confirmation, and "leads a life in harmony with the faith and the role to be undertaken." Moreover, the sponsor cannot be impeded by some canonical penalty. Ideally, this sponsor at Baptism should also be the sponsor for Confirmation. Note that the mother and father of the child cannot serve as sponsors. Also note that these are the same requirements for Confirmation sponsors. (Cf. *Code of Canon Law*, #874.1).

Strictly speaking, a person only needs one sponsor for Baptism, male or female, but may have two sponsors, one male and one female. Here the *Code of Canon Law* wants to eliminate the practice of having numerous sponsors, as has occurred in some cultures (#873). Also, in the case of an emergency, such as imminent death, no sponsor is needed.

Here we should pause to clarify who qualifies as a Catholic godparent. A Catholic who does not practice the faith by regularly attending Mass or who is in an invalid marriage disqualifies himself from being a godparent. Moreover, if a person is Catholic but antagonistic to the faith, i.e. has the attitude "I am a Catholic but ... ," and would not be a good example and witness to the faith also disqualifies himself. If a person is not striving to fulfill his own obligations of Baptism and Confirmation, he will not fulfill the responsibilities of helping another to do so.

As a pastor, I am truly perturbed each time someone comes by the rectory office and wants me to sign a sponsor's certificate and attest that he is a practicing Catholic when I do not recognize him, he has not registered in the parish, and he does not attend Mass faithfully. In justice, I cannot meet such a request.

Parents need to find good practicing Catholics for godparents. Sadly, this task can be very difficult in today's world. The best place is to look for relatives, even grandparents, who have a blood relationship with the godchild and have kept the faith over the years. Good friends are also appropriate, but sometimes friendships wane, leaving the godchild without an active godparent.

Godparents should be faithful individuals who are ready to accept the responsibility of being a part of a godchild's life for the rest of his life.

What if someone would like to have a faithful Protestant friend as a sponsor? Technically, only Catholics can be godparents or sponsors. A Christian of another denomination, whether Orthodox or Protestant, however, may be a "Christian witness" to the baptism along with the Catholic godparent. The reason for this distinction and restriction is that the godparent not only is taking responsibility for the religious education and spiritual formation of the baptized person, but also is representing the Church, the community of faith, into which the person is being baptized. A Christian who is not Catholic, although perhaps a very holy Christian, cannot fully attest to the beliefs of the Catholic Church. Likewise, a Catholic can only be a Christian witness for someone who is baptized into another Christian denomination. (cf. Vatican II, *Decree on Ecumenism*, #57.)

In all, godparents serve a special role in the life of the baptized person. Therefore, each parent should choose a godparent not just because of a blood relationship or friendship; rather, a godparent should be a trustworthy witness of the faith who will help the godchild attain salvation.

WHAT IS THE RITE OF CHRISTIAN INITIATION (RCIA)?

The Rite of Christian Initiation for Adults (RCIA) is a formal program of catechetical instruction, ascetical practice (prayer and spirituality), and liturgies whereby adults – called catechumens – are formally admitted into the Church and receive the Sacraments of Initiation – Baptism, Confirmation, and Holy Eucharist. (The Sacrament of Penance is received later since baptism washes away all sin, original sin and actual sin.) The *Constitution on the Sacred Liturgy* of the Second Vatican Council decreed, "The catechumenate for adults, comprising several distinct steps, is to be restored and brought into use at the discretion of the local ordinary. By this means the time of the catechumenate, which is intended as a period of suitable instruction, may be sanctified by sacred rites to be celebrated at successive intervals of time" (#64).

This mandate first calls to mind a "restoration" of something that one time existed in the Church. St. Paul in his Letter to the Galatians mentioned that "the man instructed in the Word [i.e. a catechumen] should share all he has with his instructor" (6:6), indicating a formal preparation for entrance into the Church. St. Justin Martyr (d. c. 165) in his *First Apology* described the catechumenate: "Those who are persuaded and believe in the truth of our teachings and sayings undertake to live them accordingly; they are taught to ask, with fasting, for the remission of their sins; we also praying and fasting with them. Then they are led by us to a place where there is water, and they are regenerated in the same way as we have been regenerated." Tertullian (d. c. 220) coined the title "catechumen" and reproached the pagans for not making a distinction between them and the "faithful." Remember that during this time, the Church was under persecution by the Roman Empire and was confronted with various heresies; therefore, the Church wanted a very formal, careful period of instruction to prevent the infiltration of both persecutors and heretics.

The catechumens themselves were distinguished between inquirers (*audientes*), those initially interested in the faith, and actual catechumens who had made an initial commitment to pursue the faith. The catechumenate involved several stages, each with a catechetical, ascetical, and liturgical facet, and usually lasted three years. During this time, they could attend Mass through the Liturgy of the Word, but could not participate in the Liturgy of the Eucharist. At the end of this period, the catechumens were examined, not so much for their knowledge, but to determine whether they lived the faith devoutly and had a sincere conviction of faith. If the examination was favorable, the catechumen became a candidate for baptism, received further instruction, and was baptized at the Easter Vigil Mass.

After the legalization of Christianity in 313, the catechumenate began to fall into disuse for various reasons: The fear of persecution was greatly lessened. Baptism of infants became the norm with adult baptism waning. Conversion of the barbarian invaders precluded any prolonged period of instruction. Actually, Pope Gregory the Great (d. 604) mandated only a forty day preparation period for these people. By the Middle Ages, the catechumenate had disappeared, with only traces remaining in the rites of Baptism and formal reception into the Church.

Given this brief history, the Second Vatican Council saw the need to restore the formal catechumenate for adults. In 1972, the Congregation for Divine Worship issued a new rite, approved by Pope Paul VI. As in the early Church, RCIA is a gradual process that involves the whole community of the faithful. Not only does RCIA prepare individuals for entrance into the Church, it allows the members of the Church to renew their faith.

During the course of the RCIA program, the individual follows a spiritual journey of "steps" accomplished through defined periods punctuated with formal rites. The first period is the Precatechumenate, when candidates inquire about the faith and receive evangelization. Hopefully, the person comes to that initial conversion and step of faith, aided by the grace of God. This period ends with the Rite of Acceptance into the Order of Catechumens when the candidates publicly declare their intention to enter the Church.

This Rite of Acceptance then begins the Period of the Catechumenate, during which the catechumens receive catechetical, ascetical, and liturgical training. Catechetical instruction is of the utmost importance: "This catechesis leads the catechumens not only to an appropriate acquaintance with dogmas and precepts but also to a profound sense of the mystery of salvation in which they desire to participate" (RCIA, #75). During this time, the catechumens should undergo a conversion of mind and action, becoming acquainted with the teachings of the faith and acquiring a spirit of charity. The sponsors and parish community assist the catechumens by their example and support. At Sunday Mass, the catechumens receive special exorcisms, blessings, and anointings following the homily; however, after the Liturgy of the Word, they leave the Church. The Catechumenate may extend over a prolonged period of time, even years if necessary.

The Rite of Election closes the Period of Catechumenate. This rite normally coincides with the first Sunday of Lent. At this rite, upon the testimony of sponsors and catechists and the catechumens' affirmation of their intention to join the Church, the Church makes its "election" of these catechumens to receive the Sacraments of Initiation. In the presence of the Bishop (or his delegate), they inscribe their names in the Book of the Elect at the Cathedral as a pledge of fidelity. Now the catechumens are called "the elect" or "the *illuminandi*" ("those who will be enlightened"). They now begin a Period of Purification and Enlightenment – the final, intense preparation for the reception of the Sacraments of Initiation. On the next five Sundays of Lent, three scrutinies (rites for self-searching and repentance) and the presentations of the Creed and Lord's Prayer take place. This period concludes with the celebration of the Sacraments of Initiation at the Easter Vigil.

After the Easter Vigil, the newly baptized and confirmed members of the Church (technically called neophytes) enter the Period of Postbaptismal Catechesis or Mystagogy. The neophytes grow in their understanding of the mysteries of the faith and strengthen their bonding with the rest of the faithful. They should enter more fully into the life and unity of the Church. This period normally ends around Pentecost.

The RCIA is a spiritually moving process beneficial to the whole parish community. We must keep in our prayers those individuals in our parish RCIA program.

Didn't the Sacrament of Anointing of the Sick used to be called "Extreme Unction"? Why did they change the name? Where did the sacrament come from? When should a person receive this sacrament and how many times?

During His public ministry, Jesus healed people – the blind, the lame, the lepers, the deaf and mute, the hemorrhaging, and the dying. His healing touched both body and soul. In most of the accounts of the healing miracles, the ill person comes to a deeper conviction of faith, and the witnesses know that "God has visited His people" (Luke 7:16). These healings, however, foreshadowed the triumphant victory of our Lord over sin and death through His own passion, death, and resurrection.

The healing ministry of our Lord continues through His Church. Jesus instructed the apostles and sent them out on mission: "With that, they went off, preaching the need of repentance. They expelled many demons, anointed the sick with oil, and worked many cures" (Mark 6:12-13). At the Ascension scene, Jesus echoed this instruction to the apostles and declared that "the sick upon whom they lay their hands will recover" (Mark 16:18). At Pentecost, the Holy Spirit conferred great gifts upon the Church, including healing: St. Paul recognized, "Through the Spirit one receives faith; by the same Spirit another is given the gift of healing, and still another miraculous powers" (I Corinthians 12:9-10). The Apostle St. James provided a clear teaching regarding the Sacrament of the Anointing of the Sick: "Is there anyone sick among you? He should ask for the priests of the Church. They in turn are to pray over him, anointing him with oil in the name of the Lord. This prayer uttered in faith will reclaim the one who is ill, and the Lord will restore him to health. If he has committed any sins, forgiveness will be his" (James 5:14-15). In all, the Church has been continually mindful of our Lord's command, "Heal the sick" (Matthew 10:8).

Various Church Fathers attest to the use of this sacrament in the early Church. St. Augustine (d. 430) wrote that he "was accustomed to visit the sick who desired it in order to lay his hands on them and pray at their bedside," and from his writings it is probable that he anointed them with blessed oil. Pope Innocent I (d. 417), in his letter of instruction to Decentius, affirmed that the Letter of St. James clearly refers to the sacrament and that the bishop must bless the oil, a bishop or priest must administer the sacrament, and the sacrament complements the sacrament of Penance, conveying the forgiveness of sin.

About the twelfth century, this sacrament became commonly known as "Extreme Unction," perhaps for two reasons: First, this anointing concluded the series of sacramental anointings during a person's spiritual life – beginning at Baptism and followed by Confirmation and perhaps Holy Orders, and concluding with Extreme Unction. Second, this anointing more and more was used for those in extremis or at the point of death.

Responding to the Protestant's denial of this sacrament, the Council of Trent decreed in its *Doctrine on the Sacrament of Extreme Unction* (1551), "This sacred anointing of the sick was instituted by Christ our Lord as a true and proper sacrament of the New Testament. It is alluded to indeed by Mark, but is recommended to the faithful and promulgated by James, the apostle and brother of the Lord."

The Second Vatican Council addressed the usage of the sacrament in its *Constitution on the Sacred Liturgy* (1963): "'Extreme Unction,' which may also and more fittingly be called 'Anointing of the Sick,' is not a sacrament for those only who are at the point of death. Hence, as soon as one of the faithful begins to be in danger of death from sickness or old age, the fitting time for him to receive this sacrament has certainly already arrived" (#73). Moreover, the Council highlighted the healing ministry of the

Church and the salvific healing of our Lord: "Through the sacred anointing of the sick and the prayer of her priests, the entire Church commends the sick to the suffering and glorified Lord, imploring for them relief and salvation. She exhorts them, moreover, to associate themselves freely with the passion and death of Christ" (*Dogmatic Constitution on the Church*, #11). The Council recommended that a continuous rite be prepared which would include confession, anointing, and viaticum.

In 1972, Pope Paul VI released his Apostolic Constitution *Sacram Unctionem infirmorum* which prescribed that a priest first lay his hands on the head of the sick person in silence, and then anoint his forehead and hands with the blessed Oil of the Infirm: While anointing the forehead, he prays, "Through this holy anointing, may the Lord in His love and mercy help you with the grace of the Holy Spirit," and then while anointing the hands, "May the Lord who frees you from sin save you and raise you up." (The ritual provides that in accord with local custom or culture as well as the condition of the sick person, a priest may anoint other parts of the body, for example the area of pain or injury.) If circumstances warrant it, the Sacrament of Penance precedes the anointing, which is then followed by the reception of Holy Communion which serves as the "viaticum" for passing over to eternal life. (Please note that only a priest can administer this sacrament.)

The Sacrament of Anointing of the Sick confers the particular healing gift of the Holy Spirit: Through this grace, the whole person is healed. He is strengthened to face the condition of infirmity or old age with courage and peace of heart, to trust in the will of the Lord, to resist the temptations of the Devil, and to overcome anxiety over death. Sins are forgiven and any penance is completed. A person receives the strength to unite himself more closely to the passion of our Lord, atoning for his own sins as well as for those of all of the faithful. This sacrament also prepares us to depart from this life with courage and in the hope of seeing our Lord face to face. Finally, the sacrament may also convey a physical healing in accord with God's will. (Cf. *Catechism*, #1520-23.)

We must remember that the Sacrament of Anointing of the Sick is not simply a "Last Rites" sacrament. Anyone who is prudently judged seriously ill should be anointed. A person may be anointed before serious surgery. The elderly may be anointed to help alleviate the burden and anxiety of old age. Those who have lost consciousness or the use of reason should also be anointed if they would have asked for the sacrament if they had been able to do so. Usually, a person only receives the sacrament once during an illness, but may receive it again if his condition deteriorates.

While the sacrament should not be restricted to "point of death" cases alone, we should not trivialize it either. For instance, I remember once a parishioner asked if I would anoint her. Since she looked very well, I asked her if she was going to have surgery. She replied, "No, I am flying on an airplane tomorrow." After some catechesis on my part, she made a good confession rather than being anointed. (However, given some airlines today, maybe anointing would be appropriate.)

Also, one should not wait to the last minute to have a loved one anointed. Once I was called in the middle of the night to anoint a dying person. Afterwards I was talking with the family, and I discovered the person had been in the hospital over a week. By delaying, the person could have died without the benefit of the sacrament. If a person dies, the priest cannot anoint the dead body from which the soul has already departed; rather, he would offer the prayers for the dead.

In all, Christ has given the Church a beautiful sacrament for the healing of body and soul. We must be mindful of our duty to insure that our loved ones have the benefit of this sacrament, especially as they prepare to leave this life to be joined to our Lord.

THE LAST
THINGS

WHAT IS HEAVEN?

Each time we recite the Creed, we profess, "We believe in one God, the Father almighty, creator of Heaven and earth." Heaven then designates both the firmament of creation and God's dwelling place. Scholars even debate whether the word *Heaven* derives from the Hebrew root *ham*, meaning "to cover" (as in the case of a firmament above the sky) or from *himin*, meaning "home" (God's dwelling place). Either way, Sacred Scripture supports both meanings.

Nevertheless, we focus on Heaven as the dwelling place of God. In faith, each of us looks to our ultimate union with God in Heaven. Jesus in the Beatitudes exhorted His followers, "Be glad and rejoice, for your reward is great in Heaven" (Matthew 5:12). At the Last Supper, the night before His own death, our Lord comforted the apostles: "Do not let your hearts be troubled. Have faith in God and in me. In my Father's house there are many dwelling places; otherwise, how could I have told you that I was going to prepare a place for you?" (John 14:1-2). By His passion, death, and resurrection, Christ atoned for sin and opened the gates of Heaven for us. Therefore, St. Paul wrote, "We know that when the earthly tent in which we dwell is destroyed, we have a dwelling provided for us by God, a dwelling in the heavens, not made by hands but to last forever" (II Corinthians 5:1).

Interestingly, the Book of Revelation provided a physical description of Heaven: the New Jerusalem with walls of jasper, gates of pearls, and streets of gold. However, we must be mindful that such imagery conveys the inexpressible, incomprehensible beauty of Heaven rather than intends to be a literal description.

Moving beyond the "place" of Heaven, Sacred Scripture also emphasizes Heaven as the state of existence for the soul's perfect happiness in union with God and with all of the saints and angels. Heaven is identified as "the city of the living God, the heavenly Jerusalem" (Hebrews 12:22). The quality of life in Heaven is described as "everlasting life" (Matthew 19:16), "the joy of the Lord" (Matthew 25:21), "the crown of life" (James 1:12), "a crown of glory" (I Peter 5:4) and "the wealth of His glorious heritage" (Ephesians 1:18). Here is a blessed community of those who have loyally served the Lord in this life and now have been perfectly incorporated into His mystical body, continuing to fulfill His will. However, even these descriptions cannot fully capture the blessedness of heaven: "No eye has seen, nor ear heard, nor the heart of man conceived, what God has prepared for those who love Him" (I Corinthians 2:9). Little wonder St. Paul said, "I long to be freed from this life and to be with Christ, for that is the far better thing" (Philippians 1:23).

Here in heaven, one enjoys the beatific vision, seeing God as He is "face to face." Again St. Paul wrote, "Now we see indistinctly, as in a mirror; then we shall see face to face" (I Corinthians 13:12). Pope Benedict XII (1336) defined in *Benedictus Deus*, "The souls of all the saints ... and other faithful who have died after receiving Christ's holy baptism (provided they were not in need of purification when they died, ... or, if they then did need or will need some purification, when they have been purified after death, ...) already before they take up their bodies again and before the general judgment ... have been, are, and will be in heaven, in the heavenly Kingdom and celestial paradise with Christ, joined to the company of the holy angels. Since the Passion and death of our Lord Jesus Christ, these souls have seen and do see the divine essence with an intuitive vision, and even face to face, without the mediation of any creature."

St. Ambrose (d. 397) conveyed the beatific vision in less complicated language: "How great will your glory and happiness be, to be allowed to see God, to be honored with sharing the joy of salvation and eternal light with Christ your Lord and God, ... to delight in the joy of immortality in the Kingdom of Heaven with the righteous and God's friends."

However, in no way does the enjoyment of the beatific vision mean to imply some static existence. Archbishop Fulton Sheen stated, " ... It is the mystery of the Trinity which gives the answer to the quest for our happiness and the meaning of Heaven. Heaven is not a place where there is the mere vocal repetition of alleluias or the monotonous fingering of harps. Heaven is a place where we find the fullness of all the fine things we enjoy on this earth. Heaven is a place where we find in its plentitude those things which slake the thirst of hearts, satisfy the hunger of starving minds, and give rest to unrequited love. Heaven is the communion with perfect Life, perfect Truth, and perfect Love" (*The Divine Romance*). In essence, the soul in Heaven still fulfills the will of God and lives, in the fullest sense of the term, with God in a union of love.

The *Catechism* summarized this discussion well: "This perfect life with the Most Holy Trinity – this communion of life and love with the Trinity, with the Virgin Mary, the angels, and all the blessed – is called 'Heaven.' Heaven is the ultimate end and fulfillment of the deepest human longings, the state of supreme, definitive happiness" (#1024). With God's grace, we must strive continually to convert our lives and grow in holiness, so that one day we too may enter into the heavenly rest of the Lord.

DOES HELL EXIST?

Sacred Scripture clearly attests to a place of eternal damnation called "Hell" or sometimes referred to as "Gehenna." Examples include the following: Jesus said that the angry man who holds his brother in contempt "risks the fires of Gehenna" (Matthew 5:22). Our Lord warned, "Do not fear those who deprive the body of life but cannot destroy the soul. Rather, fear him who can destroy both body and soul in Gehenna" (Matthew 10:28). Jesus said, "If your hand is your difficulty, cut it off! Better for you to enter life maimed than to keep both hands and enter Gehenna with its unquenchable fire" (Mark 9:43). Using a parable of the weeds and the wheat to describe the final judgment, Jesus foretold, "The angels will hurl [the evildoers] into the fiery furnace where they will wail and grind their teeth" (Matthew 13:42). Similarly, when Jesus spoke of the last judgment where the sheep will be separated from the goats, He will say to the wicked, "Out of my sight, you condemned, into that everlasting fire prepared for the devil and his angels!" (Matthew 25:41). Finally, in the Book of Revelation, each person is judged individually and the evildoers are cast into "the fiery pool of burning sulphur, the second death" (Revelation 20:13-14; 21:8).

Just for clarification, Gehenna was a valley south of Jerusalem which was infamous for pagan sacrifices of children by fire. The prophet Jeremiah cursed the place and predicted it would be a place of death and corruption. In later rabbinic literature, the term identified the place of eternal punishment with tortures and unquenchable fire for the wicked.

Therefore, the Church has consistently taught that Hell indeed exists. Those souls who die in a state of mortal sin immediately descend to eternal punishment in Hell. The punishment of Hell is primarily the eternal separation from God. Here one suffers the sense of loss – the loss of God's love, the loss of life with God, and the loss of happiness: True love, life, and happiness are rooted in God, and each person longs for them. However, only in Him will man find his fulfillment. (Cf. *Catechism* #1035).

The damned person also suffers pain. Given the descriptions of "fire," the apostolic constitution *Benedictus Deus* (1336) of Pope Benedict XII said that the souls would "suffer the pain of Hell," and the Council of Florence (1439) decreed that the souls would be "punished with different punishments."

Some Saints have had visions of Hell. Blessed Sister Faustina described Hell as follows: "Today I was led by an Angel to the chasms of Hell. It is a place of great torture; how awesomely large and extensive it is! The kinds of tortures I saw: The first torture that constitutes Hell is the loss of God; the second is perpetual remorse of conscience; the third is that one's condition will never change; the fourth is the fire that will penetrate the soul without destroying it – a terrible suffering, as it is a purely spiritual fire, lit by God's anger; the fifth torture is continual darkness and a terrible suffocating smell, and despite the darkness, the devils and souls of the damned see each other and all the evil, both of others and their own; the sixth torture is the constant company of Satan; the seventh torture is horrible despair, hatred of God, vile words, curses, and blasphemies. These are the tortures suffered by all the damned together, but that is not the end of the sufferings. There are special tortures of the senses. Each soul undergoes terrible and indescribable sufferings, related to the manner in which it has sinned. There are caverns and pits of torture where one form of agony differs from another. I would have died at the very sight of these tortures if the omnipotence of God had not supported me. Let the sinner know that he will be tortured throughout all eternity, in those senses which he made use of to sin. I am writing this at the command of God, so that no soul may find an excuse by saying there is no Hell, or that nobody has ever been there, and so no one can say what it is like."

We must remember that God does not predestine anyone to go to Hell or desire for anyone to be damned. God lovingly bestows the actual grace to us which enlightens the intellect and strengthens the will so that we can do good and turn away from evil. However, a person in his informed intellect and with consent of his will can choose to do evil, to commit the mortal sin, and thereby to turn away from God. If a person does not repent of mortal sin, does not have any remorse, and persists in this state, then that person's rejection of God will continue for eternity. In a sense, people put themselves in Hell.

Pope John Paul II in *Crossing the Threshold of Hope* (pp. 185-6) addressed the question, "Can God, who has loved man so much, permit the man who rejects Him to be condemned to eternal torment?" Citing Sacred Scripture, the Holy Father in his answer repeats the unequivocal teaching of our Lord. He also reminds us that the Church has never condemned a particular person to Hell, not even Judas; rather, the Church leaves all judgment to God. However, the Pope, through a series of questions, asserts that the God of Love is also the God of Justice, who holds us responsible for our sins and punishes them accordingly.

Therefore, to believe in Hell does not entail being ignorant, neurotic, or self-loathing, as some misguided people would suggest today; actually, we would be ignorant, neurotic, or self-loathing to think there is no Hell. Perhaps we would see less violence, abuse, and corruption in our world if more people believed in Hell. We must instead pray for the grace to resist temptation and follow the way of the Lord while at the same time always seeking forgiveness for any failing. In speaking of the journey of the Pilgrim Church, Vatican II in the *Dogmatic Constitution on the Church* (#48) advised, "Since we know neither the day nor the hour, we should follow the advice of the Lord and watch constantly so that, when the single course of our earthly life is completed, we may merit to enter with Him into the marriage feast and be numbered among the blessed and not, like the wicked and slothful servants, be ordered to depart in the eternal fire, into the outer darkness where 'men will weep and gnash their teeth.'" For this very reason, we pray in the first Eucharistic Prayer of the Mass, "Father accept this offering from your whole family. Grant us your peace in this life, save us from final damnation, and count us among those you have chosen."

DO WE STILL BELIEVE IN PURGATORY?

Vatican II's *Dogmatic Constitution on the Church* asserted, "This sacred council accepts loyally the venerable faith of our ancestors in the living communion which exists between us and our brothers who are in the glory of heaven or who are yet being purified after their death; and it proposes again the decrees of the Second Council of Nicea, of the Council of Florence, and of the Council of Trent" (#51). Moreover, the *Catechism* clearly affirms the Church's belief in purgatory and the purification of the soul after death (cf. #1030-32).

As Vatican II stated, the Church has consistently believed in a purification of the soul after death. This belief is rooted in the Old Testament. In the Second Book of Maccabees, we read of how Judas Maccabees offered sacrifices and prayers for soldiers who had died wearing amulets, which were forbidden by the Law; Scripture reads, "Turning to supplication, they prayed that the sinful deed might be fully blotted out" (12:43) and "Thus, [Judas Maccabees] made atonement for the dead that they might be freed from the sin" (12:46). This passage gives evidence of the Jewish practice of offering prayers and sacrifices to cleanse the soul of the departed. Rabbinic interpretation of Scripture also attests to the belief. In the Book of the Prophet Zechariah, the Lord spoke, "I will bring the one third through fire, and I will refine them as silver is refined, and I will test them as gold is tested" (13:9); the School of Rabbi Shammai interpreted this passage as a purification of the soul through God's mercy and goodness, preparing it for eternal life. A similar passage is found in Wisdom 3:1-12. In Sirach 7:33, "Withhold not your kindness from the dead" was interpreted as imploring God to cleanse the soul. In sum, the Old Testament clearly attests to some kind of purification process of the soul of the faithful after death.

The New Testament has few references about a purging of the soul or even about Heaven for that matter. Rather the focus is on preaching the gospel and awaiting the second coming of Christ, which only later did the writers of Sacred Scripture realize could be after their own deaths. However, in Matthew 12:32, Jesus' statement that certain sins "will not be forgiven either in this world or in the world to come," at least suggests a purging of the soul after death. Pope St. Gregory (d. 604) stated, "As for certain lesser faults, we must believe that, before the Final Judgment, there is a purifying fire. He who is truth says that whoever utters blasphemy against the Holy Spirit will be pardoned neither in this age nor in the age to come. From this sentence we understand that certain offenses can be forgiven in this age, but certain others in the age to come." The Council of Lyons (1274) likewise affirmed this interpretation of our Lord's teaching.

The early Church preserved the belief in offering prayers for the purification of the soul. Pope St. Gregory said, "Let us not hesitate to help those who have died and to offer our prayers for them." St. Ambrose (d. 397) preached, "We have loved them during life; let us not abandon them in death, until we have conducted them by our prayers into the house of the Lord." Moreover, the Church has affirmed this belief many times, as Vatican II stated.

The key to this answer, however, is to see the beauty behind the doctrine of Purgatory. We believe that God gave us a free will so that we could choose between right and wrong, good and evil. Our free will allows us to make the one fundamental choice – to love God. An act of the free will also entails responsibility. When we choose not to love God and thereby sin, we are responsible for that sin. God in His justice holds us accountable for such sins, but in His love and mercy desires us to be reconciled to Himself and our neighbor. During our life on this earth, if we really love God, we examine our consciences, admit our sins, express contrition for them, confess them, and receive absolution for them in the Sacrament of Penance. We perform penances and other sacrifices to heal the hurt caused by sin. In so doing, we are continually saying "yes" to the Lord. In a sense our soul is like a lens: when we sin, we cloud the lens, it gets dirty, and we lose the focus of God in our lives. Through confession and penance, God cleanses the "lens" of our soul. When we die, if we leave this life fundamentally loving God, dying in His grace and friendship, and free of mortal sin, we will have eternal salvation and attain the beatific vision – we will see God for who He is. If we die with venial sins or without having done sufficient penance for our sins, God in His love, mercy, and justice will not only hold us accountable for our sins but also purify our souls, "cleanse the lens" so to speak. After such purification, the soul will then be united with God in Heaven and enjoy the beatific vision.

Protestants have difficulty with the doctrine of Purgatory for basically two reasons: First, when Martin Luther translated the Bible into German in 1532, he removed seven books of the Old Testament, including the two Books of Maccabees, Sirach, and Wisdom, where at least implicitly the purification of the soul is found. Second, John Calvin preached that we had lost our free will due to original sin and that God had predetermined whether a soul was saved or damned; therefore, if we cannot choose to sin and if our eternal destiny is predetermined, who needs a purgatory? In all, the Protestant leaders cast aside centuries of Christian Church teaching when they denied the doctrine of purgatory.

In *Crossing the Threshold of Hope*, Pope John Paul II related God's "living flame of Love" spoken of by St. John of the Cross with the doctrine of Purgatory: "The 'living flame of love,' of which St. John speaks, is above all a purifying fire. The mystical nights described by this great Doctor of the Church on the basis of his own experience corresponds, in a certain sense, to Purgatory. God makes man pass through such an interior purgatory of his sensual and spiritual nature in order to bring him into union with Himself. Here we do not find ourselves before a mere tribunal. We present ourselves before the power of love itself. Before all else, it is Love that judges. God, who is Love, judges through love. It is love that demands purification, before man can be made ready for that union with God which is his ultimate vocation and destiny."

WHAT IS THE LAST JUDGMENT AND
THE SECOND COMING OF JESUS?

The New Testament has various references to the second coming of our Lord and the last judgment. Immediately one thinks of the Book of Revelation, also known as the Apocalypse, which focuses on those "end times" but employs cryptic symbolism and imagery. In all, the various signs predicting the second coming and the depictions of it can easily cause confusion. Perhaps, this is why different cults have emerged over the centuries which isolated themselves from the rest of society in preparation for an imminent Second Coming.

As Catholics, we are mindful and profess in our Creed that Christ will come again to judge the living and the dead. Vatican Council II's *Dogmatic Constitution on the Church* stated, "Already the final age of the world is with us and the renewal of the world is irrevocably under way; it is even now anticipated in a certain real way, for the Church on earth is endowed already with a sanctity that is real though imperfect" (#48). To try to grasp the when, what, and how of this Second Coming and Last Judgment, we really need to glean the various passages in Sacred Scripture and see how our Church has interpreted them. In all, the Second Coming and Last Judgment are united in one drama.

Our Lord in the gospel spoke of His Second Coming. He indicated that various signs would mark its advent: Mankind will suffer from famine, pestilence, and natural disasters. False prophets who claim to be the Messiah will deceive and mislead people. Nations will wage war against each other. The Church will endure persecution. Worse yet, the faith of many will grow cold, and they will abandon the faith, even betraying and hating one another. (cf. Matthew 24:4-14 and Luke 17:22-37.)

St. Paul described a "mass apostasy" before the Second Coming, which will be led by the "son of perdition," "the Man of Lawlessness," "the adversary who exalts himself above every so-called god proposed for worship." This "lawless one" is part of the work of Satan, and with power, signs, wonders, and seductions will bring to ruin those who have turned from the truth. However, "the Lord Jesus will destroy him with the breath of His mouth and annihilate him by manifesting His own presence." (Cf. II Thessalonians 2:3-12.) The *Catechism* affirms, "God's triumph over the revolt of evil will take the form of the Last Judgment after the final cosmic upheaval of this passing world" (#677).

Our Lord will come suddenly: "The Son of Man in His day will be like the lightning that flashes from one end of the sky to the other" (Luke 17:24). St. Peter predicted, "The day of the Lord will come like a thief, and on that day the heavens will vanish with a roar; the elements will be destroyed by fire, and the earth and all its deeds will be made manifest" (II Peter 3:10).

Death will be no more. The dead shall rise, and those souls who have died will be united again to their bodies. All will have a glorious, transformed, spiritualized body. As St. Paul said, "He will give a new form to this lowly body of ours and remake it according to the pattern of His glorified body ... " (Philippians 3:21).

At this time, the Last or General Judgment will occur: Jesus said, "Those who have done right shall rise to life; the evildoers shall rise to be damned" (John 5:29). Our Lord described this judgment as follows: "When the Son of Man comes in His glory, escorted by all of the angels of Heaven, He will sit upon His royal throne, and all the nations will be assembled before Him. Then He will separate them into two groups, as a shepherd separates sheep from goats" (Matthew 25:31-32). Here each person will have to account for his conduct, and the deepest secrets of his soul will come to light. How well each person has responded to the prompting of God's grace will be made clear. Our attitude and actions toward our neighbor will reflect how well we have loved our Lord: "As often as you did for one of my least brothers, you did it for me" (Matthew 25:41).

Our Lord will judge us accordingly. For those who have died and already have faced the Particular Judgment, their judgment will stand. For those living at the time of the Second Coming, they will receive judgment. Those who have rejected the Lord in this life, who have sinned mortally, who have no remorse for sin and do not seek forgiveness, will have condemned themselves to Hell for all eternity: "By rejecting grace in this life, one already judges oneself, receives according to one's works, and can even condemn oneself for all eternity by rejecting the Spirit of love" (*Catechism*, #678). The souls of the righteous will enter heavenly glory and enjoy the beatific vision, and those who need purification will undergo it.

We do not know when this second coming will occur. Jesus said, "As to the exact day or hour, no one knows it, neither the angels in Heaven nor even the Son, but only the Father. Be constantly on the watch! Stay awake! You do not know when the appointed time will come" (Mark 13:32-33). Given the world situation of lawlessness, apathy, and apostasy, and even the explosion of reported apparitions and messages of our Blessed Mother, we better stay awake and keep watch.

WHAT DO WERE MEAN BY THE
"RESURRECTION OF THE DEAD"?

In the gospels, Jesus had predicted three times that He would be arrested by the chief priests and scribes, suffer, be condemned to death, and be crucified; however, He also predicted that He would be "raised up" on the third day (cf. Matthew 16:21, 17:22-23, 20:17-19). The predictions came true. On Easter Sunday morning, when Mary Magdalene and other women, St. Peter and St. John went to the tomb, they found it empty. The angel proclaimed, "You are looking for Jesus of Nazareth, the one who was crucified. He has been raised up; he is not here" (Mark 16:6). Jesus had risen body and soul from the dead.

Later, Jesus appeared to the apostles and others. He would appear and disappear suddenly. He could be embraced (Matthew 28:9). He showed the wound marks of His hands and side to the apostles, and invited St. Thomas to examine them with his fingers (John 20:19ff). He was not always easily recognizable, as in the appearance to Mary Magdalene (John 20:11ff) or to the apostles by the Sea of Galilee (John 21:1ff). Jesus also shared meals with His apostles (John 21:9ff, Luke 24:36ff) and other disciples (Luke 23:13). In all, Jesus affirmed He was not some ghost or some resuscitated corpse: Jesus said, "Look at my hands and my feet; it is really I. Touch me, and see that a ghost does not have flesh and bones as I do" (Luke 24:29).

Therefore, through the resurrection, our Lord has a radically transformed or glorified existence. Glorification means that Jesus was fully and perfectly spiritualized and divinized without loss of His humanity.

When we die, our soul stands before God in the Particular Judgment, and we have to account for our lives – good and bad, omissions and commissions. God will then judge the soul worthy of Heaven, Hell, or Purgatory. The body, committed to the earth, will decay.

At the end of time, however, we too will share in the resurrection of the dead, also known as the resurrection of the body. St. Paul addressed this issue: "Perhaps someone will say, 'How are the dead to be raised up? What kind of body will they have?' A nonsensical question! The seed you sow does not germinate unless it dies. So is it with the resurrection of the dead. What is sown in the earth is subject to decay, what rises is incorruptible. What is sown is ignoble, what rises is glorious. Weakness is sown, strength rises up. A natural body is put down and a spiritual body comes up" (I Corinthians 15:35-36, 42-44). The Fourth Lateran Council consequently (1215) decreed, Christ "will come at the end of the world ... and all will rise with their own bodies which they now have so that they may receive according to their works, whether good or bad."

At this time, through the power of Christ's resurrection, the just shall rise, the souls shall be reunited with their bodies, and their bodies will be glorified – radically transformed and made superior to their present condition. The bodies of the wicked and "godless" will also rise again in incorruptibility and immortality, but they will not be glorified; rather, these bodies will rise as they had been on earth, but more in the sense of an identity rather than an amalgamation of parts at any one time.

Traditionally, theology has described the glorified and perfected bodies as having the characteristics of identity, entirety, and immortality. The bodies of the saints – the faithful in Heaven and Purgatory – will also have four "transcendent qualities": impassibility, or freedom from physical evil, death, sickness, and pain; clarity, or freedom from defects and an endowment with beauty and radiance; agility, whereby the soul moves the body and there is freedom of motion; and subtility, whereby the body is completely spiritualized under the dominion of the soul. These transcendent qualities actually capture the substance of St. Paul's First Letter to the Corinthians: what is corrupt rises to incorruption; what is ignoble, to glory; what is weakness, to strength; and what is a natural body, to a spiritual body.

Nevertheless, we must admit that this "glorification" exceed our understanding and even our imagination. We believe it becaus Christ promised this resurrection of the body: "For an hour is com ing in which all those in their tombs shall hear His voice and com forth. Those who have done right shall rise to live; the evildoer: shall rise to be damned" (John 5:28-29).

CAN CATHOLICS BE CREMATED?

While cremation is definitely becoming more and more popular, it is actually something new to Catholic Christian tradition. The early Church retained the Jewish practice of bodily burial and rejected the common pagan Roman practice of cremation. The basis for this rule was simply that God has created each person in His image and likeness, and therefore the body is good and should be returned to the earth at death (Genesis 3:19). Moreover, our Lord Himself was buried in the tomb and then rose in glory on Easter. Therefore, Christians buried their dead both out of respect for the body and in anticipation of the resurrection at the Last Judgment. St. Paul reminds us, "The Lord Himself will come down from heaven at the word of command, at the sound of the archangel's voice and God's trumpet; and those who have died in Christ will rise first" (I Thessalonians 4:16).

The Church's stance against cremation was also reinforced by those who mocked the belief in the resurrection of the body. Many of the early martyrs were burned at the stake and then their persecutors scattered their ashes as a sign of contempt for this Christian belief.

After the legalization of Christianity in the 4th century, cremation generally ceased in the Roman Empire. As Christian culture continued to spread, even in those missionary lands, regular bodily burial became the norm, even in cultures that had once practiced cremation. Due to the religious belief of the people, the civil authorities also outlawed cremation: For example Charlemagne made cremation at capital offense in 789. The only exception given to this rule was when there may have been a mass death and the spread of disease threatened.

In the nineteenth century, cremation again arose in Europe due greatly to the Freemasonry movement and the rationalist philosophy which denied any notion of the supernatural or spiritual, particularly the immortality of the soul, the afterlife, and the resurrection of the body. The concern for hygiene and the conservation of land also prompted a revival. Many began to view cremation as an acceptable funeral custom. Nevertheless, largely motivated by the affront to the Catholic faith posed by cremation, the Church officially condemned the practice in 1886.

The old 1917 *Code of Canon Law* (#1203) prohibited cremation and required the bodies of the faithful to be buried. Again, an exception was given in times of mass death and the threat of disease. Those individuals who had directed their bodies to be cremated were denied ecclesiastical burial.

In 1963, the Church clarified this regulation. The Sacred Congregation for the Doctrine of the Faith (then known as the Holy Office) issued an instruction *Piam et Constantem* stating, "The constant pious practice among Christians, of burying the bodies of the faithful departed, has always been the object of solicitude on the part of the Church, shown both by providing it with appropriate rites to express clearly the symbolic and religious significance of burial, and by establishing penalties against those who attacked this salutary practice." The Church permitted cremation in cases of necessity, but prohibited it for anyone who was making a stand against the faith.

The new *Code of Canon Law* (1983) stipulates, "The Church earnestly recommends that the pious custom of burying the bodies of the dead be observed; it does not, however, forbid cremation unless it has been chosen for reasons which are contrary to Christian teaching" (#1176). Therefore, a person may choose to be cremated if he has the right intention. However, the cremated remains must be treated with respect and should be interred in a grave or columbarium.

A pastoral problem with cremation has concerned their presence at the funeral Mass and then their placement afterwards. Until recently, the cremains could not be present for the funeral Mass. On March 21, 1997, the Sacred Congregation for Divine Worship and the Discipline of the Sacraments granted an indult authorizing each local bishop to set a policy regarding the presence of the cremains for the funeral Mass. Appropriate prayers and liturgical directives have been issued to accommodate this situation. The Sacred Congregation emphasized that the cremains must be treated with respect and must be interred after the funeral Mass either in a columbarium or in the ground with an appropriate marking memorializing the deceased. The keeping of the cremains at home or the scattering of them at sea, in the air, or in the garden is not permitted.

As a priest, I believe that the entire Catholic funeral liturgy – the vigil service, the Mass of Christian Burial, and the Final Committal and Burial – offers to us a great reminder of our faith and aids in our healing. The regular liturgical prayers and actions are designed to honor the body. Moreover, the body best reminds us of that person who entered a new life at Baptism, becoming a "temple of the Lord," was anointed at Confirmation, was nourished with the Holy Eucharist, and has now gone, we hope and pray, to the fulfillment of that life and eternal rest. While the death of someone we love is always hard to face, there is something good and comforting when we gather as a faith community in the presence of our Lord and the body of the deceased, and offer that loved one back to God. Unfortunately, on more than one occasion, I have dealt with families who have had the deceased loved one cremated, and later regretted the action, even feeling great guilt. I always recommend for people who want to be cremated or want to have their deceased loved one cremated that they do so after the funeral Mass and then inter the remains properly.

While cremation is permitted and the indult allows the presence of the cremains at the funeral Mass, the preference remains to bury the body of the deceased loved one.

MARY, OUR BLESSED MOTHER

WHAT IS THE IMMACULATE CONCEPTION?

A persistent confusion seems to exist over the "Immaculate Conception." Some people mistakenly think the term is related to Mary's conception of Christ by the power of the Holy Spirit. However, the Immaculate Conception is the belief that "the most Blessed Virgin Mary was, from the first moment of her conception, by a singular grace and privilege of almighty God and in view of the merits of Christ Jesus the Savior of the human race, preserved immune from all stain of original sin ... " (*Ineffabilis Deus*).

In examining the history surrounding this belief, we see the beauty of a Church founded by Christ, whose faithful followers struggle to grasp ever more clearly the mystery of salvation. This struggle is guided by the Holy Spirit, whom Jesus called "The Spirit of Truth," who "will instruct you in everything and remind you of all that I told you" and "will guide you to all truth" (cf. John 14:17, 15:26, 16:13).

Part of the "struggle" with the Immaculate Conception is that there is no specific, crystal-clear scriptural citation for it. Nevertheless, the references in the Gospels to the Blessed Mother and her role in the mystery of salvation intimate this belief. In the Gospel of Luke, we find the beautiful passage of the Annunciation, where Archangel Gabriel said to Mary (in our familiar wording), "Hail Mary, full of grace. The Lord is with you. Blessed are you among women" (Luke 1:28). While some scripture scholars haggle over "how full is full," the testimony of St. Gabriel definitely indicates the exceptional, singular holiness of the Blessed Mother. St. Gabriel recognized that the Lord is with her even more than with himself, an angel. She is blessed among all women, even among all people. When one considers the role Mary was to play in the life of our Lord – whether His incarnation, His childhood, or His crucifixion – she must have been outstanding in holiness, truly "full of grace" in accepting and in fulfilling her role as the Mother of the Savior, in the fullest sense of Mother. We believe, therefore, this exceptional, grace-filled holiness extended to the very beginning of her life, her conception.

On the practical side, if original sin is inherited through our parents, and Jesus took on our human nature in all things except sin, then Mary had to be free of original sin. Sin could not touch our Savior. The question then arises, "How is Christ the Savior of Mary?" Actually much of the debate concerning the Immaculate Conception during the Middle Ages focused on this problem. Duns Scotus (d. 1308) posited one solution saying, "Mary more than anyone else would have needed Christ as her Redeemer, since she would have contracted original sin ... if the grace of the Mediator had not prevented this." Quoting the *Dogmatic Constitution on the Church*, the *Catechism* adds, "The 'splendor of an entirely unique holiness' by which Mary is 'enriched from the first instant of her conception' comes wholly from Christ: she is 'redeemed, in a more exalted fashion by reason of the merits of her Son'" (#492). In essence, since Mary was chosen to share intimately in the life of Jesus from her conception, He was indeed her Savior from her conception.

Perhaps one reason why the discussion over the Immaculate Conception was prolonged is because the early Church was outlawed and under persecution until the year 313, and then had to address various problems surrounding Jesus Himself. More reflection about Mary and her role occurred after the Council of Ephesus (431) solemnly affirmed Mary's divine motherhood and gave her the title, "Mother of God" in that she conceived by the power of the Holy Spirit and bore Jesus who is the second person of the Holy Trinity, consubstantial with the Father. Several of the early Church Fathers including St. Ambrose (d. 397), St. Ephraem (d. 373), St. Andrew of Crete (d. 740), and St. John Damascene (d. 749) meditated on Mary's role as Mother, including her own grace-filled disposition, and wrote of her sinlessness. A feast day in honor of the Immaculate Conception has been celebrated in the Eastern part of the Church at least since the sixth century.

As time passed, further discussion arose about this belief. In 1849, Pius IX asked the bishops throughout the Church what they themselves, their clergy, and the people felt about this belief and whether they would want it defined solemnly. Of 603 bishops, 546 responded favorably without hesitation. Of those opposing, only 5 said the doctrine could not be solemnly defined, 24 did not know whether this was the opportune time, and 10 simply wanted a condemnation of any rejection of the doctrine. On December 8, 1854, Pius IX solemnly defined the dogma of the Immaculate Conception in his bull *Ineffabilis Deus*.

Finally, it is also interesting that in several apparitions of our Blessed Mother, she herself has attested to her Immaculate Conception: On December 9, 1531 (the date for the Solemnity of the Immaculate Conception in the Spanish Empire) at Guadalupe, Mary said to Juan Diego, "I am the perfect and perpetual Virgin Mary, Mother of the true God, through whom everything lives ... ," indicating a freedom from all sin. In 1830, Mary told St. Catherine Laboure to have the Miraculous Medal struck with the inscription, "Mary conceived free from sin, pray for us who have recourse to thee." Lastly, when she appeared to St. Bernadette at Lourdes in 1858, Mary said, "I am the Immaculate Conception."

In a homily on the Solemnity of the Immaculate Conception delivered in 1982, Pope John Paul II wrote, "Blessed be God the Father of our Lord Jesus Christ, who filled you, Virgin of Nazareth, with every spiritual blessing in Christ. In Him, you were conceived Immaculate! Preselected to be His Mother, you were redeemed in Him and through Him more than any other human being! Preserved from the inheritance of original sin, you were conceived and came into the world in a state of sanctifying grace. Full of grace! We venerate this mystery of the faith in today's solemnity. Today, together with all the Church, we venerate the Redemption which was actuated in you. That most singular participation in the Redemption of the world and of man, was reserved only for you, solely for you. Hail O Mary, Alma Redemptoris Mater, dear Mother of the Redeemer."

WHAT IS THE ASSUMPTION
OF THE BLESSED MOTHER?

Addressing a jubilant crowd of over 500,000 people packed into St. Peter's Square, Pope Pius XII solemnly defined in *Munificentissimus Deus* on November 1, 1950 that "the Immaculate Mother of God, the ever-virgin Mary, having completed the course of her earthly life, was assumed body and soul into heavenly glory." Although the solemn definition may have been at the midpoint of the twentieth century, the belief in the Assumption of our Blessed Mother exemplifies the dynamism of revelation and the Church's ongoing understanding of it as guided by the Holy Spirit.

Granted, the word Assumption does not appear in Sacred Scripture. For this reason, many fundamentalists who literally interpret the Bible would have a difficulty with this belief. Nevertheless, we must first pause and reflect on the role of our Blessed Mother in the mystery of salvation, for this provides the foundation for the belief in the Assumption. We firmly believe that from the first moment of her conception, Mary was free of all sin including Original Sin by a special favor of Almighty God. The Archangel Gabriel recognized her as "full of grace," "blessed among women," and "one with the Lord." Mary had been chosen to be the Mother of our Savior. By the power of the Holy Spirit, she conceived our Lord, Jesus Christ, and through her, true God became also true man: "The Word became flesh and dwelt among us." During her lifetime, although the Gospel citations are limited, Mary always presented our Lord to others: to Elizabeth and her son, John the Baptist, who leapt for joy in the womb at the presence of the Lord still in His own mother's womb; to the simple shepherds as well as the wise Magi; and to the people at Cana when our Lord acquiesced to His mother's wish and performed the first miracle. Moreover, Mary stood at the foot of the cross with her Son, supporting Him and sharing in His suffering through her love as only a mother could do. Finally, she was with the Apostles at Pentecost, when the Holy

Spirit descended and the Church was born. Therefore, each of us can step back and see Mary as the faithful servant of God who shared intimately in the birth, life, death, and resurrection of our Lord.

For these reasons, we believe that the promises our Lord has given to each of us of sharing eternal life, including a resurrection of the body, were fulfilled in Mary. Since Mary was free of original sin and its effects (one of which is corruption of the body at death), since she shared intimately in the life of the Lord and in His passion, death, and resurrection, and since she was present at Pentecost, this model disciple appropriately shared in the bodily resurrection and glorification of the Lord at the end of her life. (Note that the solemn definition does not specify whether Mary physically died before being assumed or just was assumed; it simply states, "Mary, having completed the course of her earthly life ... .") The *Catechism*, also quoting the Byzantine Liturgy, states, "The Assumption of the Blessed Virgin is a singular participation in her Son's resurrection and an anticipation of the resurrection of other Christians: 'In giving birth you kept your virginity; in your Dormition you did not leave the world, O Mother of God, but were joined to the source of Life. You conceived the living God and, by your prayers, will deliver our souls from death'" (#966).

This belief in the Assumption of our Blessed Mother has been longstanding in our Church. We must remember that the early Church was preoccupied with resolving questions about Christ, particularly His incarnation and the hypostatic union (the unity of His divine and human natures in one person). However, in addressing these questions, the Church gradually defined the titles of Mary as Mother of God and as the New Eve, and the belief of the Immaculate Conception, all of which form the basis for the Assumption.

In *Munificentissimus Deus*, Pope Pius XII cited various Church Fathers to trace the longstanding tradition of the belief of the Assumption' St. John Damascene (d. 749), St. Andrew of Crete (d. 740), St. Modestus of Jerusalem (d. 300), and St. Gregory of Tours

(d. 594), to name a few. Bishop Theoteknos of Livias (c. 550-650) delivered one of the most comprehensive early sermons concerning the Assumption: "For Christ took His immaculate flesh from the immaculate flesh of Mary, and if He had prepared a place in heaven for the Apostles, how much more for His mother; if Enoch had been translated and Elijah had gone to Heaven, how much more Mary, who like the moon in the midst of the stars shines forth and excels among the Prophets and Apostles? For even though her God-bearing body tasted death, it did not undergo corruption, but was preserved incorrupt and undefiled and taken up into heaven with its pure and spotless soul."

St. John Damascene also recorded an interesting story concerning the Assumption: "St. Juvenal, Bishop of Jerusalem, at the Council of Chalcedon (451), made known to the Emperor Marcian and Pulcheria, who wished to possess the body of the Mother of God, that Mary died in the presence of all the Apostles, but that her tomb, when opened, upon the request of St. Thomas, was found empty; wherefrom the Apostles concluded that the body was taken up to heaven" (*Second Homily on the Dormition of Mary*). In all, the Patristic Fathers defended the Assumption on two counts: Since Mary was sinless and a perpetual virgin, she could not suffer bodily deterioration, the result of original sin, after her death. Also, if Mary bore Christ and played an intimate role as His mother in the redemption of man, then she must likewise share body and soul in His resurrection and glorification.

The Byzantine Emperor Mauritius (582-602) established the celebration of the Dormition of the Blessed Virgin Mary on August 15 for the Eastern Church. (Some historians speculate that the celebration was already widespread before the Council of Ephesus in 431.) By the end of the sixth century, the West likewise celebrated the Feast of the Assumption. While the Church first emphasized the death of Mary, gradual shifts in both title and content occurred, so that by the end of the eighth century, the Gregorian Sacramentary had prayers for Assumption Day.

The Feast of the Assumption gives each of us great hope as we contemplate this one facet of the beautiful woman of faith, our Blessed Mother. Mary moves us by example and prayer to grow in God's grace, to be receptive to His will, to convert our lives through sacrifice and penance, and seek that everlasting union in the Heavenly Kingdom. In 1973, the National Conference of Catholic Bishops in their letter *Behold Your Mother* stated, "Christ has risen from the dead; we need no further assurance of our faith. Mary assumed into heaven serves rather as a gracious reminder to the Church that our Lord wishes all whom the Father has given Him to be raised with Him. In Mary taken to glory, to union with Christ, the Church sees herself answering the invitation of the heavenly Bridegroom."

WHY DO WE CALL MARY TOWER OF DAVID, TOWER OF IVORY, HOUSE OF GOLD, ARK OF THE COVENANT, GATE OF HEAVEN, MYSTICAL ROSE, MORNING STAR, MIRROR OF JUSTICE, SEAT OF WISDOM, AND STAR OF THE SEA?

We find these terms in the Litany of the Blessed Virgin Mary (specifically the Loreto version), which was composed in the mid-16th century. St. Peter Canisius (d. 1597) popularized the litany in 1558 when he published it to foster devotion to our Blessed Mother in response to the Protestant "Reformers" who had attacked such devotion. The litany represents a compilation of titles praising our Blessed Mother that were used at services at the Shrine of Loreto in Italy from the thirteenth century.

Most of the titles in question are associated with the prophecies and symbolism of the Old Testament which foreshadow the role our Blessed Mother played in the mystery of salvation. Several of these center on her sanctity and maternity. For instance, the *Tower of David* stood prominently and strongly on the highest summit of the mountains surrounding Jerusalem. Such a tower was part of the defense mechanism of the city. From it, warnings would be given of approaching enemies. Mary is compared to the Tower of David because of her holiness, being recognized as full of grace and having been conceived free of original sin. By her prayers and example, she is part of God's "defense mechanism" by which the Kingdom of God will stand undefeated and sin will always be conquered. (Cf. Song of Songs, 4:4.)

Similarly, Mary is also called the *Tower of Ivory*. This term is also used in the Song of Songs (7:5) to describe the beloved bride. (A similar term, *Ivory Palace* is mentioned in Psalm 45, verse 9, for the same reason.) Both instances foreshadow the nuptial relationship between Christ and His bride, the Church, as conveyed in St. Paul's Letter to the Ephesians. Here though we remember, as Vatican II taught, that Mary is "a type of the Church": She conceived by the power of the Holy Spirit and through her, our Savior entered into this world. As such, "the Church indeed contemplating [Mary's] hidden sanctity, imitating her charity, and faithfully fulfilling the Father's will, by receiving the Word of God in faith becomes a mother" (*Dogmatic Constitution on the Church*, #64).

The role of mother is particularly clear in the term *Ark of the Covenant*. Remember in the Old Testament the Ark of the Covenant housed the Ten Commandments, the Law of God. As the Israelites journeyed to the promised land, a cloud, signifying the presence of God, would descend upon or "overshadow" the tent where the Ark was kept. Jesus came to fulfill the covenant and the law. In the Annunciation story, Archangel Gabriel says to Mary, "The Holy Spirit will come upon you and the power of the Most High will overshadow you" (Luke 1:35), conveying the same notion. Therefore, Mary "houses" Jesus in the womb; she is the new "Ark."

From this foundation flow the other titles: Jeremiah predicted that the Messiah would be named, "The Lord our Justice" (23:6); Mary is the *Mirror of Justice* because no one better reflected the love and devotion to our Lord in His life than Mary. Because of her pure love and because she "housed" Jesus, she is called *House of Gold*. Jesus is the Wisdom of God, "the Word who became flesh and dwelt among us" (John 1:14); therefore, Mary, who bore our Lord, is called *Seat of Wisdom*.

For us, Mary is also a sign of great hope. Vatican II stated, "The Mother of Jesus in the glory which she possesses body and soul in heaven is the image and beginning of the Church as it is to be perfected in the world to come. Likewise, she shines forth on earth, until the day of the Lord shall come, a sign of certain hope and comfort to the Pilgrim People of God" (*Dogmatic Constitution on the Church*, #68). For this reason, she is called *Morning Star*, because she is a symbol of the victorious Christian who perseveres in faith, and shares in Christ's messianic authority and victory over the darkness of sin and death. The term is found in the Book of

Revelation (2:26-28): "To the one who wins the victory, who keeps to my ways till the end, I will give authority over the nations – the same authority I received from my Father. He shall rule them with the rod of iron and shatter them like crockery; and I will give him the morning star." Also in Songs of Songs (6:10) we find, "Who is this that comes forth like the dawn, as beautiful as the moon, as resplendent as the sun ... "; as the brightness of a light penetrating the early morning darkness, Mary heralds the coming of her Son, who is the light of the world (cf. John 1:5-10, 3:19).

She too is the *Gate of Heaven*. Mary is the means by which our Lord came down from heaven to free us from sin. At the end of her life, we believe that Mary was assumed body and soul into heaven, a fulfillment of everlasting life and the resurrection of the body promised by Jesus. Therefore, she is the gate through which Jesus entered this world, and gate of fulfilled promise by which we will share everlasting life.

Therefore, we look to her as the *Star of Sea*. As a star guides the sailor on the stormy sea to safe port, so Mary, through her prayer and example, guides us along our journey of life, over sometimes turbulent water, to the heavenly port.

In all, Mary is the *Mystical Rose*. The rose is considered the most beautiful flower, the flower of royalty which surpasses all others in fragrance. A rose has a delicate bloom supported by a strong stem with thorns for defense. Similarly, our Blessed Mother's soul reflects the love of God, while her person represents a strong woman of firm faith conviction ready to defend the Lord. She has the sweetness of sanctity and the beauty of virtues.

In sum, all of these titles remind us of the important role of the Blessed Mother in our Catholic spirituality. She is a model of virtue and sanctity as an individual, a spouse, a mother, and a disciple of the Lord. Moreover, she is a sign of the life to come.

WHAT DO WE MEAN WHEN WE SAY MARY WAS "EVER VIRGIN"?

We as Catholics firmly believe that Mary is "ever virgin." The *Catechism* asserts, "The deepening of faith in the virginal mother-hood led the Church to confess Mary's real and perpetual virginity even in the act of giving birth to the Son of God made man" (#499). Given this teaching, the perpetual virginity of Mary has tradition-ally been defended and examined in three parts: Mary's concep-tion of Christ (*virginitas ante partum*); her giving birth to Christ (*virginitas in partu*); and her remaining a virgin after the birth of Christ (*virginitas post partum*). This formulation was used by many of the early Church Fathers – St. Augustine, St. Peter Chrysologus, Pope St. Leo the Great, St. Gregory Nazianzus, and St. Gregory Nyssa. For example, the *Catechism* quotes St. Augus-tine's elaboration: Mary "remained a virgin in conceiving her Son, a virgin in giving birth to Him, a virgin in carrying Him, a virgin in nursing Him at her breast, always a virgin" (#510).

Mary's virginity prior to the conception of Christ is quite clear from the Gospels of St. Matthew and St. Luke where she is clearly identified as "a virgin" (cf. Luke 1:26-27, Matthew 1:18). More-over, when Archangel Gabriel announced to Mary that she would be the mother of the Messiah, she responded, "How can this be since I do not know man?" indicating her virginity.

At the other end of the spectrum is Mary's virginity after the birth of Christ. In an article concerning whether Jesus had blood brothers and sisters, this question is dealt with in detail. Succinct-ly, we as Catholics believe that Mary and Joseph did not have oth-er children after the birth of Christ. No evidence exists either in Sacred Scripture or Tradition to believe otherwise.

The troublesome part is the middle – Mary's virginity in giving birth to Christ. We remember that one of the sufferings inherited because of original sin is that of "child bearing pains": The Lord God said to Eve, "I will intensify the pangs of your childbearing;

in pain shall you bring forth children" (Genesis 3:16). Since Mary was free of original sin by her immaculate conception, she would consequently be free of "child bearing pain." In wrestling with this belief, the early Church Fathers then struggled to explain the meaning of this virginity *in partu*. The majority of Western Fathers seemed to emphasize Mary's physical integrity. For instance, Pope St. Leo the Great said, " ... She [Mary] brought Him forth without the loss of virginity, even as she conceived Him without its loss ... . [Jesus Christ was] born from the Virgin's womb because it was a miraculous birth ... ." They compared the birth of our Lord to Him miraculously emerging from the closed tomb or appearing suddenly in the upper room although the doors were locked. Some Fathers used the analogy of the birth of our Lord to a ray of sun shining through a glass: just as the glass remains "unaltered" by the ray, so did Mary by the birth of our Lord. (Even Pope Pius XII in his encyclical *Mystici Corporis* (1943) asserted, "It was [Mary] who gave miraculous birth to Christ our Lord ... .")

On the other hand, the Eastern Fathers emphasized Mary's joy and freedom from pain in giving birth to Jesus, the Son of God. They looked upon Mary as the New Eve, free of the pain of original sin. Moreover, they did not want to lose the notion of Mary being a mother in the full sense of the term. Remember, the Gospel of St. Luke simply states, "She gave birth ... " (Luke 2:7), which does not demand a miraculous birth process.

Officially, the Church has upheld the perpetual virginity of Mary. Pope Siricius in 390 wrote: "This is the virgin who conceived in her womb and as a virgin bore a son." The Council of Chalcedon (451) ratified the teaching of Pope Leo I regarding that Mary is ever-virgin. The Lateran Council (649) (not one of the general councils) stated: "If anyone does not, according to the holy Fathers, confess truly and properly that holy Mary, ever virgin and immaculate, is Mother of God, since in this latter age she conceived in true reality without human seed from the Holy Spirit, God the Word Himself, who before the ages was begotten of God the Father, and gave birth to Him without injury, her virginity remaining equally inviolate after the birth, let him be condemned." In 1555, Pope Paul IV affirmed the virginity of Mary before, during, and after the birth of the Lord. However, the Church has not defined specifically how Mary is virgin *in partu.*

In the 1950s, great controversy arose among theologians over the interpretation of virgin *in partu.* Albert Mitterer cautioned against so emphasizing the physical quality of virginity that one lost sight of the goodness of Mary's role as mother and her giving birth to Jesus. Freedom from "child bearing pain" does not necessarily entail freedom from the act of child bearing. Dr. Ludwig Ott stated, "It seems hardly possible to demonstrate that the dignity of the Son of God or the dignity of the Mother of God demands a miraculous birth."

Fr. Karl Rahner, without delving into all of the anatomical details, focused on the spiritual reality of Mary's virginity: Mary bore the Son of God. Her childbearing must have been essentially different from other women since she was free of the effects of original sin. Therefore, her virginity, childbearing, and motherhood are together in union with the will of God.

Finally, on July 27, 1960, the Holy Office (now the Sacred Congregation for the Doctrine of the Faith) warned, "Several theological studies have been published in which the delicate problem of Mary's virginity *in partu* is dealt with in unbecoming terms and, what is worse, in a manner that is clearly opposed to the traditional doctrine of the Church and to the devotional sense of the faithful." Frankly, a discussion of *virginitas in partu* which focuses on anatomical minutia not only loses sight of the beautiful theology of the incarnation but also becomes embarrassing.

In all, we need to emphasize and revere both the virginity and motherhood of Mary. The *Dogmatic Constitution on the Church* of Vatican II asserted that Christ's birth "did not diminish His mother's virginal integrity but sanctified it" (#57). Accordingly, "in the mystery of the Church, which is itself rightly called mother and virgin, the Blessed Virgin stands out in eminent and singular fashion as exemplar both of virgin and mother" (#63).

WHY IS MARY REFERRED
TO AS THE "MEDIATRIX"?

The Second Vatican Council dedicated the eighth chapter of the *Dogmatic Constitution on the Church* to our Blessed Mother. Since our Lord continues His work and saving mission through His body, the Church, the council fathers, particularly under the guidance of Pope Paul VI, decided that it was most appropriate to address the role of our Blessed Mother in this document because "she is endowed with the high office and dignity of the Mother of the Son of God, and is ... the beloved daughter of the Father and the temple of the Holy Spirit" (#53). The whole Church honors Mary as a pre-eminent and wholly unique member of the Church, and as a model in faith, hope, and charity.

Given this basis, the Vatican Council II here again repeated the titles of Mary as Advocate, Helper, Benefactress, and Mediatrix (#62). In its basic definition, a mediator is one who serves as an intermediary between two other parties. Oftentimes, the mediator assists in reconciling differences and bringing the parties to an understanding.

Examining the references to our Blessed Mother in the Sacred Scriptures, we find this role of "mediator." Mary, recognized by Archangel Gabriel as full of grace, one with the Lord, and blessed among all women, conceived by the power of the Holy Spirit and bore Jesus Christ. Through her "mediation" Jesus entered this world, true God becoming also true man. In the gospel passages in which she appears, our Blessed Mother always presented our Lord to others: the shepherds, the Magi, the priest Simeon, and the wedding party at Cana. She stood at the foot of the cross, sharing in our Lord's sufferings, and at that point He gave her to us as our Mother. Finally, Mary was with the apostles at Pentecost; she who brought Jesus into this world was there for the birth of the Church. At the end of her life, Mary was assumed body and soul into heaven, the fulfillment of the promises of eternal life of body and soul given to all of the faithful. The *Dogmatic Constitution on the Church* captured her life well in stating, "Thus in a wholly singular way she cooperated by her obedience, faith, hope and burning charity in the work of the Savior in restoring supernatural life to souls" (#61).

Therefore we could look at Mary as the Mediatrix in three senses: First, as mother of the redeemer, she was the intermediary through which the Son of God entered this world to save us from sin.

Second, by the witness of her own faith and thereby of presenting Christ to others, she aided in reconciling sinners to her Son. Mary, sinless yet knowing the suffering caused by sin, continues to call sinners to her Son. Through her example, she inspires all of us to the faith, hope, and love that our Lord wants all of us to have.

Finally, because of her assumption and role as mother for all of us, she prays for us, interceding on our behalf just as she did at Cana, asking the Lord to bestow graces to us as He wills.

This title and role of Mediatrix, however, in no way is meant to distract the faithful from Christ or erode His role as the one Mediator (#62). Christ's mediation is primary, self-sufficient, and absolutely necessary for our salvation, whereas the mediation of our Blessed Mother is secondary and dependent upon Christ. The Vatican Council stated, "In the words of the apostle [St. Paul], there is but one mediator: 'for there is but one God and one mediator of God and men, the man Christ Jesus, who gave Himself a redemption for all' (I Timothy 2:5-6). But Mary's function as mother of men in no way obscures or diminishes this unique mediation of Christ, but rather shows its power. But the Blessed Virgin's salutary influence on men originates not in any inner necessity but in the disposition of God. It flows forth from the superabundance of the merits of Christ, rests on His mediation, depends entirely on it, and draws of its power from it. It does not hinder in any way the immediate union of the faithful with Christ but on the contrary fosters it" (#60).

Let us continually implore our Blessed Mother's prayers. May her example inspire us to strive to be full of grace, seeking forgiveness for sin, and to present Christ to others in our words and deeds. As she held Christ in her womb, may we hold Christ in our hearts. In so doing, we too may become like mediators, leading others to Christ through our own witness.

DID JESUS HAVE "BLOOD" BROTHERS AND SISTERS?

This question arises because the gospels refer to the "brothers" and "sisters" of our Lord. In the New American Bible's English translation of the Gospel of St. Mark, we do indeed read about the crowd asking, "Isn't this the carpenter, the son of Mary, a brother of James and Joses and Judas and Simon? Aren't his sisters our neighbors here?" (Mark 6:3). A similar reference occurs earlier in Mark 3:31 "'His mother and brothers arrived ... .'"

The problem emerges in understanding the meaning of the word *brother*. In the original text of the gospel, we find the Greek word *adelphos*, meaning "brothers," used. However, *adelphos* does not just mean blood brothers born of the same parents. Rather, *adelphos* was used to describe brothers not born of the same parents, like a half-brother or step-brother. The word also described other relationships like cousins, nephews, uncles, etc. For example in Genesis 13:8 and 14:14-16, the word *adelphos* was used to describe the relationship between Abraham and Lot; however, these two men did not share a blood brother relationship, but one of uncle and nephew. Another instance is that of Laban, who was an adelphos to Jacob, not as a brother, but as an uncle. (In the New American translation, "kinsman" or "relative" will be used in these Old Testament cases; I do not know why this is not true in the English translation of the gospel.)

The same meanings are true for the word *sister* in Greek. For example, in I Chronicles 23:21-22, the sons of Kish married their "sisters," a literal translation of the text, but in reality they married their cousins.

Actually the confusion originates in Hebrew and Aramaic, the languages of most of the original Old Testament texts and of Christ. In these languages, no special word existed for cousin, nephew or aunt, half-brother or half-sister, or step-brother or step-sister; so they used the word *brother* or a circumlocution, such as in the case of a cousin, "the son of the brother of my father." When the Old Testament was translated into Greek and the New Testament written in Greek, the word *adelphos* was used to capture all of these meanings for male relatives. So in each instance, we must examine the context in which the title is used. In all, the confusion arises in English because of the lack of distinct terms for relatives in the Hebrew and Aramaic, and the usage of the Greek *adelphos* to signify all of these relations.

Nevertheless, other gospel passages clarify these relationships. James and Joses were the sons of Mary of Cleophas (Mark 15:40). Mary of Cleophas is described in the Gospel of John as our Blessed Mother's "sister" (John 20:25); obviously, she must have been a cousin, and James and Joses thereby cousins of our Lord. Judas was the son of James (not either of the apostles) (Luke 6:16). James the lesser was the son of Alphaeus (Luke 6:15). James the greater and John were the sons of Zebedee with a mother other than our Blessed Mother Mary (Matthew 20:20ff).

The gospels are also very clear that Mary was a virgin at the time she conceived Jesus through the power of the Holy Spirit (cf. Matthew 1:18-25, Luke 1:26-38). Remember when the Archangel Gabriel announced to Mary God's plan, she responded, "How can this be since I do not know man?" After the birth of our Lord, although the gospels do not give us many details of His childhood, no mention is made of Mary and Joseph ever having other children. Never does it refer to the "sons of Mary" or "a son of Mary," but only the son of Mary.

This point is again corroborated at the crucifixion scene: Before He dies, our Lord says to Mary, "Woman, there is your son," and then to St. John, who is definitely not a blood brother, "There is your mother." According to Jewish law, the oldest son had the responsibility of caring for the widowed mother, and that responsibility would pass to the next oldest if anything happened to the first born son. By this time, St. Joseph had died. Since Jesus, the first born, had no "blood brother," He entrusted Mary to the care of St. John, the Beloved Disciple.

Interestingly, the Orthodox Churches solve this problem over brothers and sisters by speculating that St. Joseph was a widower who had other children before he married Mary. These brothers and sisters would really then be half-brothers and half-sisters. Perhaps this notion is why St. Joseph sometimes appears elderly in paintings.

Actually, this whole confusion in not new. About 380, Helvidius suggested that the "brethren" were the children born of Mary and Joseph after Jesus. St. Jerome declared this as a "novel, wicked, and daring affront to the faith of the whole world." In his *On the Perpetual Virginity of the Blessed Mary*, St. Jerome used both Scripture and the fathers like Saints Ignatius, Polycarp, Irenaeus and Justin Martyr to refute Helvidius. Later, the First Lateran Council (649) definitively declared that Mary was "ever virgin and immaculate." Therefore, as Catholics, based on Sacred Scripture and Tradition, we do not believe that Mary and Joseph had other children and consequently that Jesus had blood brothers and sisters.

WHY DO WE CALL MARY "MOTHER OF GOD"?

To understand the title, "Mother of God," we must first clearly understand Mary's role as mother of our Savior, Jesus Christ. As Catholics, we firmly believe in the incarnation of our Lord: Mary conceived by the power of the Holy Spirit. (cf. Luke 1:26-38 and Matthew 1:18-25.) Through her, Jesus Christ – second person of the Holy Trinity, one-in-being (consubstantial) with the Father, and true God from true God – entered this world taking on human flesh and a human soul. Jesus is true God and true man. In His person are united both a divine nature and a human nature. Mary did not create the divine person of Jesus, who existed with the Father from all eternity: "In fact, the One whom she conceived as man by the Holy Spirit, who truly became her Son according to the flesh, was none other than the Father's eternal Son, the second person of the Holy Trinity. Hence the Church confesses that Mary is truly 'Mother of God' (*Theotokos*)" (*Catechism*, #495). As St. John wrote, "The Word became flesh and made His dwelling among us, and we have seen His glory: The glory of an only Son coming from the Father filled with enduring love" (John 1:14).

For this reason, sometime in the early history of the Church, our Blessed Mother was given the title "Mother of God." St. John Chrysostom (d. 407), for example, composed in his Eucharistic Prayer for the Mass an anthem in honor of her: "It is truly just to proclaim you blessed, O Mother of God, who are most blessed, all pure and Mother of our God. We magnify you who are more honorable than the Cherubim and incomparably more glorious than the Seraphim. You who, without losing your virginity, gave birth to the Word of God. You who are truly the Mother of God."

However, objection to the title "Mother of God" arose in the fifth century due to confusion concerning the mystery of the incarnation. Nestorius, Bishop of Constantinople (428-431), incited a major controversy. He stated that Mary gave birth to Jesus Christ, a regular human person period. To this human person was united the person of the Word of God (the divine Jesus). This union of two persons – the human Christ and the divine Word – was "sublime and unique" but merely accidental. The divine person dwelt in the human person "as in a temple." Following his own reasoning, Nestorius asserted that the human Jesus died on the cross, not the divine Jesus. As such, Mary is not "Mother of God," but simply "Mother of Christ," the human Jesus. Sound confusing? It is, but the result is the splitting of Christ into two persons and the denial of the incarnation.

St. Cyril, Bishop of Alexandria (d. 440), refuted Nestorius, asserting, "It was not that an ordinary man was born first of the Holy Virgin, on whom afterwards the Word descended; what we say is that, being united with the flesh from the womb, [the Word] has undergone birth in the flesh, making the birth in the flesh His own ..." (*Against Those Who do not Wish to Confess that the Holy Virgin is the Mother of God*). This statement affirms the belief asserted in the first paragraph.

On June 22, 431, the Council of Ephesus convened to settle this argument. The Council declared, "If anyone does not confess that the Emmanuel is truly God and therefore that the holy Virgin is the Mother of God (*Theotokos*) (since she begot according to the flesh the Word of God made flesh), *anathema sit*." Therefore, the Council officially recognized that Jesus is one person, with two natures, human and divine, united in a true union. Second, Ephesus affirmed that our Blessed Mother can rightfully be called the Mother of God: Mary is not Mother of God, the Father, or Mother of God, the Holy Spirit; rather, she is Mother of God, the Son, Jesus Christ. The Council of Ephesus declared Nestorius a heretic, and the Emperor Theodosius ordered him deposed and exiled. (Interestingly, a small Nestorian Church still exists in Iraq, Iran, and Syria.)

The incarnation is indeed a profound mystery. The Church uses very precise, albeit philosophical, language to prevent confusion and error. Nevertheless, we must ponder this great mystery of how our divine Savior entered this world, taking on our human flesh, to free us from sin. We must also ponder and emulate the great example of our Blessed Mother, who said, "I am the handmaid of the Lord; be it done unto me according to thy word." May we turn to her always as our own Mother, pleading, "Holy Mary, Mother of God, pray for us sinners now and at the hour of our death. Amen."

SAINTS, ANGELS, & THE DEVIL

WHAT IS THE OFFICIAL PROCESS FOR DECLARING SOMEONE A SAINT?

The official process for declaring someone a saint is called *canonization*, meaning the person is worthy of inclusion in the canon of the Mass. Prior to the year 1234, the Church did not have a formal process as such. Usually martyrs and those recognized as holy were declared saints by the Church at the time of their deaths. Before the legalization of Christianity in the year 313 by Emperor Constantine, the tombs of martyrs, like St. Peter, were marked and kept as places for homage. The anniversaries of their deaths were remembered and placed on the local Church calendar. After legalization, oftentimes basilicas or shrines were built over these tombs.

As time went on, the Church saw the need to tighten the canonization process. Unfortunately, sometimes figures of legends were honored as saints. Or once, the local church in Sweden canonized an imbibing monk who was killed in a drunken brawl – hardly evidence of martyrdom. Therefore, in the year 1234, Pope Gregory IX established procedures to investigate the life of a candidate saint and any attributed miracles. In 1588, Pope Sixtus V entrusted the Congregation of Rites (later the Congregation for the Causes of the Saints) to oversee the entire process. Beginning with Pope Urban VIII in 1634, various Popes have revised and improved the norms and procedures for canonization.

Today the process proceeds as follows: When a person dies who has "fame of sanctity" or "fame of martyrdom," the bishop of the Diocese usually initiates the investigation. (Note that the person must be dead five years before the cause of sainthood is introduced.) The bishop appoints a Tribunal to examine the evidence and to take testimony of both those who do and do not consider the person a saint. One element is whether any special favor or miracle has been granted through this candidate saint's intercession. The Church will also investigate the candidate's writings to see if there is "purity of doctrine," essentially, nothing heretical or against the faith. All of this information is gathered, and then a *transumptum*, a faithful copy, duly authenticated and sealed, is submitted to the Congregation for the Causes of the Saints.

Once the cause is accepted by the Congregation, further investigation is conducted. A Postulator is appointed who continues to gather information, and presents and discusses the cause with the judges of the Congregation. If the candidate was a martyr, the Congregation determines whether he died for the faith and truly offered his life in a sacrifice of love for Christ and the Church. In other cases, the Congregation examines to see if the candidate was motivated by a profound charity towards his neighbor, and practiced the virtues in an exemplary manner and with heroism. Throughout this investigation the "general promoter of the faith," or devil's advocate, raises objections and doubts which must be resolved. During this time, the Postulator composes a *positio*, a biography, legal brief, and scholarly position all in one.

The *positio* is then presented to a panel of nine theologians, who examine the case and vote whether the person truly exhibited "heroic virtue." Six positive votes sends the cause to the larger meeting of the Congregation of bishops and cardinals. A two-thirds positive vote then sends the cause to the Holy Father who examines the case. If the Holy Father decides that a candidate is declared to have lived life with heroic virtue, he declares him "venerable."

The next step is beatification. A martyr may be beatified and declared "blessed" by virtue of martyrdom itself. Otherwise, the candidate must be credited with a miracle. In verifying the miracle, the Church looks at whether God truly performed a miracle and whether the miracle was in response to the intercession of the candidate saint. Once beatified, the candidate saint may be venerated but with restriction to a city, diocese, region, or religious family. Accordingly, the Pope would authorize a special prayer, Mass, or proper for the Divine Office honoring the Blessed.

After beatification, another miracle is needed for canonization and the formal declaration of sainthood. Once this miracle is substantiated, the Pope may declare the person a saint. When the Holy Father canonizes, he acts infallibly: He, as the Successor of St. Peter, makes an irrevocable decision binding for the universal Church, and in this matter of faith and morals, presents and declares this person worthy of veneration.

However, we must not lose sight that this thorough process exists because of how important the saints are as examples for us, the faithful who strive to live in the Kingdom of God now and see its fulfillment in Heaven. Vatican II declared, "God shows to men, in a vivid way, His presence and His face in the lives of those companions of ours in the human condition who are more perfectly transformed in the image of Christ. He speaks to us in them and offers us a sign of this kingdom to which we are powerfully attracted, so great a cloud of witnesses is there given and such a witness to the truth of the Gospel. It is not merely by the title of example that we cherish the memory of those in heaven; we seek rather that by this devotion to the exercise of fraternal charity the union of the whole Church in the Spirit may be strengthened" (*Dogmatic Constitution on the Church*, 50).

WHY DO WE PRAY TO SAINTS?

Since the earliest days of the Church, Catholics have always venerated those holy men and women who have gone before us and are now with our Lord in heaven. Unlike most Protestant denominations, Catholics have a clear sense that we who belong to the pilgrim Church on earth are united with the Church triumphant in heaven and the Church undergoing purification in purgatory: we call this union the communion of Saints (cf. *Catechism*, #957). Together, the Church on earth, in heaven, and in purgatory form one Church, one Mystical Body of Christ.

Vatican II's *Dogmatic Constitution on the Church* emphasized that Christ founded the Church, "the society structured with hierarchical organs and the mystical body of Christ, the visible society and the spiritual community, the earthly Church and the Church endowed with heavenly riches." The Church on earth and the Church of heaven, are not two separate realities; "on the contrary, they form one complex reality which comes together from a human and a divine element" (#8).

This union, however, is not something static, but dynamic. Just as we who are members of the Church on earth help each other on the path of salvation through our prayers, good works, and example, so do the saints help us. The *Dogmatic Constitution on the Church* stated, "Being more closely united to Christ, those who dwell in heaven fix the whole Church more firmly in holiness, add to the nobility of the worship that the Church offers to God here on earth, and in many ways helps in a broader building up of the Church. Once received into their heavenly home and being present to the Lord, through Him and with Him and in Him, they do not cease to intercede with the Father for us, as they proffer the merits which they acquired on earth through the one mediator between God and men. ... So by their brotherly concern is our weakness greatly helped" (#49).

Note that the *Dogmatic Constitution on the Church* emphasized that Christ is the one mediator. Sometimes Protestants object to the

Church's devotion to saints because they misconstrue praying "to the saints" to mean diminishing the role of Jesus. While we may say, "Pray to the saints," we actually mean asking them to intercede for us – to pray with us and for us – to our Lord, who bestows all graces. To refute this very objection raised by the first Protestant leaders, the Council of Trent (1563) stressed that "it is good and useful to invoke [the saints] humbly, and to have recourse to their prayers, their help and assistance, in order to obtain favors from God through His Son, our Lord Jesus Christ, who alone is our Redeemer and Savior." Yes, we must never lose our focus on Christ. However, the saints who are alive with Christ can indeed pray for us and by their vigilant and faithful example help keep our eyes focused on Christ. If anything, these saints, who have proclaimed Christ as Redeemer and Savior in their lives, want to lead all to Him, not to distract us from Him.

The very active role of the saints in the Church comes alive in the Liturgy. Remember that during the Rites of Baptism and Ordination, the faithful chant the Litany of Saints, invoking the aid of this cloud of witnesses (Hebrews 12:1). Each time we celebrate the Holy Sacrifice of the Mass, we remember these great saints, mentioning by name at least our Blessed Mother, the patron saint of the parish, and the saint whose feast it may be. In the Preface, the priest exhorts the faithful to lift up their hearts and join with all the angels and saints in praising God. During the Eucharistic Prayer, we recall their constant intercession for us. At this time, Heaven is joined to earth once again as our Lord becomes present and dwells among us in the Holy Eucharist. Our communion with the Lord in the Blessed Sacrament unites us in communion with all the angels and saints. Therefore, we praise God for this great band of witnesses, and we must not forget to implore their aid, remembering, "Their glory fills us with joy, and their communion with us in your Church gives us inspiration and strength as we hasten on our pilgrimage of faith, eager to meet them" (Preface from the Solemnity of All Saints).

WHAT ARE RELICS?

Relics include the physical remains of a saint (or of a person who is considered holy but not yet officially canonized) as well as other objects which have been "sanctified" by being touched to his body. These relics are divided into two classes: First class or real relics include the physical body parts, clothing, and instruments connected with a martyr's imprisonment, torture, and execution. Second class or representative relics are those which the faithful have touched to the physical body parts or grave of the saint.

The use of relics has some, although limited, basis in Sacred Scripture. In II Kings 2:9-14, the Prophet Elisha picked up the mantle of Elijah, after he had been taken up to Heaven in a whirlwind; with it, Elisha struck the water of the Jordan, which then parted so that he could cross. In another passage (II Kings 13:20-21), some people hurriedly buried a dead man in the grave of Elisha, "but when the man came into contact with the bones of Elisha, he came back to life and rose to his feet." In Acts of the Apostles we read, "Meanwhile, God worked extraordinary miracles at the hands of Paul. When handkerchiefs or cloths which had touched his skin were applied to the sick, their diseases were cured and evil spirits departed from them" (Acts 19:11-12). In these three passages, a reverence was given to the actual body or clothing of these very holy people who were indeed God's chosen instruments, "Elijah, Elisha, and St. Paul. Indeed, miracles were connected with these "relics," not that some magical power existed in them, but just as God's work was done through the lives of these holy men and women so did His work continue after their deaths. Likewise, just as people were drawn closer to God through the lives of these holy men, so did they (even if through their remains) inspire others to draw closer even after their deaths. This perspective provides the Church's understanding of relics.

The veneration of relics of the saints is found in the early history of the Church. A letter written by the faithful of the Church in

Smyrna in the year 156 provides an account of the death of St. Polycarp, their bishop, who was burned at the stake. The letter reads, "We took up the bones, which are more valuable than precious stones and finer than refined gold, and laid them in a suitable place, where the Lord will permit us to gather ourselves together, as we are able, in gladness and joy, and to celebrate the birthday of his martyrdom." Essentially, the relics – the bones and other remains of St. Polycarp – were buried, and the tomb itself was the "reliquary." Other accounts attest that the faithful visited the burial places of the saints and miracles occurred. Moreover, at this time, we see the development of "feast days" marking the death of the saint, the celebration of Mass at the burial place, and a veneration of the remains.

After the legalization of the Church in 313, the tombs of saints were opened and the actual relics were venerated by the faithful. A bone or other bodily part was placed in a reliquary – a box, locket, and later a glass case – for veneration. This practice especially grew in the Eastern Church, while the practice of touching cloth to the remains of the saint was more common in the West. By the time of the Merovingian and Carolingian periods of the Middle Ages, the use of reliquaries was common throughout the whole Church.

The Church strived to keep the use of relics in perspective. In his *Letter to Riparius*, St. Jerome (d. 420) wrote in defense of relics: "We do not worship, we do not adore, for fear that we should bow down to the creature rather than to the Creator, but we venerate the relics of the martyrs in order the better to adore Him whose martyrs they are."

Here we need to pause for a moment. Perhaps in our technological age, the whole idea of relics may seem strange. Remember, all of us treasure things that have belonged to someone we love – a piece of clothing, another personal item, or a lock of hair. Those "relics" remind us of the love we continue to share with that person while he was still living and even after death. We are very proud to say, "This belongs to my mother," for instance. Our hearts are torn when we think about disposing of the very personal things of a deceased loved one. Even from an historical sense, at Ford's Theater Museum for instance, we can see things that belonged to President Lincoln, including the blood stained pillow on which he died. With great reverence then, we treasure the relics of saints, the holy instruments of God.

During the Middle Ages, the "translation of relics" grew, meaning the removal of relics from the tombs, their placement in reliquaries, and their dispersal. Sadly, abuses grew also. With various barbarian invasions, the conquests of the Crusades, the lack of means for verifying all relics, and less than reputable individuals who in their greed preyed on the ignorant and superstitious, abuses did occur. Even St. Augustine (d. 430) denounced impostors who dressed as monks selling spurious relics of saints. Pope St. Gregory (d. 604) forbade the selling of relics and the disruption of tombs in the catacombs. Unfortunately, the Popes or other religious authorities were powerless in trying to control the translation of relics or to prevent forgeries. Eventually, these abuses prompted the Protestant leaders to attack the idea of relics totally. (Unfortunately, the abuses and the negative reaction surrounding relics has led many people to this day to be skeptical about them.)

In response, the Council of Trent (1563) defended invoking the prayers of the saints, and venerating their relics and burial places: "The sacred bodies of the holy martyrs and of the other saints living with Christ, which have been living members of Christ and the temple of the Holy Spirit, and which are destined to be raised and glorified by Him unto life eternal, should also be venerated by the faithful. Through them, many benefits are granted to men by God."

Since that time, the Church has taken stringent measures to insure the proper preservation and veneration of relics. The *Code of Canon Law* (#1190) absolutely forbids the selling of sacred relics, and they cannot be "validly alienated or perpetually transferred" without permission of the Holy See. Moreover, any relic today would have proper documentation attesting to its authenticity. The *Code* also supports the proper place for relics in our Catholic practice: Canon 1237 states, "The ancient tradition of keeping the

relics of martyrs and other saints under a fixed altar is to be preserved according to the norms given in the liturgical books," (a
practice widespread since the fourth century). Many Churches
also have relics of their patron saints which the faithful venerate on
appropriate occasions. And yes, reports of the Lord's miracles and
favors continue to be connected with the intercession of a saint and
the veneration of his relics. In all, relics remind us of the holiness
of a saint and his cooperation in God's work; at the same time,
relics inspire us to ask for the prayers of that saint and to beg the
grace of God to live the same kind a faith-filled life.

WHAT ARE ANGELS?

The *Catechism* clearly affirms, "The existence of the spiritual, non-corporeal beings that Sacred Scripture usually calls 'angels' is a truth of faith. The witness of Scripture is as clear as the unanimity of Tradition" (#328). Given that we do believe in angels, we define them as pure spirits and personal beings with intelligence and free will. They are immortal beings. As the Bible attests, they appear to humans as apparitions with a human form.

Since the 4th century, nine choirs or types of angels are identified in the Bible and have been elaborated upon by various theologians: The first three choirs see and adore God directly. The seraphim, which means "the burning ones," have the most intense "flaming" love for God and comprehend Him with the greatest clarity. (Interestingly, Lucifer, which means "light bearer," was one of the seraphim whose beautiful light was changed into darkness.) The cherubim, which means "fullness of wisdom," contemplate God's divine providence and plan for His creatures. Lastly, the thrones, symbolizing divine justice and judicial power, contemplate God's power and justice.

The next three choirs fulfill God's providential plan for the universe: The dominations or dominions, whose name evokes authority, govern the lesser choirs of angels. The virtues, whose name originally suggested power or strength, implement the orders from the dominations and govern the heavenly bodies. Lastly, the powers confront and fight against any evil forces opposed to God's providential plan.

The last three choirs are directly involved in human affairs: The principalities care for earthly principalities, such as nations or cities. The archangels deliver God's most important messages to mankind, while each angel serves as a guardian for each of us. Although not official dogma, this schema became popular in the Middle Ages in the writings of St. Thomas Aquinas, Dante, Hildegard of Bingen, and John Scotus Erigina.

Nevertheless, we believe that Almighty God created the angels before the rest of creation. At some point, some angels, led by Lucifer, did rebel against God. These angels made a free choice, radically and irrevocably rejecting God and His rule. Therefore, they were cast into Hell. This event is mentioned, albeit briefly, in several passages of the New Testament: St. Peter wrote, "Did God spare even the angels who sinned? He did not! He held them captive in Tartarus [Hell] – consigned them to pits of darkness, to be guarded until judgment" (II Peter 2:4). In the Letter of St. Jude we read, "There were angels, too, who did not keep to their own domain, who deserted their dwelling place. These the Lord has kept in perpetual bondage, shrouded in murky darkness against the judgment of the great day. Sodom, Gomorrah, and the towns thereabouts indulged in lust, just as those angels did; they practiced unnatural vice. They are set before us to dissuade us, as they undergo a punishment of eternal fire." (Jude 6-7). When Jesus spoke of the Last Judgment and the need to serve the least of our brethren, He said to the unrighteous, "Out of my sight, you condemned, into that everlasting fire prepared for the devil and his angels" (Matthew 25:41). Always remember that these fallen angels – the devil and demons – had been created good, but by their own free will chose to sin and turn away from God.

A key to understanding angels is by looking at what they do. First, angels see, praise, and worship God in His divine presence. Jesus said, "See that you never despise one of these little ones. I assure you, their angels in heaven constantly behold my heavenly Father's face" (Matthew 18:10), a passage which also indicates that each of us has a guardian angel. The Book of Revelation described how the angels surround the throne of God and sing praises (cf. Revelation 5:11ff, 7:11ff). Moreover, they rejoice over the saved soul of the repentant sinner (Luke 15:10).

Second, angel comes from the Greek *angelos* which means "messenger," which describes their role in interacting with this world. St. Augustine stated that angels were "the mighty ones who do His word, hearkening to the voice of His word." Throughout Sacred Scripture, the angels served as messengers of God, whether delivering an actual message of God's plan of salvation, rendering justice, or providing strength and comfort. Here are a few examples of their role as messengers in the Old Testament: After the Fall of Adam and Eve and their expulsion, the cherubim guarded the entrance to the Garden of Eden (Genesis 3:24). Angels protected Lot and his family in Sodom and Gomorrah (Genesis 19). The angel stopped Abraham as he was about to offer Isaac in sacrifice (Genesis 22). An angel guarded the people on the way to the Promised Land (Exodus 23:20). In the New Testament, an angel appeared to the centurion Cornelius and prompted his conversion (Acts 10:1ff); and an angel freed St. Peter from prison (Acts 12:1ff). In all, Hebrews 1:14 captured their role well: "Are they not all ministering spirits, sent to serve those who are to inherit salvation?"

Sacred Scripture identifies by name three angels, who are the great messengers of God – Sts. Michael, Raphael, and Gabriel. They are called archangels because of their important roles in God's plan. St. Michael, whose name means, "one who is like God," led the army of angels who cast Satan and the rebellious angels into Hell; at the end of time, he will wield the sword of justice to separate the righteous from the evil (cf. Revelation 12:7-0). St. Gabriel, whose name means "strength of God," announced to Mary that she had been chosen as the Mother of the Savior (cf. Luke 1:26-38). St. Raphael, whose name means "remedy of God," cured the blind man Tobit (cf. Tobit 5).

The angels are also our guardians. The *Catechism* states, "From infancy to death human life is surrounded by their watchful care and intercession" (#336). St. Basil (d. 379) asserted, "Beside each believer stands an angel protector and shepherd leading him to life." Most of us at an early age learned the little prayer to our guardian angel: "Angel of God, my guardian dear, to whom God's love commits me here. Ever this day be at my side, to light, to guard, to rule, to guide."

Moreover, as Catholics, we remember the important role of St. Michael in defending us against Satan and the powers of evil. Toward the end of the nineteenth century, Pope Leo XIII (d. 1903) had a prophetic vision of the coming century of sorrow and war. In this vision, God gave Satan the choice of one century in which to do his worst work. The devil chose this century. So moved was the Holy Father from this vision that he composed the prayer to St. Michael the Archangel: "St. Michael the Archangel, defend us in battle! Be our protection against the wickedness and snares of the devil. May God rebuke him, we humbly pray, and do thou, O Prince of the heavenly host, by the power of God, thrust into Hell Satan and all the other evil spirits who roam about the world seeking the ruin of souls." For many years, this prayer was recited at the end of Mass. About a year ago, our Holy Father at one of his Wednesday audiences made the strong suggestion that the recitation of the prayer be instituted at Mass once again given the great evils we see present in our world – the sins of abortion, euthanasia, terrorism, genocide, and the like.

As members of the Church, we are conscious of the angels in our liturgical practices. At Mass, in the Preface before the Eucharistic Prayer, we join with all of the angels and saints to sing the hymn of praise, "Holy, holy, holy ... ." In Eucharistic Prayer I, the priest prays, "Almighty God, we pray that your angel may take this sacrifice to your altar in heaven." In the Final Commendation of the Funeral Liturgy, the priest prays, "May the angels lead you into paradise; may the martyrs come to welcome you and take you to the holy city, the new and eternal Jerusalem." Moreover, we celebrate in our liturgical calendar the Feasts of the Archangels (September 29) and Guardian Angels (October 2).

In our daily prayers and activities, we should be mindful of these servants of God who by His love keep our lives safe from harm and guide us on the path of salvation.

WHO IS THE DEVIL?

The Catechism of the Catholic Church asserts, "Behind the disobedient voice of our first parents lurks a seductive voice, opposed to God, which makes them fall into death out of envy. Scripture and the Church's Tradition see in this being a fallen angel, called 'Satan' or the 'devil'" (#391). Throughout Sacred Scripture, we find mention of Satan, the devil. The word *Satan* comes from the Hebrew verb *satan* meaning to oppose, to harass someone; so *Satan* would be the tempter, the one to make us trip and fall, the one to turn us from God. The word *devil* is derived from the Greek *diabolos* meaning an accuser, a slanderer. Other synonyms for Satan in Sacred Scripture are the Evil One, Beelzebub, the Accuser, the Tempter, the Great Dragon, and the Ancient Serpent.

We believe that in the beginning, God created Satan as a good angel: The Lateran Council IV (1215) stated, "The devil and the other demons were indeed created naturally good by God, but they became evil by their own doing." These angels irrevocably chose through their free will to rebel against God and not to serve Him. For this rebellion, they were cast into Hell. Sacred Scripture attests to this belief: Our Lord, speaking of the Final Judgment, said, "Then [the Son of Man] will say to those on His left: 'Out of my sight, you condemned, into that everlasting fire prepared for the devil and his angels'" (Matthew 25:41). St. Peter wrote, "Did God spare even the angels who sinned? He did not! He held them captive in Tartarus [the term in Greek mythology to indicate the place of punishment in the underworld] ... " (II Peter 2:4). St. John added, "The man who sins belongs to the devil, because the devil is a sinner from the beginning" (I John 3:8). In sum, God created the devil as good, God punished him for his sin, and God allows his present activity. The *Catechism* admits, "It is a great mystery that providence should permit diabolical activity, but 'we know that in everything God works for good with those who love Him'" (#395).

Our Lord identified Satan in various ways. He called Satan the Prince of this World: Satan uses material things to distract us from

God. He tempts us to adore the material, the sensual, and the powerful rather than to adore God. He lures us into a sense of false security of thinking we can build our own little kingdom here and now without any need of God.

Jesus referred to Satan as the Father of Lies: The devil perverts the truth, as he did with Eve. He fills our minds with doubts. He provides all the rationalizations why something is right even though our Lord and the Church teach it as wrong.

Satan is the Prince of Darkness: He lurks about and is crafty. He fills us with the pessimistic thoughts, the bad thoughts, and the hateful thoughts. He shows us all the hurts, frustration, and troubles of this world and of our own lives hoping to lead us to despair.

Finally, Jesus called him the Murderer: The devil seeks to kill the grace of God in our soul, and then take our soul to hell.

Given these titles and roles, it is little wonder that Christian art has depicted Satan as an ugly, horrible beast with horns. Even in the morality plays of the Middle Ages, Satan could appear in disguise, but was always recognized by his limp, a sign of his fall from heaven.

Nevertheless, we are confident that the power of God will always triumph over that of Satan; good, over evil; and love, over hatred. St. John reminds us, "It was to destroy the devil's works that the Son of God revealed Himself" (I John 3:8).

We take the presence and power of Satan seriously. We continue to ask the candidates in our Baptismal liturgy, "Do you reject Satan? And all his works? And all his empty promises?" We must make that rejection everyday. If Satan tempted our Lord in the desert, he surely will tempt us. He knows how we are weak and when we are vulnerable. St. Peter warned, "Stay sober and alert. Your opponent the devil is prowling like a roaring lion looking for someone to devour" (I Peter 5:8). Moreover, when we do commit sin, we must sincerely repent of it and seek forgiveness, never allowing Satan to gain a foothold into our lives.

Archbishop Fulton Sheen provided us with a keen insight into Satan: "Do not mock the Gospels and say there is no Satan. Evil is too real in the world to say that. Do not say the idea of Satan is dead and gone. Satan never gains so many cohorts, as when, in his shrewdness, he spreads the rumor that he is long since dead. Do not reject the Gospel because it says the Savior was tempted. Satan always tempts the pure – the others are already his. Satan stations more devils on monastery walls than in dens of iniquity, for the latter offer no resistance. Do not say it is absurd that Satan should appear to our Lord, for Satan must always come close to the godly and the strong – the others succumb from a distance."

WHAT DOES THE CHURCH TEACH ABOUT FORTUNETELLERS, PSYCHIC COUNSELORS, AND WITCHES?

As Catholics, we remember that the first commandment states, "I am the Lord thy God. Thou shalt not have any gods before me." When asked what was the greatest commandment, our Lord Jesus Christ, repeating the precept found in Deuteronomy, said, "You shall love the Lord your God with your whole heart, with your whole soul, and with all of your strength" (Matthew 22:37). While God can choose to reveal the future to His prophets or saints, we as individuals must always have trust in His divine providence. St. Paul reminds us, "We know that God makes all things work together for the good of those who love Him, who have been called according to His decree" (Romans 8:28). While we may have that passing curiosity of what will happen in the future, we anchor our lives in the Lord, trusting in His love and care.

To try to discover the future through palm reading, tarot cards, or some other form of fortune-telling, or to try to control the future through black magic, witchcraft, or sorcery violates the first commandment. Sacred Scripture has many condemnations of these activities: In the Old Testament we find, "You shall not let a sorceress live" (Exodus 22:17), "Whoever sacrifices to any god, except to the Lord alone, shall be doomed" (Exodus 22:19), "A man or a woman who acts as a medium or fortuneteller shall be put to death by stoning: they have no one but themselves to blame for their death" (Leviticus 20:27), and "Let there not be found among you anyone who immolates his son or daughter in the fire, nor a fortuneteller, soothsayer, charmer, diviner, or caster of spells, nor one who consults ghosts and spirits or seeks oracles from the dead. Anyone who does such things is an abomination to the Lord ... " (Deuteronomy 18:10-12).

The New Testament also addresses this issue: St. Paul condemned sorcery (Galatians 5:19). In Acts of the Apostles, St. Paul rebuked Elymas, the magician, calling him "son of Satan and enemy of all that is right" (Acts 13:8ff), and St. Peter rebuked Simon Magus, a magician, who wanted to buy the powers of the Holy Spirit to make himself more powerful (Acts 8:9ff). In the Book of Revelation, Jesus declared, "As for the cowards and traitors to the faith, the depraved and murderers, the fornicators and sorcerers, the idol-worshipers and deceivers of every sort – their lot is the fiery pool of burning sulphur – the second death" (Revelation 21:8).

Particular concern must be given to witchcraft, which involves both unraveling the future as well as trying to control the future. Granted, the television show "Sabrina" or the older one "Bewitched" may have light-heartedly built a story around witches and witchcraft. Nevertheless, witchcraft involves producing certain effects which are beyond one's natural powers through the assistance of powers (the occult) other than those of God. Commonly, witchcraft involves a pact with the devil or at least some imploring of evil spirits for assistance. The annals of witchcraft include rites to awaken the dead, arouse passion in a person, and bring disaster or even death upon an enemy. Satanism in particular, gives homage to the Prince of Darkness, and even celebrates a "Black Mass," which parodies our Mass but commits sacrilegious and blasphemous actions. Even if one talks of "white magic" or "white witchcraft," the practitioner is invoking powers not of God in ways outside those of prescribed religion.

Adhering to the revelation of Sacred Scripture, the Church has over the centuries formally condemned witches and witchcraft, and has judged fortune-telling, tarot card reading, and the like as sinful. The *Didache* (*The Teaching of the Twelve Apostles*, c. 80) warned, "You shall not practice magic." The Council of Ancyra (314) imposed a five-year penance on anyone who consulted a magician. Early Irish canons penalized with excommunication anyone for engaging in sorcery until forgiveness had been sought and penance performed. Pope Gregory XV (1621) declared that persons who had made a pact with the devil or practiced black magic which caused the death of another should be arrested and condemned to death by the secular court.

However, one must remember that the Church also strived to prevent witch-hysteria or crazed witch-hunts, like those in colonial Salem: For example, Pope Nicholas I (866) prohibited the use of torture in obtaining confessions, although it was permitted by civil law and common judicial practice. Pope Gregory VII (1080) forbade accused witches to be put to death for supposedly causing storms or crop failures. Pope Alexander IV (1258) restricted the Inquisition to investigating only those cases of witchcraft which were clearly linked with charges of heresy. Nevertheless, despite the official precautions, torture was sometimes used and innocent people sometimes were put to death. As it is so easy to look back in hindsight, one can see that some cases were more of delusion and of the psychological nature.

The *Catechism of the Catholic Church* in discussing the first commandment repeats the condemnation of divination: "All forms of divination are to be rejected: recourse to Satan or demons, conjuring up the dead or other practices falsely supposed to 'unveil' the future. Consulting horoscopes, astrology, palm reading, interpretation of omens and lots, the phenomena of clairvoyance, and recourse to mediums all conceal a desire for power over time, history, and, in the last analysis, other human beings, as well as a wish to conciliate hidden powers. They contradict the honor, respect, and loving fear that we owe to God alone" (#2116). Any practice which utilizes occult powers – whether to inflict harm or to manifest some good – are condemned as contrary to true religion. These practices are generally considered mortal sins. Any invocation of the devil would clearly be considered mortal sin.

However, practices like horoscopes or palm reading may be considered venial sins if they are performed through ignorance or stupidity, for fun or pleasure, and without firm conviction. Nevertheless, even the simplest practices can seduce us to a banality of evil. Do not forget the story of the exorcism of the little boy which served as the basis for the book *The Exorcist* began with his use of a Ouija board.

We believe, as St. John wrote, "God is love" (I John 4:16). God so loved the world that He gave His only Son that whoever believes in Him may not die but may have eternal life" (John 3:16). Jesus is the light of the world, shining through the darkness (John 1:4-5). He is the way, the truth, and the life (John 14:6). To invoke Satan or any other power, to enter the darkness (the occult) for any assistance, or to attempt to usurp powers which belong to God alone is a defiance of the authority of Almighty God. To commit such acts is to turn away from God and place our own souls in jeopardy.

MORAL
ISSUES

WHAT DO WE MEAN BY
"FOLLOW YOUR CONSCIENCE"?

"Follow your conscience" is a sound moral precept. However, this phrase must be understood in its proper context. Remember that the conscience is the capacity of the intellect to judge here and now a situation, to apply knowledge of what is good and true to that situation, and then to direct the will to do what is good and to avoid what is evil. Not only is conscience prospective in that it looks at what is to be done, it is also reflective in that it looks back and assesses what has been done.

The key to a conscience "operating" properly is its formation. Conscience is not something that operates in a vacuum and determines on its own what is right and wrong. Rather, conscience applies the truth, God's universal, absolute truth. We call this truth law. Pope John Paul II in his encyclical *The Splendor of Truth* stated, "Acknowledging the Lord as God is the very core, the heart of the Law, from which the particular precepts flow and towards which they are ordered" (#11). Classically, we identify the primary source of God's law as the eternal law: "The supreme rule of life is the divine law itself, the eternal objective and universal law by which God out of His wisdom and love arranges, directs and governs the whole world and the path of the human community" (Vatican II, *Declaration on Religious Liberty*, #3).

This "supreme rule of life" is illuminated in both the natural law and the divine positive law. Natural law is not a biological or physical law. Instead, the natural law can be known through reason. As a person contemplates his bodily and spiritual nature, of what it means to be a good person, or how society ought to be structured, he can discern the divine plan. This natural law expresses the purposes, rights, and duties of an individual. For example, the absolute respect for the sanctity of human life arises from the dignity proper to the individual that any rational person can discern through reason, not simply through a natural drive or instinct to preserve one's life. Since God is the creator of all things, this contemplation and discernment truly reflects the eternal law of God.

On the other hand, divine positive law refers to those truths expressed directly by God. Take for example the 10 Commandments: These are not suggestions, but commandments of God which bind us to obedience. We would find other laws or principles revealed in Sacred Scripture, such as again the sanctity of human life, of marriage, and of sexuality. Interestingly, when we think about this for a moment, one could derive at least the last seven of the 10 Commandments through the use of reason even if Moses had never received them: It is reasonable and proper for human dignity not to steal, commit adultery, and so on. Therefore, the natural law and divine positive law support one another and enable us to live according to the eternal law of God.

The Church's Magisterium preserves these laws and gives further guidance to particular moral issues. In our world, we are confronted by very complicated moral situations, such as euthanasia, bioethics, and modern warfare. These issues are not specifically addressed in Sacred Scripture, and the average person could find it very difficult to discern a right course of action on his own, no matter how good his reasoning abilities. The Magisterium, guided by the Holy Spirit, "the Spirit of Truth" (John 15:17) whom Jesus said, "will instruct you in everything" (John 15:26), renders binding moral guidance so that the Catholic faithful can live authentic Christian lives in accord with the eternal law of God.

In this understanding of law and truth, albeit very brief, we find a God who has revealed how we ought to live as one made in His image and likeness, as one redeemed by Christ, and as a baptized member of the Church. The duty of conscience is to learn these "laws" of God and integrate them into our lives. Vatican II asserted, "In the depths of his conscience man detects a law which he does not impose on himself but which holds him to obedience. Always summoning him to love good and avoid evil, the voice of conscience can when necessary speak to his heart more specifically: 'do this and shun that.' For man has in his heart a law written by

God. To obey it is the very dignity of man; according to it he will be judged" (*Pastoral Constitution on the Church in the Modern World*, #16).

Therefore, "follow one's conscience" properly understood means forming our conscience according to God's law and then living life as God wants it to be lived. When our conscience reflects back on our actions and we find that we have violated God's laws – we have sinned – we ought to be moved with contrition to seek forgiveness. St. Bonaventure said, "Conscience is like God's herald and messenger; it does not command things on its own authority, but commands them as coming from God's authority, like a herald when he proclaims the edict of the king. This is why conscience has binding force."

Unfortunately in our world, many people do think that "follow one's conscience" means to do whatever "I" think is best as some isolated, autonomous, human being. I then become the standard of truth. They think God's commandments and the Church's teachings may be nice guidelines but are not binding. How wrong! Remember Jesus said, "If you wish to enter life, keep the commandments" (Matthew 19:17), and "You will live in my love if you keep my commandments" (John 15:10). St. John emphasized, "The man who claims, 'I have known him,' without keeping his commandments is a liar; in such a one there is no truth." Conscience does not establish the law, but conforms to and applies God's law to actions.

Moreover, some equate a correctly formed conscience with sincerity. I remember once overhearing a couple of my college students arguing over the notion of premarital sex. One said that it was wrong because the Bible said so and because such people did not take full responsibility for the love and life involved in the action. The other said, "What is right for you may not be right for me. Your values are yours, and mine our mine. What I decide is right." Wrong! I could not help but enter into the conversation. I said, "If you follow that principle and make morality relative, I could say, 'I believe that black people are inferior and there should be segregation.' [The relativist student happened to be African American.] Then I could get enough votes and make it law. Would that be right?" I had him stumped. Of course it would not be right because it violates the eternal law of God. This is why apartheid was wrong no matter how many Afrikaaners sincerely believed it was right. A sincere conscience is an erroneous one if it does not reflect the law of God.

Yes, we follow our conscience, but only a properly formed conscience. We struggle with God's law. Sometimes we may not fully understand the teachings of the Church especially in our modern moral situation when we are bombarded with the counter gospel. Nevertheless, in faith we submit our wills and say, "I believe. I will follow." Rather than just "going off" and doing whatever may seem popular, easy, and pleasing, we put aside pride and in love follow Christ. The grace of our Lord will strengthen us and the Holy Spirit will bring us to understanding one day. Only then can we say we are living with dignity and in the freedom of children of God.

WHAT IS THE DIFFERENCE BETWEEN MORTAL AND VENIAL SIN?

The *Catechism* reminds us, "Sin is an offense against reason, truth, and right conscience; it is failure in genuine love for God and neighbor caused by a perverse attachment to certain goods. It wounds the nature of man and injures human solidarity. It has been defined [by St. Augustine] as 'an utterance, a deed, or a desire contrary to the eternal law'" (#1849).

Traditionally, Catholic moral theology has distinguished between a mortal and a venial sin. In the First Letter of St. John, we read, " ... All wrongdoing is sin, but not all sin is deadly" (5:17). The notion of a "deadly" or mortal sin is found in other parts of Sacred Scripture as well: For instance, St. Paul in Galatians (5:19-21) asserted, "It is obvious what proceeds from the flesh: lewd conduct, impurity, licentiousness, idolatry, sorcery, hostilities, bickering, jealousy, outbursts of rage, selfish rivalries, dissensions, factions, envy, drunkenness, orgies, and the like. I warn you, as I have warned you before: those who do such things will not inherit the kingdom of God!" (cf. also Romans 1:28-32, I Corinthians 6:9-10, and Ephesians 4:3-8). Therefore, Sacred Scripture explicitly identifies certain sins which kill the grace of God in our soul and deprive a person of eternal salvation.

The *Catechism* presents the three criteria that must be satisfied for a sin to be mortal: First, the act committed must be considered grave or serious matter. Mortal sins are heinous in the eyes of God. Throughout the moral section of the *Catechism*, sins are noted as "gravely sinful": for example, "The fifth commandment forbids direct and intentional killing as gravely sinful" (#2268). Second, the sinner must have full knowledge of the sinful character of the act; in other words, he must be acting with an informed intellect and must know this act violates God's eternal law. Third, the sinner must give full consent of the will, meaning that he has reflected on doing the action and deliberately wants to do it.

Mortal sin destroys our union with God and the presence of sanctifying grace in our souls. Because these are heinous actions in the eyes of God, for a person to knowingly and willingly commit them indicates a turning away from the love of God. Anyone conscious of a mortal sin must undergo an interior conversion and then receive forgiveness and absolution through the Sacrament of Penance. Until making a good confession and receiving sacramental absolution, anyone conscious of being in a state of mortal sin cannot receive Holy Communion, except under extraordinary circumstances, e.g. no possibility of going to confession (cf. *Catechism*, #1457). Moreover, an unrepentant person guilty of mortal sin objectively risks eternal damnation in Hell; however, "although we can judge that an act is in itself a grave offense, we must entrust judgment of a person to the justice and mercy of God" (*Catechism*, #1861).

On the other hand, venial sin denotes either an act of a less serious matter, or one which involves grave matter but is performed without full knowledge or complete consent of the will. Unlike mortal sin which involves a complete turning away from God's love, venial sin wounds our relationship with God. The periodic confession of venial sins is also highly recommended as part of a good spiritual regimen. Actually, all sin is serious since it hurts our relationship with our Lord. Moreover, even venial sin can lead to mortal sin or become habitual if not corrected. A practice of regular confession helps the individual better form the conscience, recognize faults and weaknesses, resist temptations, and receive God's grace to heal and strengthen the soul. St. Teresa of Avila said, "Always fear when some fault you commit does not grieve you. For in regard to sin, even venial, you know that the soul must feel great sorrow ... . For the love of God, take care never to grow careless about venial sin, however small ... . There is nothing small if it goes against so great a sovereign."

With this in mind, we can also approach the subject of fundamental option, an easily misunderstood topic today. The idea of fundamental option is that each person makes a basic choice to love

God, to accept His truth, and to be His disciple. That choice though is lived-out each day of our lives by the individual choices we make to do good. In this sense, fundamental option makes sense.

Sadly, some individuals misconstrue fundamental option in such a way that there are no particular mortal sins. Instead, the one "mortal sin" which would take a soul to Hell is for a person to willingly, knowingly reject God and His love entirely. Such a stance would reduce fundamental option to some psychological game, whereby a person says, "I love God. I do not reject God. My individual choices or particular actions do not affect my total being. Therefore, although I committed adultery, or murdered someone, or fornicated, or robbed the bank, [or committed any other mortal sin], God still loves me, I love God, and I am going to heaven." Think again! While only God can probe the depths of our soul and judge a person, those actions are objectively mortal sins. To choose mortal sin indicates a contempt for the divine law. To commit such actions evidences a lack of love for God and for neighbor. In essence, particular mortal sins show a rejection of God. Our Holy Father, John Paul II, wrote, "It thus needs to be stated that the so-called fundamental option ... is always brought into play through conscious and free decisions. Precisely for this reason, it is revoked when man engages his freedom in conscious decisions to the contrary, with regard to morally grave matter. To separate the fundamental option from concrete kinds of behavior means to contradict the substantial integrity or personal unity of the moral agent in his body and in his soul" (*The Splendor of Truth*, #67). Therefore, mortal sin can radically change the person's fundamental option. (Cf. *Reconciliatio et Paenitentia*, #17).

As we continue our spiritual journey in this life, we must not only renew each day the "fundamental" choice we have made for our Lord, but also repent of any sin and turn to our Lord for forgiveness. Let us also pray for those, especially those in our family, who have gone astray and are not living a life with our Lord, that they will turn to the Lord, seek forgiveness, and come to a new life in Him.

WHAT IS WRONG WITH THE "PRO-CHOICE" STAND CONCERNING ABORTION?

The pro-abortion movement has made great gains using the "pro-choice" label. First, the "pro-choice" label numbs our moral sensitivity because its masks that anyone really is for abortion and diverts our attention from the act itself. Secondly, the idea of being "pro-choice" seems to appeal to Americans who cherish freedom and the idea of being free to choose rather than being forced to do anything.

In arguing against this "pro-choice" position, one must first focus on the heart of the choice – a child. Proceeding from a purely, scientific approach, we know that when conception occurs, a new and unique human being is created. The DNA genetic code attests to this uniqueness. (Why else has DNA coding become so important in identifying criminals?) Moreover, from that moment of conception, the child continues to develop and to grow: the child is born, matures to adolescence and then adulthood, and eventually dies. Note though that this is all the same person who was conceived: all that has been added is nourishment, time, and hopefully a lot of love. Therefore, our Church teaches, "From the time that the ovum is fertilized, a life is begun which is neither that of the father nor of the mother; it is rather the life of a new human being with his own growth. It would never be made human if it were not human already" (*Declaration on Procured Abortion*, #12).

Moving beyond science to the level of faith, we also believe that almighty God creates and infuses an unique and immortal soul into that body. This soul, our spiritual principle, is what gives each person that identity of being made in God's image and likeness. (Cf. *Catechism*, #363-368). Even if there were some doubt that God infused the soul at conception or some doubt that the conceived child were truly a person, "it is objectively a grave sin to dare to risk murder. 'The one who will be a man is already one'" (*Declaration on Procured Abortion*, #13).

We find in Sacred Scripture testimony to the sanctity of life in the womb: The Lord said to the mother of Sampson, "As for the son you will conceive and bear, no razor shall touch his head, for this boy is to be consecrated to God from the womb!" (Judges 13:5). Job said, "Did not he who made me in the womb make him? Did not the same One fashion us before our birth?" (Job 31:15). In Psalm 139:13, we pray, "Truly you have formed my inmost being; you knit me in my mother's womb." The Lord spoke to Jeremiah, "Before I formed you in the womb I knew you, before you were born I dedicated you, a prophet to the nations I appointed you" (Jeremiah 1:5).

For Christians the sanctity of life in the womb and the belief that this truly is a person is further corroborated by the incarnation: Mary conceived by the power of the Holy Spirit, and Jesus Christ true God entered this world becoming also true man. Even though Jesus was still in the womb of His blessed mother, St. Elizabeth and St. John the Baptist, also in the womb, rejoiced at the presence of the Lord. Would anyone dare suggest Jesus was not a person in the womb of His mother? Little wonder in the *Didache* (*The Teaching of the Twelve Apostles*) – the first manual of doctrine, liturgical laws, and morals written about the year 80 – we find the moral prohibition, "You shall not kill by abortion the fruit of the womb and you shall not murder the infant already born."

Given that the heart of the choice involves an unique, human person, the choice of action becomes clear: to preserve and safeguard the life of this person in the womb or to destroy it. Since this is a person, the latter choice does not involve simply the termination of a pregnancy or the removal of a fetus; rather, the latter choice involves the direct killing of an innocent person, a deliberate murder. Therefore, the act of abortion is an intrinsically evil act. The Second Vatican Council asserted, "Life must be protected with the utmost care from the moment of conception: abortion and infanticide are abominable crimes" (*Pastoral Constitution on the Church in the Modern World*, #51).

We do not have the right to choose evil, no matter what the circumstances are or even if some sort of "good" may arise. To purposefully choose to do evil is an affront to God Himself, in whose image and likeness we are made. Here it is not as though one is choosing between two good actions; instead, one is defending the sanctity of human life in the face of evil. To say one is "pro-choice" in this matter is no different in saying one is "pro-choice" for apartheid, Nazi concentration camps, or Jim Crow segregation laws – "I am personally against it, but everybody should choose." Pope John Paul II stated, "Anyone can see that the alternative here is only apparent. It is not possible to speak of the right to choose when a clear moral evil is involved, when what is at stake is the commandment, 'Do not kill!'" (*Crossing the Threshold of Hope*, p. 205).

In those difficult, tragic situations – rape and incest (which result in conception at best 2% of the time depending upon which set of statistics one examines), a young teenage pregnant mother, or a deformed or handicapped child – we must remember the child is still an innocent human being who through no fault of his own was conceived. Here sharing in the cross of our Lord becomes a reality without question. In these cases, we as members of the Church must support both the mother and the child through our prayers and by opening our hearts, homes, and wallets to their needs. We must make the sacrifice to preserve human life. We must always choose what is good in the eyes of God.

WHAT IS WRONG WITH THE
"MORNING AFTER PILL" OR *RU-486?*

Since the advent of the "Pill," medical technology has made further developments in the area of artificial birth control. Technically, the original pills were anovulants made of an extremely high dosage of synthetic hormones. Taken orally, these anovulants suppressed ovulation and thereby prevented conception. Studies have shown that while the original pills were very effective in preventing ovulation, the medical side effects were disastrous, e.g. the high incidence of cancer, heart problems, and blood clots.

In response, some pharmaceutical firms lowered the dosage and developed a "double barreled" type of "contraceptive" which not only suppressed ovulation but also, in case that failed and conception did occur, prevented the implantation of the newly conceived life. Essentially these new "contraceptives" made the lining of the uterus (the endometrium) hostile to the conceived life and caused its expulsion from the body. Therefore, these drugs which prevent the implantation are not really contraceptives, which prevent conception, but abortifacients, which expel a conceived new life.

The *Ethical and Religious Directives for Catholic Health Facilities* (1971) stated, "Abortion, that is the directly intended termination of pregnancy before viability, is never permitted nor is the directly intended destruction of a viable fetus. Every procedure whose sole immediate effect is the termination of pregnancy before viability is an abortion, which, in its moral context, includes the interval between conception and implantation of the embryo" (#12). Therefore, abortifacients are declared morally wrong under the teachings concerning abortion.

Here lies the problem of RU-486 (named after "Roussel Uclaf" manufactured by Hoechst A.G.). RU-486, a synthetic hormone, blocks the hormone progesterone which prepares the uterus to receive the newly conceived life. As a result, the newly conceived life is expelled from the uterus. Researchers report a 96% effectiveness rate when RU-486 is used in conjunction with another drug Prostaglandin.

Remember the Second Vatican Council asserted, "Life must be protected with the utmost care from the moment of conception: abortion and infanticide are abominable crimes" (*Pastoral Constitution on the Church in the Modern World*, #51). The *Declaration on Procured Abortion* (1974), released in response at least partially to the infamous *Roe v. Wade* decision, affirmed that life is sacred from conception and that directly intended abortion is an intrinsically evil act.

This position is grounded first on scientific knowledge of conception and DNA: "From the time the ovum is fertilized, a life is begun which is neither that of the father nor of the mother; it is rather the life of a new human being with his own growth. It would never be made human if it were not human already" (*Declaration on Procured Abortion*, #12). Just think – each of us is the same person that was conceived. All that has been "added" is nourishment, time, and hopefully a lot of love. We are the same person who was conceived, who was born, who matures, and who will someday leave this life for eternal life.

Secondly, we firmly believe that almighty God alone creates and gives each person an immortal soul. While during the course of Church history, theologians have debated exactly when God infuses the soul, the Church has always taken the safest moral course because of the sacredness of life. With the ability of medical science to identify the sperm and ovum and their functions, and to understand the process of conception and DNA, the safest moral position would be that God infuses the soul at conception. Moreover, "even if a doubt existed concerning whether the fruit of conception is already a human person, it is objectively a grave sin to dare to risk murder" (#13). Therefore, the act and results of an abortifacient drug such as RU-486 is no different in its morality than a surgical abortion procedure.

The evil of RU-486 is particularly seductive. The drug seemingly amoralizes the act: No one has to undergo a surgical procedure. No one sees the results. No one has to really consult anyone about terminating a pregnancy; a woman simply can use this like any oral drug. No one even has to speak of an abortion – this is officially labeled a contraceptive. No one has to worry about conceiving a child; the pill takes care of everything. However, the individual mother will always know and carry the burden alone.

Jesus said, "Everyone who practices evil hates the light; he does not come near it for fear his deeds will be exposed. But he who acts in truth comes into the light, to make clear that his deeds are done in God" (John 3:20-21). RU-486 lurks in the darkness.

WHAT DOES THE CHURCH TEACH
ABOUT PREMARITAL SEX?

The Catholic Church continues to teach that sexual love between a man and woman is reserved to marriage. We find this teaching in the creation account of Genesis, Book 1, Chapter 1 of Sacred Scripture: First, God creates man in His own image and likeness, making them male and female (Genesis 1:27). In the next verse, the Bible reads, "God blessed them, saying, 'Be fertile and multiply; fill the earth and subdue it'" (Genesis 1:28). Before the man and woman come together as husband and wife, and before they express their love as husband and wife, they are first blessed by God.

Only in marriage do we find God's blessing upon the act of sexual love, or what is better termed marital love. This physical expression of love in marriage is a sacred sign of a husband and wife's covenant of life and love that they share in union with God. This marital love signifies the vows freely exchanged between each other and thereby reflects the faithful, permanent, exclusive, and self-giving love they have promised to each other and to God. This understanding is evident in Jesus' response to the Pharisees' question regarding divorce: "Have you not read that at the beginning the Creator made them male and female and declared, 'For this reason a man shall leave his father and mother and cling to his wife, and the two shall become as one'? Thus they are no longer two but one flesh. Therefore let no man separate what God has joined" (Matthew 19:4-6). Through the Sacrament of Holy Matrimony, God blesses the couple joined in this sacred bond and generously bestows grace so that they may assume the duties of marriage in mutual and lasting fidelity.

Moreover, the marital love of husband and wife which unites them as "one flesh" may overflow and participate in God's creative love: a child may be born from their love. Here again, God gives abundant graces so that the husband and wife can fulfill their duties as father and mother. Therefore, in accord with God's design, sexual love is reserved to marriage.

Think though of this issue from the perspective of the child, who may be conceived by an act of sexual love: A child has the inviolable right to life from the moment of conception until death. He has the right to be born. He has the right to two loving parents who are husband and wife, who have pledged their total love to each other, and who have the means to provide for raising a child. He has the right to be considered as a gift from God, not as an "unplanned pregnancy," an "accident," or a "burden." In essence, a child has the right to the best family possible'a family filled with love. (Cf. *Donum vitae*, II, 8.) Here again, just using our reason, we can conclude that sexual love ought to be reserved to marriage.

Taking sexual love outside the context of marriage is contrary to the dignity of each person and of marriage. Our Holy Father, Pope John Paul II lamented the decline in respect for marital love in his encyclical *The Gospel of Life*: "Sexuality too is depersonalized and exploited: from being the sign, place and language of love, that is, of the gift of self and acceptance of another, in all the other's richness as a person, it increasingly becomes the occasion and instrument for self-assertion and the selfish satisfaction of personal desires and instincts" (#23).

Given this teaching, little wonder the Bible has grave condemnations against both fornication, "carnal union between an unmarried man and an unmarried woman" (*Catechism*, #2353), and adultery, "when two partners, of whom at least one is married to another party, have sexual relations, even transient ones ... " (*Catechism*, #2381). Jesus said, "Wicked designs come from the deep recesses of the heart: acts of fornication, theft, murder, adulterous conduct, greed, maliciousness, deceit, sensuality, envy, blasphemy, arrogance, and obtuse spirit. All these evils come from within and render a man impure" (Mark 7:21-23; cf. also Matthew 15:19). St. Paul warned, "Can you not realize that the unholy will not fall heir to the kingdom of God? Do no deceive yourselves: no fornicators, idolaters, or adulterers, no sexual perverts, thieves, misers or drunkards, no slanderers, or robbers will inherit God's kingdom" (I Corinthians 6:9-10). In the last judgment scene depicted in the

Book of Revelation, God said, "As for the cowards and traitors to the faith, the depraved and murderers, the fornicators and sorcerers, the idol-worshipers and deceivers of every sort – their lot is the fiery pool of burning sulphur, the second death!" (Revelation 21:8). God's upholding of the sacredness of marital love is clearly evidenced in the blatant condemnation of the sins against it.

Sadly, in our society, we see the act of marital love trivialized. Whether we would turn to pornography or even to a comedy show, the act of marital love is oftentimes portrayed as a selfish expression without any sense of permanence, fidelity, or exclusivity. The act is reduced simply to an immediate, fleeting pleasure without any sense of responsibility to each other or to the possible child conceived. The couple easily forgets that the action could conceive a child and that they could become "Mommy and Daddy." And what then? Would the child be aborted? Would he be raised by one parent, by grandparents, or by two parents "forced" to get married?

We see the tragedy that occurs when we deviate from God's plan. Many people have thought they were in love with someone else, gave themselves to that person in the most intimate expression of human love, and then were later discarded. Many people heard the phrase, "I want you," but all the person really wanted was a body, not a person; a sensation, not a commitment of life and love. Many people speak of "making love," without realizing we cannot make love: God Himself is love, we can only live in His love in accord with His design (I John 4:16). Yes, the eyes of many people today reveal an internal emptiness which comes from spending oneself on a fleeting pleasure rather than on building upon a marriage and a family.

In response, the Church calls people to live the virtue of chastity. Chastity respects the dignity of our human sexuality and the sacredness of marital love. In chastity, a person strives for mastery over feelings and passions, respects the sacredness of marital love, and takes responsibility for his actions. This virtue, moreover, gives great freedom: freedom from slavery to passions; freedom from any sexually transmitted disease, so easily contracted in this age because of promiscuity; freedom from loss of a good reputation and being known as "easy," "a slut" or "a womanizer"; freedom from painful memories or regrets of past relationships; and freedom from mortal sin and eternal punishment. St. Paul challenges us to live in the freedom of God's children. Granted, the temptations of this world are great. By the grace of God, we can live in such freedom, respecting the sacredness of marital love.

WHAT IS THE CHURCH'S TEACHING ON CONTRACEPTION?

This question concerns probably one of, if not the most controversial moral teachings of Catholicism. This topic is definitely the one that prompts headlines and excites some people to say, "I disagree with the Church" or "The Church is wrong." I have even had Catholics report to me that when they have visited a Protestant Church, they have heard sermons denounce the Catholic Church's teaching on this subject. In marriage preparation programs, the topic sometimes ignites heated debate between couples and the presenters upholding the Church's teaching. Sadly, many Catholics simply do not understand the Church's teaching on this issue. Moreover, many priests have failed to address this subject from the pulpit – whether in a positive, rational way or at all. So we need to put aside our prejudices and our misconceptions, open our minds and hearts, and approach this issue.

Marriage in the Eyes of God and the Church

Before addressing the issue of contraception per se, one must first understand the Church's moral teaching concerning marriage. The Church does not simply deliver a moral teaching in isolation; rather, the moral teaching is undergirded by a moral framework of how life ought to be lived in the eyes of God. In this case, the moral framework is what God has revealed concerning marriage.

In the creation account of Genesis, we find the beautiful truth, "God made man in His image; in the divine image He created him; male and female He created them" (Genesis 1:27). In this one verse, we find an intrinsic goodness and dignity to each human being. We also recognize a goodness to our human sexuality'both man and woman are made in God's image and likeness, and both masculinity and femininity are equally good. Yes, man and woman are different – anatomically, physiologically, and even psychologically (as admitted by many psychologists, even "feminist" ones). These differences do not indicate inequality, instead complementarity.

With this truth, we must also view our human life not just by the confines of this world, but also with a view to a supernatural and eternal destiny. God has made us for Himself, and we hope one day to find this life fulfilled in the Kingdom of Heaven.

In the next verse of Genesis (1:28), we read, "God blessed them, saying, 'Be fertile and multiply; fill the earth and subdue it.'" Here is marriage, a God-given, God-designed institution. If we could think of the best way to realize that "image and likeness of God," it would then be in marriage. In this sacred union, man and woman – each made in God's image and likeness with their similarities and their uniqueness – come together as one.

The second creation account of Genesis reinforces this idea: Here, God takes the rib from the man to create "a suitable partner," whom the man recognizes as "'This one, at last, is bone of my bones and flesh of my flesh; this one shall be called "woman" for out of "her man" this one has been taken.' That is why a man leaves his father and mother and clings to his wife, and the two of them become one body" (2:23-24). Pope John Paul II reflected that in marriage "man" in the moment of communion truly becomes the image of God, "an image of an inscrutable divine communion of Persons."

Our Lord, Jesus Christ, in the gospel affirmed the teaching of Genesis. When asked by the Pharisees about divorce, Jesus replied, "Have you not read that at the beginning the Creator made them male and female, and declared, 'For this reason a man shall leave his father and mother and cling to his wife, and the two shall become as one'? Thus, they are no longer two but one flesh. Therefore, let no man separate what God has joined" (Matthew 19:3ff).

Given this basis in Sacred Scripture, we hold marriage as a sacrament in our Catholic belief. Vatican II's *Pastoral Constitution of the Church in the Modern World* (#47-52) spoke beautifully about marriage: Marriage is a partnership of life and love designed by God and endowed by Him with its own proper laws, with various benefits, and with various ends in view. Both husband and wife "surrender themselves to each other" and give their "irrevocable personal consent." Marriage involves a mutual giving of two persons, which entails total fidelity and permanence.

Moreover, the love of husband and wife which binds them together as one overflows, and they may participate in creation, giving birth to children. Through the sacrament they live and the bountiful graces offered by our Lord, couples are fortified to fulfill their duties to each other and their family. As such, marriage is clearly the foundation of the family and the whole human race.

Therefore, we speak of marriage not as a contract but as a covenant. Just as God made a covenant of life and love with His people of the Old Testament through Abraham and Moses, just as Christ made the perfect, everlasting, and life-giving covenant through the blood of His cross, so marriage is a covenant, a permanent bonding of life and love. (For this reason, St. Paul frequently used the image of Christ and His Church in explaining the love of husband and wife (e.g. Ephesians 5:22ff).) Therefore, when a couple exchanges vows, they are promising a love of fidelity, permanence, exclusivity, and perpetuity to each other and God. Man and woman enter into a life-giving covenant with God as husband and wife.

Marital Love

Given our understanding of marriage and marital love, we can readily see that the most beautiful expression of love in marriage is marital love, or physical love, or sexual intercourse, or conjugal love – whatever term one prefers. Granted, love in marriage encompasses much more than the act of conjugal love. Nevertheless, this action radiates an unique and special symbolism of the sacrament of marriage – the covenant shared between the two who have become one flesh.

Interestingly, conjugal love plays an important role in understanding the Sacrament of Marriage. In our sacramental theology, we hold that a sacrament has two parts: the form, or prayer part of the sacrament; and the matter, the physical and action part of the sacrament. For instance, in performing a baptism, the matter of the sacrament is the priest pouring water over the head of the person or immersing the person in water three times; at the same time, the priest prays the form of the sacrament, "I baptize you in the name of the Father, and of the Son, and of the Holy Spirit." In marriage, the couple are the ministers of the sacrament; the priest is the official witness of the Church who also imparts God's blessing. The form of the Sacrament of Marriage is the exchange of vows; the matter of the sacrament is the consummation of the marriage, when the two people enact those vows in that physical expression of love. Therefore the Church teaches, "The acts of marriage by which the intimate and chaste union of the spouses takes place are noble and honorable; the truly human performance of these acts fosters the self-giving they signify and enriches the spouses in joy and gratitude" (*Pastoral Constitution on the Church in the Modern World*, #49).

Pope Paul VI in his encyclical *Humanae Vitae* (#9) offered a beautiful reflection on this conjugal love of marriage. The Holy Father said that marital love is a genuinely human love, because it embraces the good of the whole person and is rooted in a free giving of one spouse to the other. This love endures through joy and pain, success and failure, happiness and sorrow, uniting the couple in both body and soul. This love is also total – free of restriction, hesitation, or condition. This love is faithful and exclusive to both partners. In all, this love must be a mutually respectful action, a genuine expression of love. Unlike what is so often portrayed by the various media today, marital love is not some erotic action, rooted in selfishness, fleeting pleasure, or dominance. No, marital love is a sacred action which unites a couple with each other and God. The spirit of this teaching reflects what Jesus said at the Last

Supper, "There is no greater love than this: to lay down one's life for one's friends" (John 15:13).

Moreover, the act of marital love also participates in God's creative love. The couple who has become a new creation by becoming husband and wife, one flesh, may also bring about the creation of new life in accord with God's will. Vatican II asserted, "By its very nature the institution of marriage and married love is ordered to the procreation and education of the offspring and it is in them that it finds its crowning glory" (*Pastoral Constitution on the Church in the Modern World*, #48, cf. #50). The Council acknowledged that while not diminishing the importance of sacramental union symbolized in marital love, "it must be said that true married love and the whole structure of family life which results from it is directed to disposing the spouses to cooperate valiantly with the love of the creator and Savior, who through them will increase and enrich His family from day to day" (*Pastoral Constitution on the Church in the Modern World*, #50).

Most recently, our Holy Father, Pope John Paul II, in his encyclical *The Gospel of Life*, reflected that God's own image and likeness is transmitted through the creation of an immortal soul directly by Him. Moreover, a child is really the personification of the love of husband and wife in union with the Creator. Therefore, "it is precisely in their role as co-workers with God who transmits His image to the new creature that we see the greatness of couples who are ready 'to cooperate with the love of the Creator and the Savior, who through them will enlarge and enrich His own family day by day'" (*The Gospel of Life*, #43, quoting also *Pastoral Constitution on the Church in the Modern World*, #50).

Throughout Sacred Scripture, we find the birth of children as a blessing from God and a sign of the living covenant between God and husband and wife. For example, Moses delivered the law of the covenant, declaring: "As your reward for heeding these decrees and observing them carefully, the Lord, your God, will keep with you the merciful covenant which He promised on oath to your fathers. He will love and bless and multiply you; He will bless the fruit of your womb and the produce of your soil, your grain and wine and oil, the issue of your herds and young of your flocks, in the land which He swore to your fathers He would give you. You will be blessed above all peoples; no man or woman among you shall be childless nor shall your livestock be barren" (Deuteronomy 7:12-14). Clearly life, fruitfulness, and fertility were cherished as goods granted by God.

Because of this decree and the understanding that the procreative aspect of marital love is a sacred gift, "barrenness" or infertility was a true cross to bear for a couple. For example, in the Old Testament, in the story of Hannah, wife of Elkanah, we read of how she grieved at not being able to have a child although she had a beautiful loving marriage. Sacred Scripture reads, "Hannah rose ... and presented herself before the Lord; at the time, Eli, the priest was sitting on a chair near the doorpost of the Lord's temple. In her bitterness, she prayed to the Lord, weeping copiously, and she made a vow, promising, 'Oh Lord of hosts, if you look with pity on the misery of your handmaid, if you remember me and do not forget me, if you give your handmaid a male child, I will give him to the Lord for as long as he lives; neither wine nor liquor shall he drink, and no razor shall ever touch his head'" (I Sam 1:9-11). The Lord heard the plea of Hannah, and she conceived and bore a son, Samuel.

In the New Testament, we read the story of Elizabeth and Zechariah, who were "just in the eyes of God" and "upheld the commandments of the Lord." However, in their old age, they remained childless. By God's will, they conceived a child, John the Baptist. Elizabeth said, "In these days the Lord is acting on my behalf; He has seen fit to remove my reproach among men." (Cf. Luke 1:5-25.) Following this line of thought, Vatican II asserted, "Indeed children are the supreme gift of marriage and greatly contribute to the good of the parents themselves" (*Pastoral Constitution on the Church in the Modern World*, #50).

Therefore, we must not separate the unitive dimension of marital love from the procreative. Both dimensions are intrinsically good. Both dimensions are inherent in the act of marriage. Even if a couple is infertile, the act of marriage still retains the character of being a communion of life and love. We must constantly keep in focus the covenant of life and love a couple shares with each other in union with God.

The Church's Teaching on Contraception

Given this understanding about the sacrament of marriage, Pope Paul VI in his encyclical *Humanae Vitae* stated, "Each and every marriage act must remain open to the transmission of life (#11). The Holy Father continued, "This particular doctrine, expounded on numerous occasions by the Magisterium, is based on the inseparable connection, established by God, which man on his own initiative may not break, between the unitive significance and the procreative significance which are both inherent to the marriage pact" (*Humanae Vitae*, #12).

With the introduction of a contraceptive means (artificial or not) to the marital act, the procreative dimension is purposefully suppressed and ignored. The unitive dimension, therefore, is separated from the procreative. Just as a forced act of physical love by one spouse upon the other violates the unitive dimension of marital love, the impairment of the capacity to transmit human life violates the procreative dimension. Here note that contraception involves an impairment or a suppression of one inherent dimension of an action as God has designed it. Essentially, God has designed marital love to be both unitive and procreative; to suppress or to violate either one contradicts the design of God.

Nevertheless, we have witnessed the proliferation of the use of artificial birth control in particular. As Pope John Paul II, as well as Pope Paul VI, have repeatedly warned, what has consequently evolved in society is a contraceptive mentality, the removal of conjugal love from the Sacrament of Marriage, and in many cases – especially outside the context of marriage – the reduction of conjugal love to simply a sex act without genuine love. In *The Gospel of Life*, Pope John Paul II lamented about the effects of contraception: "Sexuality too is depersonalized and exploited: from being the sign, place, and language of love, that is, of the gift of self and acceptance of another, in all the other's richness as a person, it increasingly becomes the occasion and instrument for self-assertion and the selfish satisfaction of personal desires and instincts. Thus, the original import of human sexuality is distorted and falsified, and the two meanings, unitive and procreative, inherent in the very nature of the conjugal act, are artificially separated: in this way, the marriage union is betrayed and its fruitfulness is subjected to the caprice of the couple. Procreation then becomes the 'enemy' to be avoided in sexual activity: if it is welcomed this is only because it expresses a desire, or indeed the intention, to have a child 'at all costs,' and not because it signifies the complete acceptance of the other and therefore an openness to the richness of life which the child represents" (#23).

Here we must pause to examine another dimension of the problem with some forms of contraception. Most artificial birth control pills today are such that they have a "double-barrel" effect. On one hand, they serve as a contraceptive in suppressing ovulation; on the other hand, if ovulation occurs and conception takes place "by accident," they also make the lining of the uterus hostile to implantation, thereby expelling the conceived life. Remember that once conception occurs, an unique, precious individual has been created who has the right to life. Consequently, these pills are really abortifacients, having the same effect as the IUD (intrauterine device). Actually, this "double barrel" effect is the sad selling point for the drug RU486, commonly called "the morning after pill."

Moreover, we must also consider the possible side effects of these pills to the health of the woman. In examining the *Physician's Desk Reference* for various oral contraceptives available, the small-print list of possible health complications include, to name a few, myocardial infarction, thrombosis, cerebrovascular disorders, birth defects, and various forms of cancer (breast, cervical, ovarian, and uterine). Tragically, many doctors do not inform the woman of these health risks when prescribing these drugs. Actually, Planned Parenthood of America stated that more women die each year from complications arising from taking contraceptive pills than from complications in pregnancy and childbirth. Since each individual has an obligation for maintaining his health, any drug which consistently changes the normal functioning of the body and which carries these risks would be morally objectionable.

So what is a couple who has serious issues facing their marriage, such as a medical problem or economic constrictions, to do? The Church has always taught that a couple must act as responsible parents: "The couple must fulfill their role as cooperators of God's creative love with responsibility: they must respect the divine providence of God, consider their own good and the good of their children, born and yet to be born, weigh their own situation and needs on the spiritual and material levels, and look to the good of family, society, and Church" (*Pastoral Constitution on the Church in the Modern World*, #50). A husband and wife, with a vision of being responsible parents, must decide if now is the time to have a child. There may be serious reasons for postponing a pregnancy – even indefinitely – because of health, financial burdens, or other serious reason.

However, one must be careful not to distort what is a "serious" reason. Pope John Paul II stated, "The decision about the number of children and the sacrifices to be made for them must not be taken only with a view to adding comfort and preserving a peaceful existence. Reflecting upon this matter before God, with the graces drawn from the Sacrament, and guided by the teaching of the Church, parents will remind themselves that it is certainly less serious to deny their children certain comforts or material advantages than to deprive them of the presence of brothers and sisters who could help them to grow in humanity and to realize the beauty of life at all ages and in all its variety" (1979).

Natural Family Planning

If a couple thinks serious reasons do indeed exist for postponing a pregnancy, the Church teaches that a couple may take advantage of "the natural cycles of the reproductive system" *Humanae Vitae*, #16). We know that a woman can only conceive a child during the period of ovulation. Therefore, a couple may resort to expressing their love only when they are in the infertile phases of their cycle. This method of regulating birth is called *Natural Family Planning*, a safe and effective means which is morally acceptable and which preserves the covenant love of marriage.

Actually one of the earliest forms of natural family planning is breast feeding. If a woman breast feeds her baby consistently, she probably would not conceive for 18-24 months. Actually, many tribal people naturally regulate births this way.

In the 1930s, Calendar Rhythm was developed. This method was effective if the woman had regular cycles and if she was properly instructed. Actually, rhythm is about as effective as condoms or other barrier methods of birth control. Nevertheless, Calendar Rhythm was unreliable for many couples. Perhaps this unreliability is why many joked, "What do you call a couple who uses rhythm? Answer: Parents."

However, modern Natural Family Planning is technically called the Sympto-Thermal Method. This method relies on three signs of fertility in the woman: basal temperature pattern, cervical mucus pattern, and physical changes in the position of the cervix. These three signs inform a couple when the wife is in ovulation and possibly could conceive a child if the couple engages in marital love. Ironically, while many doctors prescribe artificial means to prevent a pregnancy, they prescribe the techniques of Natural Family Planning to help a couple who is having trouble conceiving a child identify the period of ovulation and thereby know when the possibility of conception is the greatest. Moreover, if one is worried about effectiveness, the Sympto-Thermal Method is proven to be as effective as "the Pill" and more effective than barrier methods if used properly.

Immediately, some people may honestly ask, "What is the difference between Natural Family Planning and other forms of contraception? Both seem to do the same thing." While both means may have the same intent – postponing pregnancy – the difference lies in the means themselves. With Natural Family Planning, couples keep their covenant of life and love intact. They use only the means given to them by God, which are intrinsic to who they are. In expressing their marital love, they are mindful that this action not only unites them as husband and wife, but also may participate in God's creative love. Rather than suppress and ignore one dimension, they respect both dimensions. Therefore, if they decide for a serious reason to postpone a pregnancy, then both husband and wife make the decision and both share in the sacrifice of not expressing their marital love during the period of ovulation. Natural Family Planning is also safe, and the burden is shared by both husband and wife. Moreover, the couple is open to the providence of God's will: if a child should come who was "not planned," so be it – that is God's will and God's gift; whereas with contraceptives, where the couple has everything nicely planned and is in control, the surprise pregnancy oftentimes spells disaster. Remember that one of the arguments for legalized abortion is to correct "unplanned pregnancies."

Pope John Paul II addressed the anthropological and moral differences between contraception and Natural Family Planning in his encyclical, *The Christian Family in the Modern World*: "The choice of the natural rhythms involves accepting the cycle of the person, that is the woman, and thereby accepting dialogue, reciprocal respect, shared responsibility and self-control. To accept the cycle and to enter into dialogue means to recognize both the spiritual and corporal character of conjugal communion, and to live personal love with its requirement of fidelity. In this context the couple comes to experience how conjugal communion is enriched with those values of tenderness and affection which constitute the inner soul of human sexuality, in its physical dimension also. In this way sexuality is respected and promoted in its truly and fully human dimension, and is never 'used' as an 'object' that, by breaking the personal unity of soul and body, strikes at God's creation itself at the level of the deepest interaction of nature and person" (#32).

Actually, Natural Family Planning has had great successes. For example, in 1960, the government of Mauritius, a small island country in the Indian Ocean east of Madagascar, wanted to commence a major contraceptive campaign to control the population. The bishop published a pastoral letter denouncing these plans. After discussing the issue with government officials, in 1963, an education program was started for Natural Family Planning. Doctors educated training couples who in turn taught the method to other couples. Today they train 2,000 couples each year. Each parish has a special program for educating couples in preparation for marriage, and 85% of couples married in the Church complete that training. In all, 20% of women of child-bearing age use Natural Family Planning, of whom Hindus and Moslems account for 62%. Moreover, artificial methods are on the decline. The effectiveness of Natural Family Planning has been a convincing argument against legalizing abortion in the country. What Bishop Margeot fears today is the coalition of governments – America, Japan, and Northern Europe – and foundations – Rockefeller and Packard – who are striving to impose artificial birth control throughout Africa, which in each case has eventually led to abortion.

While this column cannot give a full explanation of Natural Family Planning, I would suggest that any couple who is interested take the course. Rather than just brush aside the Church's teaching, investigate the teaching and inquire about Natural Family Planning. Ask the couples what the difference between the two methods actually is. Moreover, if used properly, Natural Family Planning is almost 100% effective with a .004 pregnancy rate (U.S. Department of Health, Education and Welfare (1978)) versus "the pill," which is 97% effective, or the condom, which is 79-88% effective

(*Contraceptive Technology*). Courses for Natural Family Planning are offered in dioceses throughout the country.

Nevertheless, this whole issue concerns that covenant love between husband and wife, and God. It deals with the creation of life in union with God. Therefore, concerning the regulation of births, Vatican II stated, "It is the married couple themselves who must in the last analysis arrive at these judgments before God" (*Pastoral Constitution on the Church in the Modern World*, #50). However, any faithful Catholic must first take into account the teaching of the Magisterium. As has been emphasized, marriage is serious, marital love is serious, the creation of life is serious. The means of contraception are intrinsically evil (*Catechism*, #2370). Thereby the violation of marital love through the use of contraceptive practices is objectively a serious, mortal sin. Granted, grave circumstances may exist which in turn may reduce the culpability of a couple in this matter. If a couple is struggling with this issue, I advise them to see a priest or talk with one of the couples who teaches Natural Family Planning. Oftentimes, the teaching couple has used the artificial means and can best explain to another couple the differences between the methods and guide them through this issue.

Nevertheless, one cannot cavalierly dismiss the consistent teaching of the Church on this issue. We cannot simply consider good intentions or motives. Moreover, we cannot just go to the "Yellow Pages" to find the priest or theologian who will give us the answer we want to hear. We have to be honest and wrestle with the truth and by the grace of God conform to it. As Pope John Paul II asserted, "As Teacher, [the Church] never tires of proclaiming the moral norm that must guide the responsible transmission of life. The Church is in no way the author or the arbiter of this norm. In obedience to the truth which is Christ, whose image is reflected in the nature and dignity of the human person, the Church interprets the moral norm and proposes it to all people of good will, without concealing its demands of radicalness and perfection" (*The Christian Family in the Modern World*, #33).

The Church's Teaching in Light
of Sacred Scripture and Tradition

In explaining the Church's teaching about contraception, many people mistakenly think that this teaching is relatively new, something which occurred with *Humanae Vitae* in 1968. Other people, from a more fundamentalist bent, want to know if there is any basis in Sacred Scripture for these teachings. In reviewing both Sacred Scripture as well as the history of our Church's teaching in this area, one finds a very positive and solid foundation.

Concerning "What does the Bible have to say?" the very positive presentation concerning creation, marital love, and covenant emerges from the texts of Sacred Scripture. However, we also discover references to any violation of the unitive-procreative dimensions of marital love and to the divine consequences which followed. In Genesis, we find the story of Onan, the second son of Judah, who married Tamar, the widow of his older brother Er. (The Levirate law of Judaism prescribed that if the oldest brother died, the next oldest, single brother would marry his widow to preserve the family line.) The Bible reads, "Onan, however, knew that the descendants would not be counted as his; so whenever he had relations with his brother's widow, he wasted his seed on the ground, to avoid contributing offspring for his brother. What he did greatly offended the Lord, and the Lord took his life." (Cf. Genesis 38:1ff). Here is a basic form of contraception – withdrawal, and clearly a sin in the eyes of God.

Interestingly, the Protestant tradition cited this story as a basis for condemning any form of contraception. Luther commented, "Onan ... spilled his seed. That was a sin greater than adultery or incest, and it provoked God to such fierce wrath that He destroyed him immediately" (*Commentary on Genesis*). In another work, he wrote, "For Onan goes in to her, that is, he lies with her and copulates, and when it comes to the point of insemination, spills the semen, lest the woman conceive. Surely at such a time the order of nature established by God in procreation should be followed" (*Works*).

Calvin also commented on the story of Onan: "The voluntary spilling of semen outside of intercourse between man and woman is a monstrous thing. Deliberately to withdraw from coitus in order that semen may fall on the ground is doubly monstrous. For this is to extinguish the hope of the race and to kill before he is born an hoped-for offspring" (*Commentary on Genesis*). Interestingly, two of the leaders of the Protestant movement both condemned a practice which suppressed the procreative dimension of marital love.

History further illuminates the Church's position on this subject. Anthropological studies show that means of contraception existed in antiquity. Medical papyri described various contraceptive methods used in China in the year 2700 BC and in Egypt in the year 1850 BC. Soranos (AD 98-139), a Greek physician from Ephesus, described seventeen medically approved methods of contraception. Also at this time, abortion and infanticide were not uncommon practices in the Roman Empire.

The early Christian community however, upheld the sanctity of marriage, marital love, and human life. In the New Testament, the word *pharmakeia* appears, which some scholars link to the contraception issue. *Pharmakeia* denotes the mixing of potions for secretive purposes, and from Soranos and others, evidence exists of artificial birth control potions. Interestingly, *pharmakeia* is oftentimes translated as "sorcery" in English. In the three passages in which *pharmakeia* appears, other sexual sins are also condemned: lewd conduct, impurity, licentiousness, orgies, "and the like" (e.g. Galatians 5:19-21). This evidence highlights that the early Church condemned anything which violated the integrity of marital love.

Further evidence is found in the *Didache*, also called the *Teachings of the Twelve Apostles*, written about the year AD 80. This book was the Church's first manual of morals, liturgical norms, and doctrine. In the first section, two ways are proposed – the way of life and the way of death. In following the way of life, the *Didache* exhorts, "You shall not murder. You shall not commit adultery. You shall not seduce boys. You shall not commit fornication.

You shall not steal. You shall not practice magic. You shall not use potions. You shall not procure abortion, nor destroy a new-born child. You shall not covet your neighbor's goods ... ." Again scholars link such phrases as "practice magic" and "use potions" with artificial birth control.

In all, the Catholic Church as well as other Christian denominations condemned the use of contraceptive means until the twentieth century. The first Christian denomination to approve contraception was the Church of England or Episcopalian Church. At the August 14, 1930 Lambeth Conference of Bishops of the Anglican Church, a resolution was passed which allowed the use of methods to limit the size of families "where there is a clearly-felt moral obligation to limit or avoid parenthood." The "primary and obvious method" was considered "complete abstinence from intercourse ... in a life of discipline and self-control lived in the power of the Holy Spirit"; however, other methods could also be used, namely artificial means. Bishop Brent gave an impassioned plea stating that if the resolution passed, soon contraception would be allowed for any reason and the decision would give way to selfish rationalization. Interestingly, following the Lambeth Conference decision, T. S. Eliot commented, "The world is trying the experiment of attempting to form a civilized, but non-Christian mentality. The experiment will fail, but we must be very patient in waiting its collapse" (*Thoughts after Lambeth*).

In response to the Church of England's approval of contraception, Pope Pius XI issued his encyclical *Casti Connubii* on December 31, 1930, stating, "Since, therefore, openly departing from the uninterrupted Christian tradition some recently have judged it possible solemnly to declare another doctrine regarding this question, the Catholic Church, to whom God has entrusted the defense of the integrity and purity of morals, standing erect in the midst of the moral ruin which surrounds her, in order that she may preserve the chastity of the nuptial union from being defiled by this foul stain, raises her voice in token of her divine ambassadorship and through our mouth proclaims anew: any use whatsoever of matrimony exercised in such a way that the act is deliberately frustrated in its natural power to generate life is an offense against the law of God and of nature, and those who indulge in such are branded with the guilt of a grave sin."

The Church faced increasing pressure regarding the use of contraceptive means with the marketing of the anovulant pill. In response, Vatican Council II stated in the *Pastoral Constitution in the Modern World*, "In questions of birth regulation, the sons and daughters of the Church, faithful to these principles, are forbidden to use methods disapproved of by the teaching authority of the Church in its interpretation of the divine law" (#51). However, Pope Paul VI had transferred the investigation of new questions concerning this matter to a special commission (originally established by Pope John XXIII in March, 1963) for the study of population, the family, and births. The Holy Father would then review their findings and render judgment. The commission included married couples and those of various competencies in this field. Select bishops were also asked for their views; other bishops voluntarily submitted them.

On July 25, 1968, Pope Paul VI issued *Humanae Vitae* which upheld the consistent teaching of the Church based on natural law as well as divine revelation: "Each and every marriage act must remain open to the transmission of life" (#11).

Our Holy Father has continually repeated the Church's teaching. In *The Christian Family in the Modern World*, he lamented the signs of a "disturbing degradation of some fundamental values" evident in "the growing number of divorces, the scourge of abortion, the ever more frequent recourse to sterilization, the appearance of a truly contraceptive mentality" (#6).

Interestingly, in 1968 Pope Paul VI prophesied grave consequences from contraception: increased marital infidelity and a lowering of moral standards; increased lack of respect for women, including seeing a woman as a sex object and as an instrument to satisfy sexual pleasures rather than seeing her as a partner in marriage; and the danger of empowering public authorities to regulate the lives of others. Thirty years later, these warnings have become realities: Statistics show the rapid increase of divorce, from a rate of 25% in 1965 to 50% in 1975 during the first five years of marriage. By the year 2000, 50% of American teenagers will have lived a significant part of their lives without a father figure. Moreover, Dr. Robert Michaels of Stanford University found a direct, positive correlation between the growing rate of divorce and the rate of contraception. (Interestingly, couples who use Natural Family Planning have a much lower divorce rate: 0.6% according to the Couple to Couple League, and 2-5% according to research conducted by California State University.)

Any person can attest to the deterioration of the moral quality of television and movies during this time. Pornography has become increasingly prevalent, with 630 million pornographic video rentals reported each year in the United States. The availability of pornography and sexual contacts through the internet is alarming.

Crimes of rape continue to rise each year. The news is replete with cases alleging sexual harassment. This year alone, we have been appalled by several cases where unmarried teenage parents killed their newborn child.

Finally, the intrusion of government into family planning has become more prevalent. Some municipal or state governments, such as Maryland and Kansas, have attempted to begin programs which pay women to use Norplant (the five-year contraceptive implanted in a woman's arm) to control the pregnancies of teenagers and welfare recipients; foreign countries like Peru have introduced sterilization programs and have compelled poor citizens to be sterilized. International policy set by the affluent Western nations to help developing Third World countries oftentimes include mandatory population control provisions, including artificial birth control and abortion. Little wonder, Pope John Paul II declared Pope Paul VI's *Humanae Vitae* a "truly prophetic proclamation" (*Familiaris Consortio*, #29).

Interestingly, Dr. William May in 1968 signed a statement with numerous other theologians dissenting from *Humane Vitae*. He has long since recanted. In 1988, on the 20th anniversary of the encyclical, he said, "I was beginning to see that if contraception is justifiable, then perhaps artificial insemination, test-tube reproduction, and similar modes of generating life outside the marital embrace are morally justifiable too ... . I began to realize that the moral theology invented to justify contraception could be used to justify any kind of deed. I saw that it was a consequentialist, utilitarian kind of argument, that it was a theory which repudiated the notion of intrinsically evil acts. I began to realize how truly prophetic the Pope had been, and how providential it was that he had been given the strength to resist the tremendous pressures brought to bear upon him" (*Columbia*, June 1988). Now ten years later, articles concerning *in vitro* fertilization, surrogate motherhood, and cloning appear regularly in the news media. One has to ask, "Where are we headed as a society?"

Conclusion

Pope Paul VI concluded *Humanae Vitae* with the statement that the Church is to be "a sign of contradiction." So indeed she is in upholding the sanctity of marriage and the error of contraception. Yes, the Church is going against the popular culture of the age. Nevertheless, St. Paul's words originally addressed to the Romans should resound in our own ears: "Do not conform yourselves to this age but be transformed by the renewal of your mind, so that you may judge what is God's will, what is good, pleasing and perfect" (Romans 12:2).

WHAT IS THE CHURCH'S POSITION ON PRENATAL DIAGNOSIS AND FETAL RESEARCH?

Before approaching fetal research per se, we must first be clear about what, or better who, the fetus is. The Catholic Church has continually asserted that a human being must be respected as a person from the moment of conception, the very first instance of existence. The *Declaration on Procured Abortion* stated, "From the time that the ovum is fertilized, a new life is begun which is neither that of the father nor of the mother; it is rather the life of a new human being with his own growth. It would never be made human if it were not human already. To this perpetual evidence ... modern genetic science brings valuable confirmation. It has demonstrated that, from the first instant, the program is fixed as to what this living being will be: a man, this individual-man with his characteristic aspects already well determined. Right from fertilization is begun the adventure of human life, and each of its great capacities requires time ... to find its place and to be in a position to act" (#12-13). Moreover, we believe that almighty God creates and infuses an immortal soul, which truly gives each of us that identity of one made in His image and likeness. Therefore, we must respect the unborn child as a person whose life is sacred and whose rights must be protected.

Given this perspective, we can now address issues and the governing principles concerning prenatal diagnosis and fetal research. The Sacred Congregation for the Doctrine of the Faith addressed these issues in its *Instruction on Respect for Human Life in Its Origin and on the Dignity of Procreation* (*Donum vitae*), released in 1987. (These principles are affirmed in the *Catechism*, #2274-75.) First, prenatal diagnosis provides information about the health of the fetus still in the womb, and thereby may enable physicians to anticipate and to correct more readily and earlier any problems. Various methods of fetal diagnosis currently exist: Amniocentesis involves withdrawing some of the amniotic fluid from the womb and then doing an analysis which can identify certain genetic problems, such a cystic fibrosis. Sonography allows physicians to see the child in the womb. Many new techniques using biochemical, cytogenic, or molecular biologic means have been developed which permit early fetal diagnosis. Prenatal diagnosis is morally acceptable "if it respects the life and integrity of the embryo and the human fetus and is directed towards its safeguarding or healing as an individual ... " (*Donum vitae*, I, 2). However, prenatal diagnosis is not moral if it is performed with the intention of aborting a child if some malformation or hereditary illness is detected: "A diagnosis must not be the equivalent of a death sentence" (ibid).

The new *Ethical and Religious Directives for Catholic Health Care Services* (1994) present these principles succinctly: "Prenatal diagnosis is permitted when the procedure does not threaten the life or physical integrity of the unborn child or the mother, and does not subject them to disproportionate risks; when the diagnosis can provide information to guide preventive care for the mother or pre- or postnatal care for the child; and when the parents, or at least the mother, give free and informed consent. Prenatal diagnosis is not permitted when undertaken with the intention of aborting an unborn child with a serious defect" (#50).

The real problem occurs when prenatal diagnosis reveals an abnormality in the child, such as Down's Syndrome or some physical malformation. The temptation in our world then becomes "Terminate the pregnancy. Abort the child." Actually, since the 1973 Supreme Court decision *Roe v. Wade* which legalized abortion, pressure upon physicians to make accurate prenatal diagnoses has grown and consequently has increased the legal penalties and settlements for failure to accurately diagnose and report any abnormality. Obstetricians regularly use prenatal diagnosis and then inform parents of the findings to protect themselves from malpractice suits. Many health care plans insist on prenatal diagnosis, and then in the case of an abnormality, apply pressure to terminate the pregnancy, which is more "cost effective" than treating the abnormality for perhaps a prolonged period of time after birth. Nevertheless, despite this knowledge, we must not lose sight that each person remains an unique individual made in the image and likeness of God. Moreover, the criterion of what is normal versus abnormal can be very subjective, depending upon who is in control.

Without question, parents must agonize when the prenatal diagnosis reveals an abnormality. Suddenly, this information about the baby they wanted so much now sparks a host of questions: "What will happen to my child? What kind of life will he have? What will the treatments entail? How could this happen to us? How can we possibly care for this child?" Especially in our world today, the temptation to abort may enter the parent's mind. However, to succumb to such a temptation and take the life of the child would leave the parents with tremendous grief, hurtful memories, and guilt.

To give the child with an abnormality life is a generous and heroic act of love. Surely, our Lord will give His grace to the couple to sustain their decision. Moreover, each member of the Church must also assist these families through prayers and charitable assistance. We must remember always that whatever we do for the least of our brethren, we do for Christ Himself (Matthew 25:40). We cannot simply give exhortations about the right to life, or talk or sing songs about good works; each of us must take responsibility for these children and support their families.

What then can we do morally when an unborn child is diagnosed with a medical problem? Medical interventions on unborn children are judged moral as long as they respect the life and integrity of the child, do not involve "disproportionate risks," and are directed to the child's healing, improvement of health, and survival. Here, the free and informed consent of parents is required, who must act in the best interests of their child. For instance, a procedure to correct a health problem from a hereditary disease is morally permissible even while the child is still in the womb. The more serious the problem and the greater urgency to correct it determines how much risk can be accepted. However, experimental treatment must not be performed on an unborn child just for the sake of experimentation; rather, any experimental treatment should be therapeutic to the child with, as best as possible, a moral certainty of not causing harm to his life and integrity. (Cf. *Donum vitae*, I, 4.)

However, we have moved from the realm of therapeutic treatment to experimental research on unborn children. The danger here is that we can lose sight of the unborn child as a person and view him as a laboratory research animal. We have slipped into this mentality primarily because our civil law, as stated in *Roe v. Wade*, does not consider the unborn child a "person." Moreover, the present capabilities of *in vitro* fertilization have compounded the problem, reducing a conceived child to "genetic material" isolated in a petri dish. Nevertheless, here again the Church asserts clear moral guidance concerning fetal research:

Any production of human beings for the sake of experimentation, research, or the harvesting of organs is morally wrong. Such actions reduce a human being to simply disposable biological material. (Cf. *Donum vitae*, I, 5.)

Any medical research or observation which jeopardizes the health or life of the unborn child is morally wrong. (Cf. *Donum vitae*, I, 5.)

Procedures designed to influence the genetic inheritance of a child, which are not therapeutic, are morally wrong. To try to correct a genetic disorder, such as cystic fibrosis, is morally permissible, whereas to manipulate the genetic structure to produce human beings selected by sex or some other quality is wrong. Attempts to produce a "breed" of humans through cloning, twin fission, or parthenogenesis outside the context of marriage or parenthood is immoral. Such procedures violate the dignity of the human being, attacking his personal integrity and identity. (Cf. *Donum vitae*, I, 6.)

"The corpses of human embryos and fetuses, whether they have been deliberately aborted or not, must be respected just as the remains of other human beings" (*Donum vitae*, I, 4). Any kind of commercial trafficking of corpses or organs in morally wrong.

These teachings reflect "Catholic common sense." If we say, "Yes, the unborn child at the moment of conception is an unique individual, made in God's image and likeness, with a body and a soul," then these principles make sense. If we say, "No," then we will permit uncontrolled research and plunge ourselves into the realm of genetic manipulation, organ harvesting and trafficking, human breeding, and unrestrained experimentation. A few recent cases demonstrate what happens when we choose the latter answer.

In 1991, Anissa Ayala, a 19 year-old suffering from leukemia, received a bone marrow transplant from her 13 month old sister, Marissa, who was purposefully conceived to be a bone marrow donor. While still in the womb, physicians analyzed Marissa's tissue and determined that she would be an acceptable donor for her older sister. What if her tissue had not been compatible with that of her sister? Would she have been aborted, and would the parents then try to conceive another compatible donor? Dr. Robert Levine at Yale University School of Medicine commented, "It seems to me that when a primary motive for conceiving a child is to produce tissue or an organ, we are getting very close to seeing this new being as a means to another end."

Take this a step further. Currently, fetal brain tissue is used to treat patients suffering from Parkinson's disease, an incurable neurodegenerative disease. Fetal brain cells are extracted and transplanted to supply the needed brain chemical Dopamine, a neurotransmitter. Tissue harvests of at least 14 fetal brains are required for best results. This procedure is still very much experimental, and the benefits still inconclusive. However, the fetal brain tissue is suctioned out while the fetus (13 to 18 weeks old) is still living; so the transplantation does not come from a clinically dead person, but from a clinically alive person. Obviously, the procedure kills the unborn child. Researchers are finding other ways in which "parts" of unborn children may be beneficial to those born. This research questions parameters concerning producing babies and aborting them simply to sell fetal tissue.

Take it a step further. Although current federal law prohibits the sale of human organs, abortion clinics regularly receive a processing fee of $50 to $150 per child from research laboratories. Here lies the beginnings of a very lucrative business.

Take it a step further. The success of organ transplants depends upon the freshness and, in the case of a fetus, the developmental stage of the organ. Therefore, one can easily predict later abortions for the sole purpose of harvesting organs for transplantation. With the legalization of partial birth abortions, this practice may soon become easier.

And in the end, the more one propagandizes the use of fetal tissue, the easier it is to think of this procedure as a good, which justifies abortion and looks at the unborn child simply as a blob of tissue. As Catholics, we must courageously defend the basic respect for all human life, born and unborn. All forms of prenatal diagnosis or fetal research must proceed from this stance. The unborn, innocent, defenseless child cries out for our protection.

WHAT DOES THE CHURCH TEACH CONCERNING IN VITRO FERTILIZATION, ARTIFICIAL INSEMINATION, AND SURROGATE MOTHERHOOD?

Children are a gift from God. They are the blessing of the covenant love shared between husband and wife. Each child is an unique, precious individual, a union of body and soul, made in God's image and likeness. Children are a "good" of marriage, a good in which couples ought to want to share. Thereby, the *Catechism* recognizes that "couples who discover that they are sterile suffer greatly" (#2374).

A couple may find help in conceiving a child through advances in medical technology. However, we must proceed with caution: Just because a certain technology is available does not necessarily entail that it is morally good and ought to be used. As with other issues, the Church evaluates technology in aiding conception and reproduction from truth principles: " ... The respect, defense, and promotion of man; his 'primary and fundamental right' to life; his dignity as a person who is endowed with a spiritual soul and with moral responsibility, and who is called to beatific communion with God" (*Donum vitae*, Intro. 1). Never can we judge technology simply by its efficiency, its utility even at the expense of others, or some prevailing ideology.

We must also remember that each child possesses genuine rights: A child has the inviolable right to life from the moment of conception until natural death. A child has the right to be respected as a person from the moment of conception. A child has the right to be "the fruit" of the conjugal love of his parents, who are united in marriage: "The transmission of human life is entrusted by nature to a personal and conscious act and as such is subject to the all-holy laws of God: immutable and inviolable laws which must be recognized and observed" (Pope John XXIII, *Mater et magistra*). Finally, a child has the right to be born. Each of us has the responsibility of guarding these rights for the defenseless child. Never must we slip into thinking that anyone has the right to a child at any cost, or that a child is like a piece of property to be had (*Donum vitae*, II, 8).

Given this foundation, we can address the techniques of *in vitro* fertilization, artificial insemination and surrogate motherhood. First, we need to be clear about the techniques themselves (which is not easy because of the jargon): *In vitro* fertilization involves the conception of the ovum outside of the mother in a test tube or a petri dish. Usually multiple ova are harvested (through hyper-ovulation and laparoscopy), fertilized with sperm collected through masturbation, and cultivated for several days. Each embryo may be transferred one at a time for implantation into the uterus. Unfortunately, usually several attempts are made before implantation is achieved. The remaining ova are frozen for further implantation or destroyed.

Artificial insemination injects previously collected sperm into the genital tracts of the mother. This sperm is normally obtained through an act of masturbation.

Finally, surrogate motherhood involves transferring the conceived ovum into the uterus of a woman who is not the genetic mother, or impregnating a woman with the sperm of a man other than her husband. This mother will bear the child, whom she will surrender upon birth.

Moreover, the question can be further analyzed by whether the technique involved is *heterologous* (where the genetic material – the gametes – comes from at least one donor other than the spouses joined in marriage) or *homologous* (where the genetic material comes from the spouses joined in marriage).

Since heterologous *in vitro* fertilization, artificial insemination, and surrogate motherhood involve the donation and the use of genetic material of someone other than the mother or father, who are joined in marriage as husband and wife, the marriage covenant is violated. These acts, thereby, entail adultery, morally speaking. In the case of a surrogate mother who does not supply the ovum but will just bear the baby, this woman outside of the marriage covenant is receiving the embryo and bearing the child, thereby usurping the privilege of the natural mother and the right of the child to be born of a natural mother. In all, these techniques are "contrary to the unity of marriage, to the dignity of the spouses, to the vocation proper to parents, and to the child's right to be conceived and brought into the world in marriage and from marriage" (*Donum vitae* II, 2). Therefore, any case of heterologous *in vitro* fertilization, artificial insemination, or surrogate motherhood is considered "gravely immoral" (*Catechism*, #2376).

The cases of homologous *in vitro* fertilization and artificial insemination which involve the genetic material of husband and wife united in marriage may at first glance seem compassionate in helping a couple conceive their own child. Returning to the basic truth principles, problems are inherent in the techniques. Homologous *in vitro* fertilization bypasses the natural expression of marital love and conception takes place outside of the mother. Generally, the technique proceeds as follows: Sperm is gathered through an act of masturbation; several ova are gathered through laparoscopy. The conception that occurs – whether from fertilization in a petri dish or test tube – is not the fruit of the natural marriage act ordered to procreation. Keep in mind that several ova are fertilized (usually 8 to 10), but each one is an unique individual, a new human being. After being cultured about 40 hours, the embryos are transferred, one at a time, to the uterine cavity, where hopefully implantation will occur. Recent statistics indicate that pregnancy results 24.1% of the time with a delivery rate of 16.8% of the time. However, what happens to the remaining conceived ova in the petri dish? These ova are frozen or destroyed, and yet we consider them human beings with a right to life. The Church expresses legitimate fear: "Homologous IVF [*in vitro* fertilization] and ET [embryo transfer] is brought about outside the bodies of the couple through actions of third parties whose competence and technical activity determine the success of the procedure. Such fertilization entrusts the life and identity of the embryo into the power of doctors and biologists and establishes the domination of technology over the origin and destiny of the human person. Such a relationship of domination is in itself contrary to the dignity and equality that must be common to parents and children" (*Donum vitae*, #II,6).

Homologous artificial insemination involves the injection of the father's sperm into the fallopian tubes of the mother, where hopefully conception will occur. The key problem here is the method for gathering sperm, which is usually done through an act of masturbation. Masturbation is a denial of the husband's free giving of himself to his wife in their natural act of marital love, and thereby wrong.

Therefore, applying the truth principles to the techniques involved, we see the moral problems at hand. We must at this point be careful not to let a sense of compassion for a couple having difficulty conceiving a child move us to abandon the truth principles. If we would abandon these principles – which to some extent society has already done – we will have a disaster. Sadly, we have seen what can happen when the technology is allowed to function outside the moral principles:

In 1979, the Gay and Lesbian Parents Coalition International was founded as an association of families with homosexual parents, where two men have paid a woman to bear "their" child using her ovum and uterus, or two women have bought sperm for artificial insemination to conceive "their" baby.

In 1988, Dr. Lee Silver, an associate professor of biology at Princeton told the House Human Resources and Intergovernmental Resources Subcommittee of Congress of his research to adapt men and even chimpanzees and gorillas to gestate a fetus.

In 1990, the Tennessee State Circuit Court tried the case of Mary Sue Davis, who sued her estranged husband, Junior Lewis Davis, for possession of seven frozen embryos held in suspended animation. During their nine years of marriage, they had difficulty conceiving a child and so they resorted to *in vitro* fertilization. Nine ova were fertilized in a petri dish. After two unsuccessful implantations, they divorced. Mrs. Davis argued in court that the remaining embryos belonged to her and should be implanted so she could have a child; on the other hand, Mr. Davis said he no longer wanted to be the father of any of these "potential" children. To resolve this legal nightmare, the judge had to choose as the basis for his ruling either property law or child custody law. In the end, he ruled they were human beings whose best interests would be served if they were implanted and born, even though this judicial interpretation contradicted the precedents of *Roe v. Wade*, which legalized abortion and declared the unborn child a non-person.

In 1995, the Center for Reproductive Health of the University of California at Irvine was charged with giving the fertilized ova of one couple to another couple, hence allowing the latter to bear the former's child, albeit unknowingly.

In all of these immoral let alone bizarre cases, does anyone think of the child? The child simply becomes property, something to have.

Nevertheless, technology which conforms to the truth principles can be used to help couples conceive a child. Catholic hospitals have developed two morally acceptable procedures: Intrauterine Insemination (IUI) and Gamate Intra-fallopian Tube Transfer (GIFT). In Intrauterine Insemination, a husband and wife express their love in a natural way. Sperm are collected by the husband using a perforated Silastic sheath. The sperm are then transferred directly to the uterine cavity, increasing the chances for conception.

In the Gamete Intrafallopian Tube Transfer, husband and wife express their love in a natural way. Again the husband uses a perforated Silastic sheath for the gathering of sperm. Ova are gathered through laparoscopy. The gametes are kept separate, and then transferred into the fallopian tubes where hopefully conception will occur. According to statistics, conception occurs 33.5% of the time with a delivery rate of 26.3%.

Although this explanation if IUI and GIFT is simple, these procedures respect the act of marital love and the conception of the child within the mother. Here the technology assists but does not replace God's design.

Without doubt, a sterile couple who wants a child so badly bears great pain. However, this couple must unite themselves to the cross of the Lord. Here such a couple can open their hearts and homes through adoption to an unwanted child. Couples can also help others families who may face financial difficulties or face the burden of caring for a handicapped child. In the end, we must preserve the moral law, for to abandon the truth principles condemns us to disaster.

WHY DOES THE CHURCH TEACH REGARDING STERILIZATION?

Before addressing the morality of sterilization, we must first remember that each person is a precious human being made in God's image and likeness with both a body and a soul. Vatican II's *Pastoral Constitution on the Church in the Modern World* asserted, "Man, though made of body and soul is a unity. Through his very bodily condition he sums up in himself the elements of the material world. Through him they are thus brought to their highest perfection and can raise their voice in praise freely given to the Creator. For this reason man may not despise his bodily life. Rather he is obliged to regard his body as good and to hold it in honor since God has created it and will raise it up on the last day" (#14). St. Paul also reminds us that our bodies are temples of the Holy Spirit (I Corinthians 6:19), and therefore we should not degrade our bodily dignity by allowing the body to participate in the act of sin. Moreover, such sin hurts the body of the Church.

Therefore, we are responsible to care for our bodily needs with proper nourishment, rest, exercise, and hygiene. At times, we take medicine, over-the-counter as well as prescribed, to preserve our bodily health. However, we must not bring harm to our body by abusing drugs.

Circumstances arise when we need surgery. To preserve the well-being of our whole body, we can surgically remove an organ that is diseased or functioning in a way that is harmful. For instance, surgery to remove an appendix that is about to rupture is perfectly moral as is surgery to remove a mole which appears to be "pre-cancerous." However, to cut off a perfectly healthy hand and destroy not only that part but also its functions is an act of mutilation and thereby morally wrong.

With this brief outline of principles, we can turn to the matter of sterilization. Here a distinction is made between direct and indirect sterilization.

Direct sterilization means that the purpose of the procedure is simply to destroy the normal functioning of a healthy organ so as to prevent the future conception of children. The most effective and least dangerous method of permanent sterilization is through a vasectomy for a man and the ligation of the fallopian tubes for a woman. Such direct sterilization is considered morally wrong. Regarding unlawful ways of regulating births, Pope Paul VI in his encyclical *Humanae Vitae* (1968) asserted, "Equally to be condemned ... is direct sterilization, whether of the man or of the woman, whether permanent or temporary" (#14). The *Catechism* also states, "Except when performed for strictly therapeutic medical reasons, directly intended amputations, mutilations, and sterilizations performed on innocent persons are against the moral law" (#2297).

On the other hand, indirect sterilization is morally permissible. Here surgery, or drug or radiation therapy is not intended to destroy the functioning of a healthy organ or to prevent the conception of children. Rather, the direct intention is to remove or to combat a diseased or malfunctioning organ. Unfortunately, the surgery or therapy may "indirectly" result in the person being sterilized. For instance, if a woman is diagnosed with a cancerous uterus, the performance of a hysterectomy is perfectly legitimate and moral. The direct effect is to remove the diseased organ and preserve the health of the woman's body; the indirect effect is that she will be rendered sterile and never be able to bear children again. The same would be true if one of a woman's ovaries or if one of a man's testes were cancerous or functioning in a way which is harmful to overall bodily well-being. (As an aside, I do not know of any medically therapeutic reason for a vasectomy or a tubal ligation.) The caution in this discussion to uphold the morality is that the operation is truly therapeutic in character and arises from a real pathological need.

Lastly, further caution must be taken concerning the rights of the state in this area. Pope Pius XI in his encyclical *Casti connubii* (1930) warned, "For there are those who, overly solicitous about the ends of eugenics, not only give certain salutary counsels for more certainly procuring the, health and vigor of the future off-spring, ... but also place eugenics before every other end of a higher order; and by public authority wish to prohibit from marriage all those from whom, according to the norms and conjecture of their science, they think that a defective and corrupt offspring will be generated because of hereditary transmission, even if these same persons are naturally fitted for entering upon matrimony. Why, they even wish such persons even against their will to be deprived by law of that natural faculty through the operation of physicians ... ." Pope Pius XI was prophetic in his teaching, since shortly thereafter the world witnessed the eugenics program of Nazi Germany which included massive sterilization. In our world, various civil governments still toy with the idea of sterilization to solve welfare problems. Perhaps we may reach the point where health insurance companies pressure individuals to be sterilized rather than risk having children which may require expensive health care.

Pope John Paul II warned in his encyclical *The Gospel of Life* of "scientifically and systematically programmed threats" against life. He continued, " ... We are in fact faced by an objective 'conspiracy against life,' involving even international institutions, engaged in encouraging and carrying out actual campaigns to make contraception, sterilization, and abortion widely available. Nor can it be denied that the mass media are often implicated in this conspiracy, by lending credit to that culture which presents recourse to contraception, sterilization, abortion, and even euthanasia as a mark of progress and a victory of freedom, while depicting as enemies of freedom and progress those positions which are unreservedly pro-life" (#17).

In all, the Catholic teaching on this issue respects the dignity of the individual in both his person and action.

WHAT DOES THE CHURCH REALLY TEACH CONCERNING HOMOSEXUALITY?

Before addressing the moral issue of the practice of homosexuality, we must first review some basic truth principles: First, each of us, whether male or female, is made in God's image and likeness (Genesis 1:27). We must be ever mindful of the inherent dignity of each person, a dignity heightened by the incarnation of Jesus Christ. Second, in accord with God's plan, the union of man and woman as husband and wife in marriage is a sacred covenant of life and love (Genesis 1:28, Matthew 19:3ff); the complementarity of the sexes reflects the inner unity of the Creator (*Letter on the Pastoral Care of Homosexual Persons*, #4). Third, the conjugal expression of love in marriage is both unitive and procreative: a sacred symbol of the two who have become one flesh and a sacred expression which may bring human life into this world.

Given these principles, the practice of homosexuality – "relations between men or between women who experience an exclusive or predominant sexual attraction toward persons of the same sex" (*Catechism*, #2357) – is considered "intrinsically disordered" (*Declaration on Certain Problems of Sexual Ethics*, #8). An "intrinsically disordered" act defies both the goodness of God's design for how life ought to be lived and the dignity proper to each person. Please note that a distinction is made between the homosexual condition or tendency and the practice of homosexuality; the practice or act is what falls into the realm of sin.

Why does the Church preach that the practice of homosexuality is a sin? The answer is first based on the revelation found in Sacred Scripture. In Genesis, we find the story of Sodom and Gomorrah (18:16-19:29), a place where "their sin was so grave" (18:20); here, Lot has to protect his two male visitors (not knowing they were angels of the Lord) from the townsmen who desired "intimacies" with them. St. Paul also condemned the practice of homosexuality: "God delivered them up in their lusts to unclean practices; they engaged in the mutual degradation of their bodies, these men who exchanged the truth of God for a lie and worshiped and served the creature rather than the Creator ... . God therefore delivered them up to disgraceful passions. Their women exchanged natural intercourse for unnatural, and the men gave up natural intercourse with women and burned with lust for one another. Men did shameful things with men, and thus received in their own persons the penalty for their perversity" (Romans 1:24-29). In other letters, he also condemns the acts of "sexual perverts" (I Corinthians 6:10 and I Timothy 1:10). Sadly, some individuals would like to contort these passages to say they really do not condemn the practice of homosexuality but rather some other problem; such a reading is erroneous and defies the consistent teaching of the Church.

While these explicit condemnations exist, the teaching of Sacred Scripture which extols the sanctity of marriage between male and female as husband and wife and their marital love clearly provides the foundation for prohibiting the homosexual action. Secondly, the answer is based on the principles established at the outset of this article. An homosexual union defies the union of husband and wife as designed by God. Such a union cannot capture the symbolism of the two – male and female – complementing each other and becoming one flesh: In such a union they cannot be God's instruments in bringing human life into this world through the normal act of marriage. Even using our reason alone, without any reference to divine revelation, we would have to conclude that the practice of homosexuality is contrary to the natural law.

Some individuals though try to exonerate or to justify homosexual activity by saying that homosexuals do not choose their condition or that their condition is due to biological factors. Granted, homosexuals may not willfully choose their condition. Some psychiatrists and psychologists attribute homosexuality to faulty education, bad example, family environment, or a lack of normal sexual development; in these instances, proper treatment may help the person. On the other hand, other researchers assert that homosexuality is a permanent condition due to biological differences; for, instance, Dr. Simon LeVay has published research promoting such a stance, but such evidence is still considered by the academic community as being inconclusive. Nevertheless, no matter what the etiology of homosexuality may be, the act is still objectively wrong. Granted, the personal culpability may be diminished because of what causes the homosexuality and thereby how freely a person wills the action. Nevertheless, please note that in no way can we justify the homosexual action or deem it a good action; however, the degree of culpability must always be judged "prudently" (*Declaration on Certain Problems of Sexual Ethics*, #8).

While the Church continues to uphold the consistent condemnation of the practice of homosexuality, it has compassion for the homosexual person: "Pastoral care of such homosexuals should be considerate and kind" (*Declaration on Certain Problems of Sexual Ethics*, #8). "They must be accepted with respect, compassion, and sensitivity. Every sign of unjust discrimination in their regard should be avoided" (*Catechism*, #2358). "It is deplorable that homosexual persons have been and are the object of violent malice in speech or in action" (*Letter on the Pastoral Care of Homosexual Persons*, #9). All of these statements distinguish the sin from the sinner.

Recent attention has focused on the relationship between parents and their homosexual children. Parents must show compassion and mercy while upholding the truth of our faith. Parents must love their children, but not the sin of their children. The Church in no way condones the practice nor accepts that the practice can be regarded as a morally neutral "alternate lifestyle." In no way can the Church judge a quasi-marital lifestyle between two people of the same sex as something equally good as heterosexual marriage. Parents have to take strong positions to defend the truth in order to save the souls of their children. Without tolerating the sin, parents must help their children by praying for them, exhorting them to a chaste lifestyle, and directing them to proper counseling or other help – actions parents should follow for any child whether of this orientation or not.

Parents and all of the faithful must be compassionate in reconciling any sinner to the faith. I think of one case where a man had entered a homosexual union, cut off all ties with his family, contracted AIDS, and was dying. Sadly, his family refused to visit him in the hospital, saying, "He's no longer our son," even though he had been reconciled back to God and the Church. The Parable of the Prodigal Son teaches us to act differently. Yes, condemn the sin, but always seek to reconcile the sinner back to God.

In all, the Church does challenge homosexual persons to live a chaste life. Like any Christian, these persons must adhere to God's plan, strive to fulfill His will in their own lives, and unite themselves in their interior suffering to Christ. They too must embrace the cross.

In this spiritual struggle, the Church reaches out to homosexuals and does strive to help them lead such a chaste life. In 1980, a group called Courage was founded by a group of priests and psychologists for persons struggling with homosexuality. The group has five purposes: (1) To live chaste lives in accordance with the Roman Catholic Church's teachings on homosexuality. (2) To dedicate their entire lives to Christ through service to others, spiritual reading, prayer, meditation, individual spiritual direction, frequent reception of the sacraments of Penance and of the Holy Eucharist. (3) To foster a spirit of fellowship in which they may share with one another their thoughts and experiences and so ensure that none of them will have to face the problems of homosexuality alone. (4) To be mindful of the truth that chaste friendships are not only possible but necessary in celibate Christian life and to encourage one another in forming and sustaining them. (5) To live lives that may serve as good examples to other homosexuals. While these principles are directed to homosexuals, they also challenge each committed Christian. By the grace of God, each of us must strive to master ourselves, approach Christian perfection, and live in the freedom of God's children.

WHAT WOULD BE THE CRITERIA FOR A "JUST WAR" IN TODAY'S WORLD?

At first hearing, war seems antithetical to Christianity since the Fifth Commandment states, "Thou shalt not kill." However, the intent of the precept forbids the purposeful taking of human life (*Catechism*, #2307). Each person has a duty to preserve his life, and therefore has a right to legitimate self-defense. Although an act of self-defense may have a two-fold effect – the preservation of the person's life and the unfortunate taking of the aggressor's life – the first effect is intended while the second is not.

In preserving its own life, a state – citizens and their governments – must strive to avoid war and settle disputes peacefully and justly. Nevertheless, "governments cannot be denied the right of lawful self-defense, once all peace efforts have failed" (Vatican II, *Pastoral Constitution on the Church in the Modern World*, #79). Such a right does not entail a *carte blanche* permission for any and all acts of war. Just war theory establishes moral parameters for the declaration and waging of war.

St. Augustine (d. 430) was the originator of the just war theory, which St. Thomas Aquinas (d. 1274) later adapted and explicated in his *Summa Theologiae*. St. Thomas maintained that a war may be waged justly under three conditions: First, the legitimate authority who has the duty of caring for and preserving the common good must declare the war. For instance, according to our Constitution, only Congress can legitimately declare a war. A private individual, no matter how much clout he may wield, does not have the right to commit a country to war. (Please note, we could easily get into those technical qualifications of "police actions," "conflicts," and "operations," but to the best of my knowledge Congress has placed restrictions even on these areas.)

Secondly, a just cause for war must exist. St. Augustine, quoted by St. Thomas, said, "A just war is apt to be described as one that avenges wrongs, when a nation or state has to be punished, for refusing to make amends for the wrongs inflicted by its subjects, or to restore what it has seized unjustly."

Finally, St. Thomas said the warring party must have the right intention, "so that they intend the advancement of good or the avoidance of evil." St. Augustine noted, "True religion looks upon as peaceful those wars that are waged not for motives of aggrandizement or cruelty, but with the object of securing peace or punishing evil-doers, and of uplifting the good." An evil intention, such as to destroy a race or to absorb another nation, can turn a legitimately declared war waged for just cause into a wrongful act.

Obviously, since the Middle Ages, warfare has changed dramatically, as witnessed by World War II and the conflicts which have followed it. Therefore, we can expand St. Thomas' and St. Augustine's theory to the following: In preparing to wage a just war (*ius ad bellum*), a country would have to meet the following criteria:

(1) Just cause – The war must confront an unquestioned danger. "The damage inflicted by the aggressor on the nation or community of nations must be lasting, grave, and certain," asserts the *Catechism* (#2309).

(2) Proper authority – The legitimate authority must declare the war and must be acting on behalf of the people.

(3) Right intention – The reasons for declaring the war must actually be the objectives, not a masking of ulterior motives.

(4) Last resort – All reasonable peaceful alternatives must have been exhausted or have been deemed impractical or ineffective. The contentious parties must strive to resolve their differences peacefully before engaging in war, e.g. through negotiation, mediation, or even embargoes. Here too we see the importance of an international mediating body, such as the United Nations.

(5) Proportionality – The good that is achieved by waging war must not be outweighed by the harm. What good is it to wage war if it leaves the country in total devastation with no one really being the "winner"? Modern means of warfare give great weight to this criterion.

(6) Probability of success – The achievement of the war's purpose must have a reasonable chance of success.

If a country can meet these criteria, then it may justly enter war. Moreover, a country could come to the assistance of another country who is not able to defend itself as long as these criteria are met.

However, the event of war does not entail that all means of waging war are licit; essentially, the "all is fair in love and war" rule is flawed. During war, the country must also meet criteria to insure justice is preserved (*ius in bello*):

(1) Discrimination – Armed forces ought to fight armed forces, and should strive not to harm noncombatants purposefully. Moreover, armed forces should not wantonly destroy the enemy's countryside, cities, or economy simply for the sake of punishment, retaliation, or vengeance.

(2) Due Proportion – Combatants must use only those means necessary to achieve their objectives. For example, no one needs to use nuclear missiles to settle a territorial fishing problem. Due proportion also involves mercy towards civilians in general, towards combatants when the resistance stops (as in the case of surrender and prisoners of war), and towards all parties when the war is finished.

While these are "just criteria," they still are wrenching. It seems paradoxical that the Christian religion which promotes love justifies a violent action to establish justice. I do not think any good person wants war. Yet at times we – as an individual, community, or nations – must confront and stop an evil. Pope John Paul II in an address to a group of soldiers stated, "Peace, as taught by Sacred Scripture and the experience of men itself, is more than just the absence of war. And the Christian is aware that on earth a human society that is completely and always peaceful is unfortunately an utopia and that the ideologies which present it as easily attainable only nourish vain hopes. The cause of peace will not go forward by denying the possibility and the obligation to defend it."

While the criteria for waging a just war are reasonable, our modern methods of warfare complicate their application, especially in the areas of proportionality (that the good achieved by waging war must not be outweighed by the harm), discrimination (that armed forces ought to fight armed forces and strive not to bring harm to noncombatants), and due proportion (that combatants use only those means necessary to achieve their objectives and show mercy to all once combat has ceased).

The Second Vatican Council recognized, "The development of armaments by modern science has immeasurably magnified the horrors and wickedness of war. Warfare conducted with these weapons can inflict immense and indiscriminate havoc which goes far beyond the bounds of legitimate defense" (*Gaudium et Spes*, #80). The Council Fathers still had fresh in their minds the ravages of World War II. For example, the Nazis purposefully dropped the "buzz bombs" on London, leveling entire city blocks and killing citizens with the intent of breaking morale. In response, the Allies dropped incendiary bombs ("fire bombs") on Hamburg on July 27, 1943 killing 45,000, and then again on Dresden on February 14, 1945 killing 135,000; in each instance, the time lapse was just twenty-four hours. The atomic bomb exploded at Hiroshima on August 6, 1945, killing about 80,000 people and injuring more than 70,000 others.

During the Cold War, the technology of warfare "advanced," and continues to do so, so that armaments – whether nuclear, biological, or chemical – have the capability of even greater destruction than anything witnessed during World War II. For example, the Office of Technology Assessment in a 1993 study concluded that a single airplane releasing by aerosol 100 kilograms of anthrax spores (a dormant phase of a bacillus that multiplies rapidly in the body, producing toxins and rapid hemorrhaging) on a clear, calm night over the Washington metropolitan area could kill between one and three million people. Obviously adherence to the criteria of proportionality, discrimination, and due proportion is harder than ever.

While affirming the right of a country to defend itself, the Catholic Church condemns indiscriminate "total war": the state of war between two parties does not justify or make fair the use of any means to wage the war. Vatican Council II therefore asserted, "Every act of war directed to the indiscriminate destruction of whole cities or vast areas with their inhabitants is a crime against God and man, which merits firm and unequivocal condemnation" (*Pastoral Constitution on the Church in the Modern World*, #80). Unfortunately, war will always involve the loss of innocent life or the destruction of non-military property; however, the purposeful intent to commit such actions or to wage indiscriminate warfare is not morally justifiable.

To prevent the occurrence of such warfare, the Vatican Council proposed the following means: First, the community of nations ought to alleviate any arms race which not only consumes so many resources which could be used to alleviate the causes of war but also easily creates the "first strike mentality" or the "Mutually Assured Destruction" strategy. Second, international agreements should be ratified and enforced which would equitably work to reduce armaments, build trust among nations, and establish channels for resolving conflicts peacefully. Third, the community of nations should work together to eliminate conditions which jeopardize peace and thereby may cause war, such as poverty, ignorance, or substandard living conditions. Fortunately, we have seen greater progress in these areas either through the efforts of the United Nations or individual countries.

Moreover, governments must be vigilant in protecting their citizens and in working together to eliminate these means of destruction. War is not simply waged between countries. The enemy is not always known. Battles have given way to acts of terrorism. An evil person with some political agenda could obtain or produce a weapon of mass destruction which could then be used against an innocent population without notice. How ironically sad it is to think that during the Cold War, we had greater stability – the United States was pitted against the Soviet Union and each side knew the sites of missile silos and the number of warheads – whereas today some megalomaniac dictator or terrorist could use a weapon of mass destruction indiscriminately.

Jesus said, "Blessed are the peacemakers." Sometimes "making peace" may well include fighting evil, even if it means the sacrifice of life. Most importantly, the world community must eliminate the evils which prompt acts of war and destroy the weapons of mass destruction which will lead to our own mutual destruction.

WHAT DOES THE CHURCH TEACH
ABOUT CAPITAL PUNISHMENT?

The *Catechism* states, "The efforts of the state to curb the spread of behavior harmful to people's rights and to the basic rules of civil society correspond to the requirement of safeguarding the common good. Legitimate public authority has the right and the duty to inflict punishment proportionate to the gravity of the offense" (#2266). Moreover, " ... the traditional teaching of the Church does not exclude recourse to the death penalty, if this is the only possible way of effectively defending human lives against the unjust aggressor" (#2267). (These citations are from the definitive Latin edition of the *Catechism* issued on September 8, 1997, which are modifications to the original text and reflect the teaching of Pope John Paul's encyclical *The Gospel of Life*.) To understand the Church's position in this matter, we have to be clear about the foundational principles governing the teaching.

First, the state has the duty to preserve the common good and to protect its citizens from harm. Therefore, the state may declare and wage a just war against an aggressor outside of the community as well as recognize the individual's legal right of self-defense. A state may also impose just penalties on those individuals who commit crimes and threaten the well-being of society.

Second, justice demands that punishment fit the crime – the penalty must be proportionate to the injury. In this way, punishment provides for proper retribution, deterrence, and reform. As a form of retribution, punishment restores the order of justice which the criminal violated. For example, if a criminal steals something, restitution must be made, such as the return of the stolen property. The criminal may also be deprived of certain freedoms through, for instance, incarceration or fines. Just retribution strives to heal the injury caused by the crime.

Along this line of thought, punishment ought to deter future crime. If justice is rendered fairly and swiftly, specific punishments for specific crimes ought to prevent further crime by either the criminal himself or others. Punishment should not only protect society from a particular criminal but also deter individuals from committing the same crime in the future.

In the end, the punishment of a criminal should incite his reform. The criminal being punished is hopefully moved to see the error of his ways, to repent, and to change his life.

Just punishment strives to balance all three perspectives – retribution, deterrence, and reform. Note also that in applying such punishment, the state must insure to the best of its ability that the person receives a fair trial and that only a legitimate authority impose any sentence.

Following this perspective of punishment, capital punishment may be used only for heinous crimes, crimes which shake the foundations of society and which would necessitate such a severe proportionate punishment. For example, the Old Testament laws permitted the use of capital punishment for serious sins: "If anyone sheds the blood of man, by man shall his blood be shed; for in the image of God has man been made" (Genesis 9:6) and "Whoever strikes a man a mortal blow must be put to death. When a man kills another after maliciously scheming to do so, you must take him even from my altar and put him to death" (Exodus 21:12, 14). However, capital crimes in the Old Testament included not just premeditated murder, but also kidnapping, cursing or striking of parents, sorcery, sodomy, bestiality, and idolatry. These sins were so heinous in the eyes of God and so threatening to the spiritual and physical welfare of the community that justice mandated capital punishment as proper retribution. The capital sentence could inspire reform: The condemned criminal, facing the loss of his life and knowing he will appear before God in judgment, would hopefully repent. The capital sentence could also deter future crime: Removed from society permanently and sent to God for divine justice, the criminal would never inflict injury again. St. Thomas Aquinas affirmed that if the good citizens "are protected and saved by the slaying of the wicked, then the latter may be lawfully put to death." Moreover, the execution of a criminal could also deter others from committing like crimes and inspire their reform.

Please keep in mind the Old Testament does speak of God's divine mercy: "As I live says the Lord God, I swear I take no pleasure in the death of the wicked man, but rather in the wicked man's conversion, that he may live" (Ezekiel 33:11). "That he may live" though may not so much focus on physical life as it does on the spiritual life, whereby the repentant sinner would avoid eternal punishment in Hell.

Finally, capital punishment may be used to punish "malefactors," i.e. people who freely choose to commit a heinous crime. St. Thomas Aquinas asserted that through sin, a man departs from the order of reason and falls away from the dignity of being an individual made in God's image and likeness. A man who commits a heinous crime, he argued, is even worse than a brute beast and even more harmful. Such a man may be permanently extricated: Just as an infectious or diseased organ would be removed to preserve the health of the entire body, so a person who is dangerous or infectious to the community may be executed rather than corrupt or bring harm to the community.

Such a malefactor must be distinguished from an innocent person. Human life is indeed sacred in all forms and all times, and we as innocent human beings have a sacred right to life. However, the Church carefully underscores the inviolability of this right for "innocent life": In the *Declaration on Euthanasia* (1980) the Church asserted, "Nothing and no one can in any way permit the killing of an innocent human being, whether a fetus or an embryo, an infant or an adult, an old person, or one suffering from an incurable disease, or a person who is dying," and in the *Declaration on Procured Abortion* (1974) the Church asserted: "Divine law and natural reason, therefore, exclude all right to the direct killing of an innocent man." Pope John Paul II in his recent encyclical *The Gospel of Life* confirmed, " ... the direct and voluntary killing of an innocent human being is always gravely immoral" (#57). When a person freely commits such a heinous crime and is judged as a threat to society as a whole, that person relinquishes the right to life in this society, this time, this space.

Given this reasoning, the Catholic Church has upheld the right of the state to execute certain criminals. However, while recognizing the traditional teaching of the Church, the United States Catholic Bishop's Conference issued their *Statement on Capital Punishment* (1980) and asserted, " ... In the condition of contemporary American society, the legitimate purposes of punishment do not justify the imposition of the death penalty." The Bishops raised several questions: Does the goal of retribution and the restoration of order justify capital punishment, even for heinous crimes? Does capital punishment successfully deter future crime? Could not imprisonment, including for life, just as effectively protect society from a criminal, provide a chance for his genuine reform, and deter future crime? Can we insure in our justice system sentences which are fair and not discriminatory? Does not capital punishment constitute a cruel punishment which brings anguish to the criminal and his family? Lastly, the Bishops pleaded that by abolishing capital punishment, society would break "the cycle of violence" and make a positive statement about the sanctity of human life and forgiveness.

Reflecting the teaching of Pope John Paul II's *The Gospel of Life*, the *Catechism* also cautions, "If, however, nonlethal means are sufficient to defend and protect people's safety from the aggressor, authority will limit itself to such means, as these are more in keeping with the concrete conditions of the common good and more in conformity with the dignity of the human person. Today, in fact, as a consequence of the possibilities which the state has for effectively preventing crime, by rendering one who has committed an offense incapable of doing harm – without definitively taking away from him the possibility of redeeming himself – the cases in which the execution of the offender is an absolute necessity are very rare, if not practically non-existent" (#2267).

Given this teaching, many Catholics find ourselves agonizing over this issue. Those who support capital punishment because it deters crime can find corroborating sociological reports just like those who argue that it does not deter crime. While trials should be timely, inmates may be confined on death row for even twelve years as their various appeals are processed, a situation which weighs against the deterrence effect of punishment. Fairness in the trial process is another clear issue: we have seen in recent times that those defendants who can afford the "dream team" lawyers who perform before the media seem to have a clear advantage in the judicial process. Our prisons, reporting atrocious crimes within their confines and recidivism rates as high as 60% after release, have failed to reform most criminals.

Most troubling are the types of crimes that afflict innocent human beings. We face each day the actions of the McVeighs, Bundys, and Dahlmers. Some crimes are so brutal that one must ask, "What kind of a human being could possibly commit such a crime?" Perhaps some individuals have become so filled with evil, blinded to truth and good, and have no remorse for the crimes they have committed, that, as St. Thomas Aquinas would posit, they must be extricated from society like a diseased organ.

Moreover, capital sentences and executions are rare. In Virginia in 1994, there were 23,947 convictions for violent crime. Of these, 55 criminals were sentenced to death, or .2% Moreover, only two criminals were executed, or .008%

Jurisdictions are now constructing state-of-the-art prisons which could eliminate the death penalty and effectively remove a criminal from society. Currently, the Commonwealth of Virginia is building two new "super maximum" security prisons, one at Big Stone Gap and one at Pound. Both will hold 1,267 inmates. Those in the special segregated population will be confined individually 23 hours a day in a 7-by-12 foot cell. The narrow slat for a window will have smoked glass so the prisoner cannot see outside the cell. The prisoner will have an exercise period of one hour a day, pacing by himself in a narrow concrete yard. These segregated prisoners will have no group activities and no educational or vocational programs. The worst criminals will have no reading materials. When visitors are allowed, no physical contact will be allowed. Does this hellish existence show love, promise reform, or reflect real improvements in our penal system, or uphold the dignity of the person?

Moreover, each year we hear of how criminals like Charles Manson are eligible for parole and could be allowed to return to society. Can there be true peace when families of victims and other citizens live in fear that the criminal may soon return?

The issue of capital punishment is very difficult indeed. We as Catholics do uphold the sanctity of human life. We also realize that at times life regrettably must be taken to establish peace and protect society – we must go to war, defend our own lives, and stop crime. The concerns surrounding capital punishment are real and must be continually addressed to insure justice. Any good Catholic, as a believer and as a citizen, must wrestle with these issues and decide what will best promote justice.

WHAT IS THE CHURCH'S TEACHING ON EUTHANASIA?

Pope Pius XII, who witnessed and condemned the eugenics and euthanasia programs of the Nazis, was the first to explicate clearly this moral problem and provide guidance. In 1980, the Sacred Congregation for the Doctrine of the Faith released its *Declaration on Euthanasia* which further clarified this guidance, especially in light of the increasing complexity of life-support systems and the promotion of euthanasia as a valid means of ending life. Addressing the increasing momentum of the euthanasia movement, Pope John Paul II in his encyclical *The Gospel of Life* (#64) warned against the "alarming symptoms of the 'culture of death' ... which sees the growing number of elderly and disabled people as intolerable and too burdensome." The *Catechism* (#2276-2279) provides a succinct explanation of our Catholic teaching on this subject.

Before addressing the issue of euthanasia itself, we must first remember that the Catholic Church holds as sacred both the dignity of each individual person and the gift of life. Therefore, the following principles are morally binding: First, to make an attempt on the life of or to kill an innocent person is an evil action. Second, each person is bound to lead his life in accord with God's plan and with openness to His will, looking to life's fulfillment in Heaven. Finally, intentionally committing suicide is a murder of oneself and considered a rejection of God's plan. For these reasons, Vatican Council II condemned "all offenses against life itself, such as murder, genocide, abortion, euthanasia, and willful suicide ... " (*Pastoral Constitution on the Church in the Modern World*, #27).

Given these principles, we believe that each person is bound to use ordinary means of caring for personal health. Here one would think of proper nourishment – food and water – and ordinary medical care. Ordinary means would be those which offer reasonable hope of benefit and are not unduly burdensome to either the patient or the family.

A person may, but is not bound to, use extraordinary mean those means which primarily are not considered ordinary medic care. In our world today, however, exactly what constitutes extr ordinary medical care becomes harder and harder to define. Fc instance, accepting an artificial heart is clearly experimental an would be extraordinary, whereas the usage of a respirator or venti lator is oftentimes standard procedure to aid the patient's recovery

To help navigate through this confusing area of extraordinar means, the focus should be on whether the treatment provides rea sonable hope of benefit to the patient and what the degree of bur den is to the patient and his family. Factors to consider in making this decision would be the type of treatment, the degree of complexity, the amount of risk involved, its cost and accessibility, and the state of the sick person and his resources. One would weigh the proportion of pain and suffering against the amount of good to be done.

Given this notion of health care, we can turn to the subject at hand. Euthanasia, literally translated as "good death" or "easy death," is "an action or omission which of itself or by intention causes death, in order that all suffering may in this way be eliminated" (*Declaration on Euthanasia*). In other words, euthanasia involves the purposeful termination of life by a direct action, such as lethal injection, or by an omission, such as starvation or dehydration.

Note that euthanasia is commonly known as "mercy killing," a misleading term. The act involves an intentional killing of an innocent person, an intrinsically evil act, no matter how good the intention may be to alleviate suffering. Pope John Paul II also asserted that euthanasia involves a false mercy, a perversion of mercy: "True compassion leads to sharing another's pain; it does not kill the person whose suffering we cannot bear" (*The Gospel of Life*, #66). Therefore, the Holy Father confirmed, "Taking into account these distinctions, in harmony with the Magisterium of my Predecessors and in communion with the bishops of the Catholic Church, I confirm that euthanasia is a grave violation of the law of God, since it is the deliberate and morally unacceptable killing of an human person" (#65).

However, euthanasia must be distinguished from the stopping of extraordinary means of health care or other aggressive medical treatment. The patient, or guardian in the case of an unconscious patient, has the right to reject outright or to discontinue those procedures which are extraordinary, no longer correspond to the real situation of the patient, do not offer a proportionate good, do not offer reasonable hope of benefit, impose excessive burdens on the patient and his family, or are simply "heroic." Such a decision is most appropriate when death is clearly imminent and inevitable. Here a person may refuse forms of treatment which at best provide a precarious and burdensome prolonging of life. In these cases, the person would place himself in God's hands and prepare to leave this life, while maintaining ordinary means of health care.

For instance several years ago, a dear priest friend of mine was diagnosed with pancreatic cancer and told he would die from the disease. Rather than undergo painful chemotherapy or radiation which would only give him perhaps 6 months more to live this life, he entered the hospice program which provided nourishment, pain medication, and excellent nursing care. He prepared himself to meet the Lord whom he served as a priest for 45 years. This decision was perfectly moral.

Another friend of mine was dying of prostate cancer which had metastasized throughout his body. When I last saw him in the hospital, he had gone into a comma and was being fed intravenously and was breathing with a respirator. His kidneys had failed. The doctors told the family that they could do nothing more and the situation was not reversible. At that point, the medical technology was not providing any hope of recovery or benefit, but rather was simply prolonging death. The family decided to turn-off the respirator, which had now become an extraordinary means, and hours later my friend went to meet his Lord. This action was morally permissible and different from purposefully terminating life.

Granted, no one enjoys suffering. However, we must remember that each of us is baptized into Christ's passion, death, and resurrection. We all share in our Lord's cross, which at times may be very painful. This suffering, however, especially at the last moments of one's life, must be seen as a sharing in our Lord's sufferings. By uniting our suffering with our Lord's, we expiate the hurt caused by our own sins and help to expiate the sins of others, just as some of the early martyrs did who offered their sufferings for sinners. Sometimes, such suffering finally heals the wounds that have divided families. In all, we must look to Christ to aid us in our suffering and guide us from this life to Himself.

None of these cases is easy. However, there is a great difference between purposely killing someone and allowing a person to die peacefully with dignity. We must remember that "what a sick person needs, besides medical care, is love, the human and supernatural warmth with which the sick person can and ought to be surrounded by all those close to him or her, parents and children, doctors and nurses" (*Declaration on Euthanasia*).

WHAT IS THE CHURCH'S TEACHING REGARDING SUICIDE?

Before addressing the act of suicide, we must first remember that God is the giver of all life. Each of us has been made in God's image and likeness (Genesis 1:27) with both a body and a soul. Therefore, life is sacred from the moment of conception until natural death, and no one can justify the intentional taking of an innocent human life.

For Christians, this teaching takes on even greater depth because our Lord entered this world and our own human condition. Our Lord knew the joy and pain, success and failure, pleasure and suffering, happiness and sorrow that come in this life. He also showed us how to live this life in the love of God and trusting in His will. Moreover, Jesus suffered, died, and rose to free us from sin and give us the promise of everlasting life. Through our baptism, we share a new life in the Lord. St. Paul reminds us, "You have been purchased, and at a price. So glorify God in your body" (I Corinthians 6:20).

Therefore, we must be mindful that the preservation of our life, body and soul, is not something discretionary but obligatory. We must preserve and nourish both our physical and spiritual life. The *Catechism* asserts, "Everyone is responsible for his life before God who has given it to him. It is God who remains the sovereign Master of life. We are obliged to accept life gratefully and preserve it for his honor and the salvation of our souls. We are stewards, not owners, of the life God has entrusted to us. It is not ours to dispose of" (#2280).

With this foundation in mind, we can see why suicide has traditionally been considered a gravely wrong moral action, i.e. a mortal sin. Our Holy Father affirmed this position in his recent encyclical *The Gospel of Life* (#66). (Please note that suicide is distinguished from the sacrifice of one's life for God or another, as in the cases of martyrdom, or of offering one's life or risking it to save another person.)

The intentional taking of one's own life is wrong for several reasons: First, in the most basic sense, each human being naturally seeks to preserve his life. To take our own life defies our natural instinct to live.

Second, suicide violates a genuine love for oneself and one's neighbors – family, friends, neighbors, and even acquaintances. Other people need us and depend upon us in ways we may not even know. When I as a priest have had to comfort the family of a suicide victim, I hope that the person somehow realizes how much he really was loved and needed. I also feel sad that this poor troubled person faced something so seemingly unbearable, insurmountable, or agonizing that he chose to withdraw from the love of God and others, and kill himself.

Finally, suicide defies the love we owe God. Sure, we all face the tough times, hardships, and sufferings. However, we are called to place ourselves in the hands of God who will never abandon us, but see us safely through this life. The words of the Our Father, "thy will be done," must be real for us. To commit suicide is to reject His lordship in our life.

Therefore, objectively, suicide is a mortal sin. (Moreover, to help someone commit suicide is also a mortal sin.) Here though we must remember that for a sin to be mortal and cost someone salvation, the objective action (in this case the taking of one's own life) must be grave or serious matter; the person must have an informed intellect (know that this is wrong); and the person must give full consent of the will (intend to commit this action). In the case of suicide, I wonder whether a person always has full consent of the will. Fear, force, ignorance, habit, passion, and psychological problems can impede the exercise of the will so that a person may not be fully responsible or even responsible at all for an action. Here again the *Catechism* states, "Grave psychological disturbances, anguish, or grave fear of hardship, suffering, or torture can diminish the responsibility of the one committing suicide" (#2282).

This qualification does not make suicide a right action in any circumstance; however, it does make us realize that the person may not be totally culpable for the action because of various circumstances or personal conditions.

Only God can read the depths of our soul. Only He knows how much we love Him and how responsible we are for our actions. We leave the judgment then to Him alone. The *Catechism* offers words of great hope: "We should not despair of the eternal salvation of persons who have taken their own lives. By ways known to Him alone, God can provide the opportunity for salutary repentance. The Church prays for persons who have taken their own lives" (#2283). Therefore, we do offer the Mass for the repose of the soul of a suicide victim, invoking God's tender love and mercy, and His healing grace for the grieving loved ones.

SPECIAL TOPICS

WHAT WAS POPE PIUS XII'S ROLE IN SAVING THE JEWS DURING WORLD WAR II?

To begin to understand Pius XII's actions during World War II, we must remember the world in which he lived. Hitler had assumed control of Germany in 1933. In July of that same year, he began not only persecuting Jews but also Christians. He infiltrated the German Evangelical Federation (the Lutheran Church), removing leaders who were opposed to his agenda. Many of these ministers died in concentration camps or prisons, like the famous Dietrich Bonhoffer.

The persecution was even more intense for the Catholic Church. Gestapo agents attended Mass and listened to every homily preached, prepared to arrest any priest attacking or criticizing the regime. Chanceries were searched for any "incriminating" documents. Communication with Rome was limited. Nazi propaganda represented the Church as unpatriotic and hoarding wealth with its clerics portrayed as idle and avaricious. By 1940, all Catholic schools had been closed, and religious instruction confined to the Church itself or at home. Meanwhile, anti-Christian teaching was imparted in the public schools.

Remember too that the first concentration camp was established in 1933 at Dacchau, outside of Munich. This camp was not so much an "extermination camp" as one for the "political" prisoners, including priests. The camp administration so feared the influence of the priests upon the rest of the prisoners that a special cellblock surrounded by barbed wire was created – Block 26, Priesterblock – to isolate them. At Dacchau alone, 2,720 priests were imprisoned (of which 1,000 died), and were subjected to the most awful tortures, including the medical experiments of the notorious Dr. Rascher.

Such persecution was not confined to Germany. For example, the Church in Poland also suffered severely. During the first four months of occupation following the September, 1939 invasion, 700 priests were shot and 3,000 were sent to concentration camps (of which 2,600 died). Countless other Catholics – priests, religious, and laity – in other countries died for the faith during the Nazi era.

Pope Pius XI, who had condemned Nazism in his 1937 encyclical *Mit Brennender Sorge*, died in February, 1939, and Pope Pius XII succeeded him as the successor of St. Peter on March 12. Think of the world and the Church Pope Pius XII had inherited!

To make matters worse, by June, 1940, Hitler controlled Europe and northern Africa, and was planning the invasion of Britain. The Vatican, officially a neutral country, was isolated. Hitler had plans to depose Pius XII, appoint his own "puppet" Pope, and move the Vatican administration to Germany, plans which would have been executed if the war would have gone in the Nazi's favor. Who then was to come to the aid of the Vatican? Pius XII, who had to insure the survival of the Church, was very much alone.

Despite the overwhelming evil of Nazism, Pius XII spoke out. After the invasion of Poland in October, 1939, he denounced the aggression of the Nazis and proposed a peace plan. In 1940, he called for the triumph over hatred, mistrust, and the spirit of "cold egoism." The following year, he pleaded for the rights of small nations and national minorities, and condemned total warfare and religious persecution.

In his Christmas message of 1942, he specifically denounced the extermination of the Jews: *The New York Times* praised this message, writing, "This Christmas more than ever Pope Pius XII is a lonely voice crying out of the silence of a continent. The pulpit whence he speaks is more than ever like the Rock on which the Church was founded, a tiny island lashed and surrounded by a sea of war ... . When a leader bound impartially to nations on both sides condemns as heresy the new form of national state which subordinates everything to itself; when he declares that whoever wants peace must protect against 'arbitrary attacks' the 'juridical safety of individuals'; when he assails violent occupation of territory, the exile and persecution of human beings for no reason other than race or political opinion; when he says that people must fight for a just and decent peace, a 'total peace' – the 'impartial' judgment is like a verdict in a high court of justice."

Besides these worldwide pleas for peace, the Vatican persistently issued communications of protest to Hitler which were attested to by von Ribbentrop at the Nuremburg war trials, who said, "I do not recollect [how many] at the moment, but I know we had a whole deskful of protests from the Vatican. There were very many we did not even read or reply to." Pope Pius XII's position was so clear to the Nazis that he was sometimes referred to as "The Chief Rabbi of the Christian world," and his papal ambassadors as "Prime Ministers for the Jews."

Pope Pius XII also acted. His Holiness allowed the Vatican diplomatic corps which were protected by diplomatic immunity to carry messages between the Allied Powers. Vatican Information Services also sent over 5 million messages for soldiers. For Jews fleeing Nazi occupied territory, the Vatican assisted them with financial resources as well as necessary paperwork. During the Nazi occupation of Rome (September, 1943 to June, 1944), Pius XII helped to raise the Gestapo's demand of 50 kilos of gold from the Jewish community for "their safety." Unfortunately, the payment did not prevent the eventual round-up of Jews. However, of the 9,500 Jews in Rome, the Nazis only captured 1,259; the rest were hidden safely in churches, monasteries, convents, and the Vatican itself.

He hid 3,000 Jews at his summer residence, Castle Gandolfo, and recruited 400 for his Swiss guards. He also lifted cloister restrictions, allowing religious houses to offer refuge for Jews. He allowed the issuance of false baptismal certificates to Jews. These deeds do not even include the general relief efforts and distribution of food coordinated by the Vatican for the city of Rome. Pinchas Lapide, a former senior Israeli government official, has proven with documentation from the Yad Vashem archives that papal relief and rescue programs saved at least 860,000 Jewish lives – more than any other agency or government, independently or together.

We too must remember that any defiance of the Nazi regime meant immediate and severe retaliation. The Catholic bishops of Holland were particularly outspoken in their protests against Nazism; for this, 80% of all Jews were arrested and deported – more than any other country in western Europe – and persecution against the Church was extremely cruel. Jean Bernard, Bishop of Luxembourg, who was detained at Dacchau, later wrote, "The detained priests trembled every time news reached us of some protest by a religious authority, but particularly by the Vatican. We all had the impression that our warders made us atone heavily for the fury these protests evoked." Cardinal Sapieha, Archbishop of Krakow, wrote to Pius XII in 1942, "We must deplore that we cannot communicate your Holiness' letters to the faithful, for that would provide a pretext for fresh persecution. We already have many who are victims because they were suspected of being in secret communication with the Apostolic See." Historian Norman Davies, scholar of Polish history, commented, "To ask why the Pope or Catholics in Poland did not do more to assist Jews, is rather like asking why Jews did nothing to assist persecuted Catholics. In a world where immediate death awaited anyone who contravened Nazi regulations both Catholic and Jew were victim." Clearly, Pius XII was burdened with speaking the truth while safeguarding the survival of the Church.

When Pope Pius XII died on October 9, 1958, Golda Meir, then Israeli delegate to the United Nations, sent official condolences: "When fearful martyrdom came to our people in the decade of Nazi terror, the voice of the Pope was raised for the victims. The life of our times was enriched by a voice speaking out on the great moral truths above the tumult of daily conflict. We mourn a great servant of peace." Dr. Raphael Cantoni, a leader in Italy's Jewish Assistance Committee added, "The Church and the Papacy have saved Jews as much and insofar as they could Christians. Six million of my co-religionists have been murdered by the Nazis ... but there would have been many more victims had it not been for the efficacious intervention of Pius XII." Therefore, for anyone to condemn so easily in hindsight Pope Pius or the Church as a whole for the course of action taken during World War II reveals an ignorance of history.

WHAT ARE THE FACTS ABOUT THE INQUISITION?

Before approaching the history óf the Inquisition, one must keep in mind two basic points: First, the Church has been entrusted by the Lord to preserve the deposit of faith and to hand on the authentic faith to later generations. At the Ascension, Christ said to the apostles, "Teach them to carry out everything I have commanded you" (Matthew 28:20). Therefore, heresy – "the obstinate post-baptismal denial of some truth which must be believed with divine and Catholic faith" (*Catechism*, #2089) – was seen as a particularly grave sin. Not only was a heretic's soul in jeopardy, but also his false teaching jeopardized the souls of others. The Church, as the guardian of souls, had to "root out" any such heresy.

Second, remember that the Roman Catholic Church was the only Church in western Europe until Martin Luther started the Protestant movement in 1517. (The Orthodox Churches had separated in the year 1054, but that schism involved parts of eastern Europe and the Middle East.) Since there was one Church, oftentimes Church and state worked together. Also, kings generally saw themselves as guardians of the faith and believed it their duty to protect their people from error. For example, King Peter of Aragon stated, "The enemies of the Cross of Christ and violators of the Christian law are likewise our enemies and the enemies of our kingdom, and ought therefore to be dealt with as such."

With this in mind, we can turn to the Inquisition. In his bull *Excommunicamus*, Pope Gregory IX formally instituted the Inquisition in 1231 as a means of repressing heresy, particularly that of the Albigensians. Prior to this time, similar mechanisms had existed: For instance, St. Augustine (d. 430) upheld the right of the state to punish the Donatist heretics for their own benefit as well as for protecting the faithful, although he also maintained that charitable and convincing instruction should be used before any corporal punishment (short of execution). The Inquisition was first established in Germany, extended to Spain in 1232, and became a general institution by 1233. The Dominicans were recruited by Conrad of Marburg, Germany to assist in the Inquisition. (Note however that St. Dominic died in 1221 and had no connection with the Inquisition, despite the claims of some misguided individuals.) Later, the Franciscans also were recruited to serve as inquisitors.

Usually, two inquisitors with equal power held directly from the Pope presided over the tribunal. At first, these inquisitors rode a circuit to hear cases of those accused as heretics. Shortly thereafter, permanent inquisitions were established with a territorial jurisdiction. For example, the Inquisition based at Paris held jurisdiction over all of France, until the 14th century when another one was held at Tours.

One must remember that one of the primary purposes of a formalized Inquisition was to insure justice and to eliminate unfounded charges or vigilante justice. The inquisitors even followed a guide, such as the *Processus inquisitionis* (1249) which outlined various acts and provided commentary about certain cases. Accordingly, an inquisitor could bring a charge against any individual who had been accused by someone or was suspected of heresy. The accused person would take an oath swearing to tell the truth and was confronted with the evidence. The accused, however, was neither informed of the identity of the witnesses nor allowed to confront them; this practice was adopted to protect the witnesses from reprisals from family or friends. On the other hand, the accused had to supply witnesses in his defense: Inquisitor Eymeric stated, "If the accused has public opinion against him, but nevertheless it cannot be proved that he has deserved his reputation as a heretic, he has only to produce witnesses who can testify to his condition and habitual residence, and who, from long knowledge can affirm that he is not heretical." Nevertheless, the accused could appeal to the Pope prior to the final judgment, and many did.

Unfortunately with the revival of Roman law, the Inquisition sometimes used torture to gain a confession. However, remember that torture was used regularly in matters involving civil law. As a matter of fact, as early as the fourteenth century, papal intervention curbed the use of torture by the Inquisition. Bernardo Gui, one of the most famous inquisitors, commented that torture was deceiving and inefficacious because it forced the confession.

If the accused was found guilty of heresy, the inquisitor had to obtain the approval of the bishop and a council of qualified consultors, lay and cleric, known as the *boni viri* ("good men") before pronouncing a sentence; this process allowed a second review of the case. Penalties for those judged as heretics but who recanted included scourging, making pilgrimages to various shrines, confiscation of property, or wearing a yellow fabric cross sewn on the front and back of one's clothing. For serious cases, imprisonment, sometimes for life, was the sentence. However, life imprisonment was not the norm: For example, inquisitor Bernard de Caux condemned only 23 out of 207 guilty heretics to life imprisonment. Moreover, those who had made false accusations were required to wear two red tongues made of cloth sewn to their clothing.

If a condemned heretic was recalcitrant and refused to repent, then he would be turned over to the state. The state, according to civil law, could impose the death penalty for heresy, which usually meant burning at the stake. Note that the Church itself could not impose the death penalty and actually pleaded for mercy in these cases. Here too remember, capital punishment was not an unusual civil punishment, even for simple theft or counterfeiting. St. Thomas Aquinas stated, "It is more wicked to corrupt the faith on which depends the life of the soul than to debase the coinage which provides merely for temporal life; wherefore if coiners and other malefactors are justly doomed to death, much more may heretics be justly slain once they are convicted."

However, the usage of the death penalty has been exaggerated. For example, Bernardo Gui during his long career (1307-1324) pronounced 930 sentences of which 139 were acquittals, 300 involved religious penances, and 42 resulted in the death sentence imposed by the state.

The Inquisition climaxed in the late 14th century. During the 1400s it continued to decline throughout most of Europe. By 1509, the Inquisition lost authority in France. It survived the longest in

Spain and in its New World colonies, until being finally suppressed in 1834. The Holy Office, established in 1542, later took over the duties of investigating heresy and became a court of final appeal.

The Spanish Inquisition seems to hold the greatest notoriety. However, evidence shows that between 1540 and 1700, only 828 persons were executed, or one out of eight cases. 90% of the accused were never tortured. Throughout the entire Spanish Empire, between 1560 and 1614, only 2% of the cases brought before the Inquisition resulted in execution.

Is the Catholic Church alone guilty of an "inquisition"? Hardly. During the Protestant revolt, Luther, Zwingli, Calvin, and the English Tudors all used and condoned torture and capital punishment for heresy. For instance, John Calvin, during his rule of Geneva between 1546-64, had 58 executed for heresy or serious sin, 73 exiled, and 900 imprisoned out of a population of 20,000. In England during the reign of Elizabeth I (1559-1603), over 250 Catholics were executed, many first suffering horrible tortures; many were sentenced to being hanged, drawn, and quartered (hanged until unconscious, disemboweled, and then cut into four pieces) and priests had the added punishment of being emasculated. Moreover, in post-Reformation Europe, Britain executed over 30,000 as witches, and Germany, over 100,000.

We cannot deny the Inquisition, and we cannot white-wash it. However, we must know the facts and the historical context in which it existed. The Inquisition was not a "Catholic event," and the methods used were the same employed by the law for civil offenses. We fortunately live in an age of toleration. Nevertheless, we must defend the truth, but as St. Augustine noted, through charitable and convincing instruction.

HOW DO CATHOLICS UNDERSTAND THE CREATION ACCOUNT OF GENESIS AND EVOLUTION?

In an address to a recent meeting of the Pontifical Academy of Sciences (1996), the Holy Father commented on the subject of evolution and recognized the progress of science in explaining the origins of life and the process of creation. However, the Pope also underscored the compatibility of scientific evidence with the truths of faith, and of science with theology: "Consideration of the method used in diverse orders of knowledge allows for the concordance of two points of view which seem irreconcilable. The sciences of observation describe and measure with ever greater precision the multiple manifestations of life ... while theology extracts ... the final meaning according to the Creator's designs." The Pope further reminded the Pontifical Academy that the truth of revelation cannot contradict truth of scientific evidence, and vice versa. Instead, the questions to be addressed are "How do the conclusions reached by the various scientific disciplines coincide with those contained in the message of revelation? And if, at first sight, there are apparent contradictions, in what direction do we look for their solution?" Before focusing on the specific issue of evolution, let us first approach the Genesis account of creation and the truths of faith we find revealed in it.

We must remember that Genesis was not meant to be a scientific explanation of how creation occurred. The first three chapters of Genesis which address creation, the fall of man, and the promise of salvation do not pretend to be a text of physics or biology which provides a scientific understanding of mankind and the world. Rather, the Genesis account of creation is a work of theology which focuses on the who, why, and what of creation. Writing centuries before the birth of our Lord, the inspired sacred authors under the guidance of the Holy Spirit wove a story to capture truths of God and His creation. Since Abraham lived approximately 1850 BC, the stories of Genesis were probably preserved orally for centuries before ever being produced in written form.

To appreciate the beauty and significance of the Genesis account, we must examine the pagan cultures surrounding the Jewish people. They lived among these various cultures, each of whom had their own religion and likewise their own creation stories. For instance, the Babylonians had a story called the *Enuma Elish*. Here the deities Apsu (male) and Tiamat (female) begot another god named Ea, who is turn had a son named Marduke. Ea slew Apsu, and Marduke then slew Tiamat. From the carcass of Tiamat, Marduke fashioned the world. Marduke also slew Kingu, Tiamat's counselor, and with his blood, fashioned mankind.

The Egyptian cult of the Sun based at the city of Heliopolis described how Atum-Re (or Ra), the sun god, was produced from Nun, the waters of chaos. Atum-Re then fertilized himself committing an act of divine masturbation and ejaculated Shu (air) and Tefnut (moisture), giving them his vital force or *ka*. Shu and Tefnut in turn produced Geb (earth) and Nut (sky), and other gods. This same story told of how humans were produced from the tears flowing from the eyes of Atum-Re.

Other Egyptian religious cults had other creation stories. The cult at Memphis told of how whatever the god Ptah had conceived in his heart and had spoken with his tongue produced all living beings. The cult of Elephantine described the god Khnum as a potter fashioning all living beings on a potter's wheel from clay. Granted, some elements from these stories are similar to ones found in Genesis, yet the difference between these stories and Genesis is vast.

Take a good look at the first Genesis account of creation, 1:1 - 2:4. Here we find an omnipotent, omniscient, all-loving, eternal, and infinite God. He creates freely according to His divine wisdom and is motivated by genuine love.

God creates all things from nothing (*ex nihilo*), creating even that from which creation is made. However, He is distinct from His creation. The Hebrew text uses the word *bara* for "create," and this word is used only for an action of God on the world. The object created is always something that is new, wonderful, and astonishing. The creative word of God is not only personal, responsible, and efficacious, but also life-giving. Recall that the Lord said to Isaiah: " ... So shall my word be that goes forth from my mouth; it shall not return to me void, but shall do my will, achieving the end for which I sent it" (Isaiah 55:11). Therefore, the created world owes not only its existence to God, but also all that it is, its nature, its purpose, and its design.

In Genesis, God creates in a very orderly fashion, following a seven-day plan. The number seven was considered a perfect number for the Jews. Although the word day normally means a twenty-four-hour period of time, it can also be used for a season, a particular time or event (e.g. "judgment day"), or a period of time. We must remember that God is infinite and thereby is not bound by time. Consequently, in Genesis, day and the seven-day sequence refer more to a designed, purposeful span of time over which God creates.

Although not a scientific account, the unfolding of creation follows a divine plan that makes logical sense from a human perspective. Most importantly, at the end of each day, God looks at creation and recognizes it as very good. This point about the goodness of creation is emphasized repeatedly to refute any notion that the material world is evil, corrupt, or depraved, as some cultures or cults thought.

Moreover, Genesis climaxes with the creation of man and woman: "God created man in His image; in the divine image He created them; male and female He created them" (1:27). This beautiful verse highlights that only man and woman reflect God's image and likeness. Moreover, both man and woman, although different, equally reflect the image and likeness of God. From this belief, we believe that God has created and given to each of us an unique and immortal soul.

Another beautiful point is in the verse that follows: Genesis reads, "God blessed them, saying, 'Be fertile and multiply; fill the earth and subdue it.'" Here we find the institution of marriage, and can posit that the fullness of being in the image and likeness of God occurs when man and woman enter into the blessed union of Holy Matrimony as husband and wife becoming one flesh. Here man and woman as husband and wife may even participate in God's creative love and bring forth new life. Moreover, man and woman are called to be good stewards, using creation wisely and for the good of all.

Immediately, we can see the differences between Genesis and the creation accounts of surrounding cultures. Genesis has no generation of a god or gods; in Genesis, God is eternal. In the other accounts, creation is the product of divine sexual activity, power struggles, murder, accident, and whim; in Genesis, God creates through His eternal Reason – His Word – and His creativity has order, design, uniqueness, and purpose. Unlike the other creation stories, Genesis emphasizes a loving God who freely created all things good, and made mankind in His image and likeness, endowing them with an unique, immortal soul. The God of Genesis is not part of creation; rather, God transcends creation, but is present to, upholds, and sustains creation which is "good" in His eyes. Finally, we must not forget that all creation, indeed the whole story of the Old Testament, is moving toward Christ and derives its true meaning from Christ through whom all things were created and who reconciled all things in His person (cf. Colossians 1:15-21). (Cf. *Catechism*, #295-301).

Given this understanding of Genesis, how then can we reconcile it with the scientific theories of "Big Bang" and evolution? First, we must remember that a theory is a statement, or "story," which tries to explain a set of phenomena. Just as Genesis is a story, albeit inspired by the Holy Spirit, which presents truths of God's creativity, Big Bang coupled with evolution form a story or theory posited to explain scientific evidence surrounding creation. According to these theories, billions of years ago, an explosion – a "Big Bang" – started the expansion of the universe which continues to this day. In essence, creation has evolved over time and will continue to evolve. One must pause however and note that the Big Bang theory presents creation by chance, error, and dissonance rather than a reasoned, ordered, designed progression. Nevertheless, scientific evidence does give some credence to this theory, and for this reason the Holy Father said, "Today ... new knowledge leads us to recognize that the theory of evolution is more than a hypothesis." Note, however, the Holy Father did not say that either theory, Big Bang or evolution, captures the whole truth surrounding creation.

To date, scientists are continually refining the Big Bang theory and evolution, especially in light of DNA research, NASA's Hubbel space-telescope findings, and recent fossil discoveries in the Namibian desert of southwestern Africa. Honest scientists would be the first to admit that they simply do not have all of the answers regarding creation. Legitimate questions still are left unanswered: "If evolution has occurred, why haven't any fish recently climbed onto the beach or an ape evolved into a human? If "Big Bang" is true with its chaotic chain reaction, how did such order come to the universe and all creation, including our own physical being? How did life ever come about, especially human life with all of its abilities to create and to think?" Such questions lead one to admit that science does not have all of the answers, and probably never will. We can accept much of the findings of science and yet tenaciously hold onto the belief of an omniscient, omnipotent, eternal God who freely and lovingly creates and continues to guide creation to its fulfillment. Even Einstein admitted that in the laws of nature "there is revealed such a superior Reason that everything significant which has arisen out of human thought and arrangement is, in comparison with it, the merest empty reflection."

What then about Adam and Eve and the evolution of human beings? Here we also struggle with science, especially those who would contend that human beings evolved from a lower life form. We also wonder how the world grew in population when according to Genesis God made Adam and Eve who had three sons – Abel, Cain, and Seth, yet later Cain has relations with his wife who seems to appear in the story (Genesis 4:17). Keep in mind that science focuses on how we came to be whereas theology is more concerned with who we are. Science again does not have all of the answers, and the Bible does not provide all the details of creation. Anthropologists continue to revise their "theories" about the development of man and the transition from *homo habilis* to *homo erectus* to *homo sapiens*. Actually, studying DNA sequences, Allan Wilson of the University of California at Berkeley, with other scientists, have posited that all living human beings share a single common female ancestor (whom they interestingly have dubbed "Eve") who lived in Africa about 200,000 years ago. (In all fairness, other anthropologists offer critiques of this theory, again showing that no one has all of the details about creation.)

Responding to the creation of human beings and evolution, Pope Pius XII in his encyclical *Humani generis* (1950) reminded us that in our Catholic faith we believe that God directly creates and infuses an unique soul to each individual. (In Pope John Paul's address, he cited *Humani generis* and underscored this truth.) Concerning Adam and his progeny, Pope Pius XII asserted, "For the faithful cannot embrace that opinion which maintains either that after Adam there existed on this earth true men who did not take their origin through natural generation from him as from the first parent of all, or that Adam represents a certain number of first parents. Now it is in no way apparent how such an opinion can be reconciled with that which the sources of revealed truth and the documents of the teachings authority of the Church propose with regard to original sin, which proceeds from a sin actually committed by an individual Adam and which through generation is passed on to all and is in everyone as his own." While "in no way is it apparent" now does not entail that it will not be later.

Reflecting on the story of Genesis and its compatibility with science, Cardinal Ratzinger said in a homily preached in 1981, "We must have the audacity to say that the great projects of the living creation are not the products of chance and error. Nor are they the products of a selective process to which divine predicates can be attributed in illogical, unscientific, and even mythic fashion. The great projects of the living creation point to a creating Reason and show us a creating Intelligence, and they do so more luminously and radiantly today than ever before. Thus we can say today with a new certitude and joyousness that the human being is indeed a divine project which only the creating Intelligence was strong and great and audacious enough to conceive of. The human being is not a mistake but something willed; he is the fruit of love. He can disclose in himself, in the bold project that he is, the language of the creating Intelligence that speaks to him and that moves him to say: 'Yes, Father you have willed me.'" From Cardinal Ratzinger's remarks, we see the need to appreciate the scientific understanding while maintaining the truths of faith.

The *Catechism* summarizes the discussion well: "Among all the Scriptural texts about creation, the first three chapters of Genesis occupy an unique place. From a literary standpoint, these texts may have had diverse sources. The inspired authors have placed them at the beginning of Scripture to express in their solemn language the truths of creation – its origin and its end in God, its order and goodness, the vocation of man, and finally the drama of sin and the hope of salvation. Read in the light of Christ, within the unity of Sacred Scripture and in the living Tradition of the Church, these texts remain the principal source for catechesis on the mysteries of the 'beginning': creation, fall, and promise of salvation" (#289).

WHAT ARE THE MASONS?

The origins of the Masons or what is officially called Freemasonry are hard to pinpoint. With the decline of cathedral building in the aftermath of the Protestant movement, the guilds of masons began accepting non-masons as members to bolster their dwindling membership. Eventually, the non-masons outnumbered the masons, and the guilds became places for the discussion of ethics and morality while retaining the secret signs, symbols, and gestures of the original guild. Four such guilds merged in 1717 in London, England to form the Grand Lodge of Freemasons. (A "freemason" was a highly skilled mason who enjoyed the privileges of membership in a trade guild.) The Masons then spread throughout the world.

Old "handbooks" of Freemasonry define the organization as "a peculiar system of morality veiled in allegory and illustrated by symbols," "a science which is engaged in the search after the divine truth," and "the activity of closely united men who, employing symbolical forms borrowed principally from the mason's trade and from architecture, work for the welfare of mankind, striving morally to ennoble themselves and others and thereby to bring about a universal league of mankind which they aspire to exhibit even now on a small scale."

James Anderson (d. 1739), a Scottish Presbyterian minister, wrote the *Book of Constitutions* in which he contrived the "traditional" albeit spurious history of Freemasonry. Masons hold that God, "the Great Architect," founded Freemasonry, and that it had as patrons, Adam and the Patriarchs. Even Jesus is listed as "the Grand Master" of the Christian Church. They credit themselves with the building of Noah's Ark, the Tower of Babel, the Pyramids, and Solomon's Temple. In all, Freemasonry borrows liberally from the history and traditions of cultic groups such as the Druids, Mithars, Egyptian priesthood, Rosicrucians, and others to weave its own history.

The Catholic Church has difficulty with Freemasonry because it is indeed a kind of religion unto itself. The practice of Freemasonry includes temples, altars, a moral code, worship services, vestments, feast days, a hierarchy of leadership, initiation and burial rites, and promises of eternal reward and punishment. While in America, most Masons are Christian and will display a Bible on their "altar," in the same lodges or elsewhere, Jews, Moslems, Hindus, or other non-Christian religions can be admitted and may use their own sacred scriptures. (In France, in 1877, the "Grand Orient" Lodge eliminated the need to believe in God or the immortality of the soul, thereby admitting atheists into their fold; this atheistic type of Freemasony spread particularly in Latin countries.)

Moreover, the rituals involve the corruption of Christianity. The cross is merely a symbol of nature and eternal life, devoid of Christ's sacrifice for sin. INRI (for Christians, *Iesus Nazarenus Rex Iudaeorum*, i.e. Jesus of Nazareth, King of the Jews) means for Masons, *Igne Natura Renovatur Integra*, i.e. "it is by fire that nature is renewed entirely," referring to the sacred fire's (truth and love) regeneration of mankind just as the sun regenerates nature in the Spring.

The rituals are also inimical to Catholicism. During the initiation rite, the candidate expresses a desire to seek "light." He is assured that he will receive the light of spiritual instruction that he could not receive in another Church. Moreover, he will gain eternal rest in the "celestial lodge" if he lives and dies according to Masonic principles. (Note also that since Masonry involves non-Christians, the use of the name of Jesus is forbidden within the lodge.)

A second difficulty with Freemasonry for Catholics involves the taking of oaths. An oath is a religious act which asks God to witness the truth of the statement or the fulfillment of a promise. Only the Church and the state for serious reason can require an oath. Under pain of death or self-mutilation, a candidate makes an oath to Freemasonry and its secrets by kneeling blindfolded in front of the altar, placing both hands on the volume of sacred law (perhaps the Bible), the square, and compass, and repeating after the "worshipful master." Keep in mind that the candidate does not yet even know all the "secrets" to which he is taking an oath. Because of to whom and to what the candidate is swearing, this oath is wrongful.

A strong anti-Catholicism also permeates Freemasonry. The two traditional enemies of Freemasonry are the Royalty and the Papacy. Masons even believe that Christ, dying on Calvary, was "the greatest among the apostles of Humanity, braving Roman despotism and the fanaticism and bigotry of the priesthood." When one reaches the thirtieth degree in the Masonic hierarchy, called the Kadosh, the person crushes with his foot the papal tiara and the royal crown, and swears to free mankind "from the bondage of Despotism and the thraldom of spiritual tyranny."

The history of Freemasonry has proven its anti-Catholic nature. In the United States, one of the leaders of Freemasonry, General Albert Pike (d. 1891), referred to the papacy as "a deadly, treacherous enemy," and wrote, "The Papacy has been for a thousand years the torturer and curse of Humanity, the most shameless imposture, in its pretense to spiritual power of all ages." In France in 1877, and in Portugal in 1910, Freemasons took control of the government for a time and enacted laws to restrict the activities of the Church particularly in education. In Latin America, the Freemasons have expressed anti-church and anti-clerical sentiment.

Since the decree *In Eminenti* of Pope Clement XII in 1738, Catholics have been forbidden to join the Masons, and until 1983, under pain of excommunication. (The Orthodox and several Protestant churches also ban membership in the Masons.) Confusion occurred in 1974 when a letter by Cardinal Franjo Seper, then Prefect of the Sacred Congregation for the Doctrine of the Faith, was interpreted to mean that Catholics could join Masonic lodges that were not anti-Catholic; the same congregation declared this interpretation as erroneous in 1981.

On November 26, 1983, with the approval of Pope John Paul II, the Sacred Congregation reiterated the ban on Catholics joining the

Masons: "The Church's negative position on Masonic association ... remains unaltered, since their principles have always been regarded as irreconcilable with the Church's doctrine. Hence, joining them remains prohibited by the Church. Catholics enrolled in Masonic associations are involved in serious sin and may not approach Holy Communion." However, neither this declaration nor the 1983 *Code of Canon Law* imposed the penalty of excommunication on Catholics belonging to the Masons.

WHO ARE THE JEHOVAH'S WITNESSES AND WHAT DO THEY BELIEVE?

The Jehovah's Witnesses were founded by Charles Taze Russell, a former haberdasher from Philadelphia, in early 1872 in Allegheny, Pennsylvania. Russell was born on February 16, 1852 in Pittsburgh, and died on October 31, 1916. He was baptized a Congregationalist, and was raised in a strict Protestant family. His later study of the Bible led him to deny the existence of hell and the doctrine of the Trinity, and to express Arian views concerning the nature of Jesus Christ, denying His divinity. In 1879, Russell founded the journal *The Watchtower* and in 1884 formed the Watchtower Bible and Tract Society. He traveled on preaching missions throughout the United States and Europe, organizing his followers, who were called Russellites, Millennial Dawnists, International Bible Students, and finally Jehovah's Witnesses. During his missionary work, he faced several scandals including the separation from his wife after eighteen years of marriage, and the accusation of fraud for selling "miracle wheat" for a very high price.

Upon Russell's death in 1916, Judge Joseph Franklin Rutherford, a Missouri lawyer who had defended Russell in several of his legal battles, succeeded him as president of the society. Rutherford officially incorporated the group in 1931 as the Jehovah's Witnesses with the legal title, "The Watch Tower Bible and Tract Society." Rutherford developed Russell's ideas into a formal doctrinal system. He also transformed the congregational structure of the sect as it was under Russell into a rigid theocracy. Rutherford laid the foundation for the sect as we know it today.

According to the Jehovah's Witnesses, there is one God, and since 1931, they have insisted that he be called "Jehovah," a corruption in the pronunciation of the Hebrew *Yahweh* which occurred about the third century BC which was carried into the King James Bible's translation of Yahweh in Exodus 6:3. The Jehovah's Witnesses say that Jesus is God's Son, but is inferior to God. They condemn the Trinity as pagan idolatry and accordingly deny Christ's divinity. Russell even claimed that the Trinity was the idea of Satan! Ironically, however, when they baptize, they use the formula, " ... In the name of the Father, and of the Son, and of the Holy Spirit."

Nevertheless, the Jehovah's Witnesses consider Jesus as the greatest witness of all, inferior to no one except Jehovah himself. Before existing as a human being, Jesus was a spiritual creature called the Logos, or Word, or even Michael the Archangel. He died as a man and was raised as an immortal spirit-Son. His passion and death were the price he paid to regain for mankind the right to live eternally on earth. Indeed the great multitude of true Witnesses hope in an earthly Paradise. (These teachings echo the heresies which the early Church condemned, beginning at the council of Nicea in 325.)

The Bible is the only source of belief and rule of conduct. However, their Bible aids seem to have more strength. They are only allowed to use their own translation of the Bible and other official publications. Unfortunately, many purposeful mistranslations exist in their version to support their tenets. For example, in the New Testament, Lord is translated "Jehovah" except where it refers directly to Christ. In the Last Supper account, they translate, "Take, eat. This is my body." to "Take, eat. This means my body." To affirm that Jesus was created, they add to Colossians 1:16, "By means of Him, everything was created ... ," the word *other*: "By means of him, all other things were created in the heaven and upon the earth ... . All other things have been created through him and for him. Also, he is before all other things and by means of him all other things were made to exist."

The Jehovah's Witnesses also deny the immortality of the soul, the existence of Hell, and the seven sacraments. (Although they have a ritual of baptism, they regard it as merely the exterior symbol of their dedication to the service of Jehovah.) They observe no feast, including Christmas, except the Memorial of the Last Supper, which they hold once a year after sundown on the fourteenth day of

Nisan (a former method of computing the date of Easter and Passover) and during which only those who consider themselves as being among the celestial 144,000 may partake of the "emblems" – the bread and wine. They refuse blood transfusions. They also refuse to salute the flag, seeing this as an act of idolatry. They also condemn smoking.

The Jehovah's Witnesses are also preoccupied with Armageddon – the final clash between the forces of good and evil. Here God will destroy the old system of creation and establish Jehovah's Kingdom. A group of 144,000 spiritual sons of God will rise to Heaven, rule with Christ, and share their happiness with the others. However, the wicked will undergo complete destruction. Russell said that this Armageddon could not happen later than 1914. (He had given specific dates and times on three earlier occasions, but was wrong.) From 1920, Rutherford proclaimed that "millions now living will never die"; he also expected the "princes of old" – Abraham, Isaac, and the others – to come back to life by 1925 as rulers over the New World. After so many mistaken predictions, the Watch Tower Society of the mid-20th century no longer specified an exact date for all of this to happen; but it repeated that "this generation will by no means pass away until all things occur." More recently, Nathan Knorr, who succeeded Rutherford in 1942 as head, predicted that the world would end in 1974; the world itself did not end, but this world did for Knorr – he died in 1974. Nevertheless, witnesses are deeply convinced that the end of the world will come within a very few years.

Each member is considered an ordained minister to give witness to Jehovah by announcing His approaching Kingdom. He may do this by door-to-door evangelization, by meeting with others for home Bible studies, or by standing at street corners to display Watch Tower literature. Preaching the good news is the only means of salvation. Ordinarily, the entry level Jehovah Witness is called a "servant." A "publisher," attends five hourly meetings a week and is to devote 10 hours a month witnessing. A "pioneer" gives 100 hours a month to the society.

The main office is in Brooklyn, New York. The Jehovah's Witnesses are highly centralized. Branch offices in important countries supervise the work and channel the distribution of publications. District and circuit servants regularly visit local congregations to meet local servants, publishers, and pioneers. Exact statistics are kept of all activities. As of 1994, about 1 million Witnesses belong to more than 22,000 congregations in some 80 countries.

WHO ARE THE MORMONS AND
WHAT DO THEY BELIEVE?

The Mormon Church, officially called the Church of Jesus Christ of the Latter Day Saints, was founded in upstate New York by Joseph Smith, who was born on December 23, 1805 in Sharon, Vermont. His parents were poor and migrated to New York about 1816. In Spring, 1820, he underwent internal religious turmoil concerning the state of his own salvation, a wrestling sparked by a religious revival which moved several of his relatives to join the Presbyterian Church. Inclined to Methodism, he sought divine guidance and later claimed to have been visited by two glorious beings – God and Jesus – who instructed him not to join any established church but to wait for the true "Church of Christ" which was about to be reestablished.

According to Smith's account, on September 21, 1823, the Angel Moroni appeared to him and revealed the existence of a gospel taught by our Lord after His resurrection to the Nephites, a branch of the House of Israel, which had fled Jerusalem prior to the Babylonian Captivity (600 BC) and had settled in America prior to its discovery by Columbus. The American Indians were the Lamanites, the degenerate remnants of the Nephites. Smith stated the Angel Moroni gave him this gospel written in a book of thin gold plates in September, 1827. (Moroni had been a Nephite prophet, the son of another prophet named Mormon, who authored the account and buried it in a hill in ancient times called Cumorah, two miles north of the village of Manchester.) Smith then translated the contents from an ancient Egyptian language with the help of two divine interpreters, Urim and Thummim, and published the *Book of Mormon* in March, 1830 at Palmyra, New York. While translating the *Book of Mormon*, Smith and his assistant Oliver Cowdery were ordained first by John the Baptist to the Aaronic priesthood giving them the authority to preach, baptize by immersion, and administer the "Sacrament of the Lord's Supper," and then ordained by Sts.

Peter, James and John to the priesthood of Melchisedech, empowering them to bestow the Holy Spirit by the laying on of hands.

On April 6, 1830 in Fayette, New York, Smith founded the Church of Jesus Christ of the Latter-day Saints, a title to distinguish themselves with the saints of former times. Smith was the first elder, prophet, seer, and revelator. He started communities in Kirtland, Ohio; Independence and Far West, Missouri; and Nauvoo, Illinois. At both Kirtland and Independence, the Mormons tried to establish "The United Order," a communal system of living. Suspected of being abolitionists and missionaries to the Indians, the Mormons were forced to leave Missouri when mobs began attacking them. In Ohio, the Mormons prospered, building their first temple and inaugurating their first foreign missionary work (1837). A year later, here too trouble arose, and again they were forced to flee the state.

They escaped to Nauvoo, Illinois. The Mormon community grew to about 20,000. Again, they built a temple, began foreign missionary work in England, and organized their own militia and court. Soon, the climate turned hostile toward the Mormons, partially due to Mormon dissenters who had left the community, and to the practice of polygamy. Joseph and his brother Hyrum were arrested and murdered in the Carthage jail by a mob that included uniformed militia on June 27, 1844.

Brigham Young (1801-1877) assumed the Church leadership and organized a migration west across Iowa reaching the Missouri River in June, 1846. After suffering through the winter, they continued the journey west on April 7, 1847. A party of 148, the Mormons arrived in Utah on July 24 and began settling. They developed a planned community, with religious and civil functions oftentimes interwoven. In 1850, Brigham Young was appointed by President Fillmore as the Governor of the Territory of Utah. By the time of Young's death in 1877, the Mormons had established 357 settlements in Utah which had a population of about 140,000.

The Mormons had difficulty with the federal government for the admission into the union because of religion and particularly the practice of polygamy, which had been openly practiced since 1852. Caution must be taken in speaking of polygamy so as not to exaggerate the "sexual" dimension: in the settling of the West, sometimes the fathers of families died, leaving no one to provide for those left behind; in the Mormon community, some men, even though they had their own family, would "adopt" these fatherless families, insuring their care. In 1863, Congress passed the Morrill Law which forbade plural marriage, a law which the Supreme Court upheld in 1879. In September, 1890, Church President Wilford Woodrull renounced polygamy as effective church teaching, and in 1896 Utah was granted statehood.

Given this overview of the history of the Mormon church, we can now turn to their beliefs and practices. Joseph Smith claimed to be the recipient of the revelation of this age. For the Mormons, their Sacred Scriptures include the Bible; *The Book of Mormon*, which is believed to be a translated pre-Columbian writing; the *Doctrine and Covenants*, which contains Smith's revelations, including the establishing of polygamy; and the *Pearl of Great Price*, which has the lost parts of the Pentateuch (the first five books of the Old Testament), Smith's writings, and articles of Mormon belief.

Mormon theology lacks a sense of the transcendent, without a clear distinction between the natural and supernatural. Mormons do believe in a personal God, but one who dwells in this time and space, and is continually self-developing and creating. Moreover, their interpretation of the Trinity is more of a tritheism (3 distinct gods – God, Jesus, and Holy Spirit – rather than three persons – Father, Son, and Holy Spirit – in one God). Jesus is the first-born of God, and He created the world with Adam, one of God's earliest "spirit children."

Like God, humans exist in a previous spirit world. All humans leave their preexistent state in the supernatural world to enter this realm and to grow in knowledge. They then continue self-developing in this world and in the next.

Mormons do not really have a concept of original sin and a deprived human nature. Rather, each person is directly responsible for all sins. Consequently, each person must strive to become godlike, for God once was like humans are now but transformed Himself into what He is now. The Mormons do affirm that to achieve this godlike status, humans need the redemption won by Jesus. Nevertheless, the idea of free agency – the exercise of one's free will – to do good and achieve this godlike status is fundamental to their belief.

After death, Mormons will progress depending upon the choices made in this life. Some individuals will face damnation, but most people will share eternal happiness at one of three levels: Telestial, Terrestrial, or Celestial. This life will be the optimal version of life experienced in this world, but without pain and suffering. Here one will be reunited with his earthly family. Mormons believe they will have an advantage in attaining everlasting happiness because they have the full truth of revelation; however, they also admit a greater jeopardy of damnation for the same reason. In the end, Jesus will return to the earth and gather the "Latter Day Saints" in recreating the world.

Worship services, called "sacrament meetings," are simple, consisting of informal talks, the singing of hymns, and the distribution of blessed bread and water signifying the covenant. Fast and Testimony Sunday occurs on the first Sunday of the month where worshipers abstain from food for twenty-four hours and offer personal testimonies at the worship meeting.

In their daily spirituality, Mormons abstain from coffee, tea, tobacco, and liquor. Mormons also practice tithing and provide relief for Church members rather than resorting to government welfare. Mormonism extols optimism, self-improvement, hard work, and respect for the law. The importance of the family is highly stressed.

Temple ceremonies, known as ordinances, are more complex and highly guarded. These ordinances include marriage for time and eternity, sealing families together for eternal association, and vicarious baptism for the dead. Only those deemed worthy by church authorities may enter temples.

The Mormon church structure includes a hierarchical priesthood embracing all males deemed worthy. A youth becomes a member of the lesser Aaronic priesthood at age 12 and advances through its three stages – deacon, teacher, and priest until age 20. He then becomes an elder, a member of the Melchizedech order which contains two high ranks – Seventies, to which men are advanced after a two-year mission experience, and then High Priest. (Young women may also serve as missionaries after age 21, but do not enter into the priesthood.)

(As an aside, when I was a senior at West Springfield High School, one of my friends was a Mormon. While the majority of us were very excited about applying to colleges, he indicated that he would first be performing missionary work for his church for two years. To this day, I greatly admire the zeal of Mormon young people in their commitment to evangelize. I have to wonder how many of our Catholic young people would be willing to make the same commitment.)

The local Church unit is the ward, which is led by an unpaid leader who is called a Bishop and who is assisted by two priestly Counselors. Several wards compose a stake. The stake is led by the Stake President, who has two priestly Counselors and a Stake High Council of Twelve Melchizedek Priesthood Brothers. Together they form a tribunal to adjudicate differences among Church members. At the top of the hierarchy is the church presidency made up of the First President, two Counselors, and the Council of the Twelve Apostles. The top 24 officials are known as the General Authorities.

The Mormon Church currently has about 3.5 million members worldwide.